MAD DOG

David Lister dedicates this book to his parents, Ian and Angie Lister, and Hugh Jordan to his deceased aunt, Margaret Noone Murray.

THE RISE AND FALL
OF JOHNNY ADAIR
AND 'C COMPANY'

David Lister and Hugh Jordan

MAINSTREAM
PUBLISHING
EDINBURGH AND LONDON

First published in Great Britain in 2003 by
MAINSTREAM PUBLISHING (EDINBURGH) LTD
7 Albany Street
Edinburgh EH1 3UG

ISBN 1 84018 791 3

A catalogue record for this book is available from the British Library

Typeset in Frutiger and Garamond

Printed in Great Britain by
Mackays of Chatham plc, Chatham, Kent

Acknowledgements

The complex and insecure world of Ulster loyalism and its violent manifestation in Protestant terrorist groups has not to date been fully explored by writers and political analysts. By contrast, all aspects of militant Irish republicanism have been studied exhaustively. We hope this book goes some way to redressing the balance by providing an insight into arguably the most feared loyalist terrorist unit of the Troubles, the unique era in which it operated and the tiny clique who led it.

To many UDA members, 'C Company' on the Shankill Road was their answer to the IRA's south Armagh brigade. Under Johnny Adair's command, they saw it as an elite unit that took the loyalist killing campaign of the early 1990s to a new level of ruthlessness. At a time when many working-class Protestants believed their culture and religion were under attack, they saw Adair as a hero who helped to take the 'war' to the doorstep of the Provisionals.

This book is the product of many months of research, which have proved deeply engrossing for both authors. David Lister would like to thank Ben Preston, the *Times*'s deputy editor, and his colleagues on the paper's newsdesk – above all Graham Paterson, John Wellman, Mike Harvey and Richard Duce. Hugh Jordan would like to thank Colm MacGinty, Jim McDowell and his other colleagues at the *Sunday World*. Both authors would like to acknowledge the support of all the staff at Mainstream Publishing, particularly Bill Campbell, Peter MacKenzie, Sharon Atherton, Tina

Hudson, Graeme Blaikie and Ailsa Bathgate, whose patience was sorely tested. Our thanks must also go to Gerry Fanning of Fanning & Kelly Solicitors, Dublin, and Ted Jones of Jones & Company, Belfast.

People who helped us at various stages, and in many ways, include: Davy Adams, Jeremy Adams, Paul Armstrong, Jilly Beattie and her mad dogs, Joan Boyd, Colin Breen, Donna and Jane Carton, Andrew Clark, Liam Clarke, Robert Cole, Adrian Cox, John Creaney QC, Jim Cusack, Martin Dillon, David Dunseith, Davy Ervine, Alan Erwin, 'Fat Graham', Geraldine Finucane, Lisa and Cathy Gormley, Thomas Harding, Deric Henderson, Joe Hendron, Angus Horner, Bob Huggins, Billy Hutchinson, Kathy Johnston, Vincent Kearney, Justin Kernoghan, the great Alan Lewis, Walter Macauley, Bob McCartney, Conor McCaughley, Henry McDonald, Lindy McDowell, Dan McGinn, Kevin Magee, Sir Patrick Mayhew, Richard Mills, Chris Moore, John Mullin, Yvonne Murphy, Ted Oliver, Barry Penrose, Jackie Redpath, David Ross, Chris Ryder, David Sharrock (the *Times*'s infamous bon viveur), Paddy and Edmund Simpson, Joe Stewart, Alan Templeton, Darwin Templeton, Bill Thompson, Stephen Walker, John Ware, Brian Wilson MP, John 'Dr Snuggles' Young and the staff at Reliable Travel in Belfast.

During a lengthy interview inside Maghaberry Prison and a series of telephone conversations, Johnny Adair blew hot and cold. When he was hot, he spoke freely and we acknowledge that contribution. We were also helped by several other prisoners and prison staff, who must remain anonymous but who provided some extraordinary gems of information. On the Shankill Road, we are grateful to Winkie and Maureen Dodds, Tracey and Agnes Coulter, Mabel Adair and her daughters Margaret, Mabel Jnr, Jeanie, Etta and Lizzie. Jackie 'Legs' Robinson, Adair's former girlfriend, provided an amazing insight into his character and never tired of answering our questions. A handful of people who grew up with Adair but subsequently lost touch with him provided some amazing glimpses into his early life.

A great many police officers, serving and retired, helped us throughout our research. Those who can be mentioned by name are Assistant Chief Constable Stephen White (currently chief of police in Basra in southern Iraq), and the retired officers Det. Supt Kevin Sheehy, Det. Sgt Alan Cormack, Det. Supt Tim McGregor, Det. Sgt Eamon Canavan, former Chief Super. George Caskey and former Chief Super. Eric Anderson. Above all, we owe a huge debt of gratitude to retired Det. Sgt Johnston 'Jonty' Brown, who knows just how priceless he is, and his wife Rebecca.

ACKNOWLEDGEMENTS

Of the many loyalists who helped us, we are most indebted to seven C Coy gunmen, none of whom have been convicted of murder but nonetheless spoke to us at length. They were among Adair's 'elite' and played central roles in his killing spree of the early 1990s. One is consistently mentioned by his real name. Four of them, who gave detailed accounts of their relationships with Adair, the methods and style of C Coy and the murders they took part in, are quoted as 'Davy', 'Pete', 'John' and 'James'. Their confessions are at times shocking, and we apologise for this to the families of their victims. However, in the interest of setting the record straight and spelling out the awful brutality of C Coy's murderous exploits, we believe this was necessary. Wherever possible we have named the killers who did Adair's dirty work, though many more could not be named for legal reasons. As well as the murders they carried out, we have also gone into detail on their partying, social lives and sexual behaviour. Throughout this book, we have helped to describe this peculiar world with first-hand accounts from the people who knew Adair best. Their words speak louder than ours.

David Lister and Hugh Jordan
September 2003

Contents

WEST BELFAST: THE SHANKILL ROAD
AND SURROUNDING AREAS

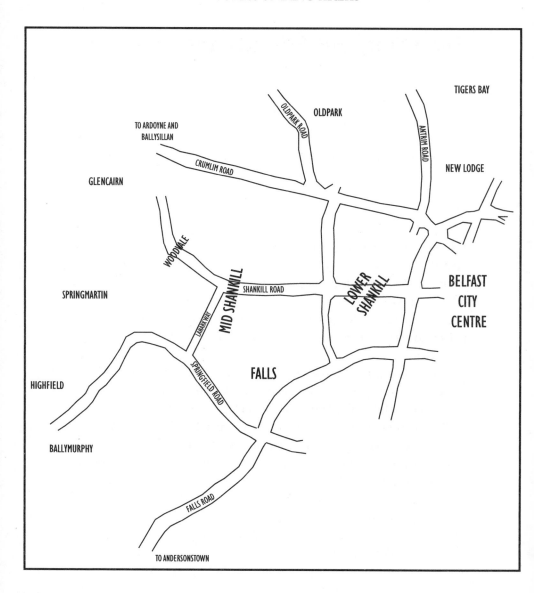

Mad Dog: His Friends and Enemies

A LIST OF MAIN CHARACTERS AND THEIR NICKNAMES

Mad Dog – Johnny Adair. Also known as 'Pitbull', 'the Wee Man' and 'Red Adair'.

Mad Bitch – Gina Adair, maiden name Crossan.

Skelly – Sam McCrory, Adair's closest friend and a C Coy gunman. Skelly is gay, a fact that has led to constant speculation about Adair's sexuality.

Big Donald – Donald Hodgen, one of Adair's oldest friends and a senior C Coy figure.

Fat Jackie – Jackie Thompson, a C Coy gunman in the early 1990s and, like Hodgen, formerly one of Adair's closest associates.

Sham – James Millar, also known as 'Boss Hogg' after the money-grabbing villain in *The Dukes of Hazzard*, the American television series. A former C Coy driver and gunman and a major drug dealer.

Winkie – William Dodds, a veteran C Coy gunman and for years one of Adair's closest allies.

Moe – William Courtney, a C Coy gunman and, like Winkie, formerly one of Adair's closest allies.

Top Gun – Stevie McKeag, Adair's most prolific gunman, who died of a cocaine overdose in September 2000.

Smickers – Gary Smith, also known as 'Chiefo'. Took over as C Coy's leading gunman following McKeag's arrest and imprisonment in 1993. Known for his unquestioning loyalty to Adair.

Spencer – Jim Spence, Adair's erstwhile 'brigadier' in west Belfast and for years a close friend.

Legs – Jackie Robinson, Adair's former girlfriend and fiancée, known for her slim figure and long legs.

King Rat – Billy Wright, the founder of the LVF. Shot dead inside the Maze Prison in December 1997. Loathed Adair with a passion.

Swinger – Mark Fulton, Wright's successor as head of the LVF and a friend of Adair. Found dead in his cell in Maghaberry Prison in June 2002.

The Mexican – Billy McFarland, the UDA's 'brigadier' for Co. Derry and north Antrim.

Doris Day – Jim Gray, the UDA's 'brigadier' in east Belfast. The derogatory nickname comes from his bleach-blond hair. His men, known for their chunky gold jewellery and extravagant lifestyles, are known as 'the Spice Boys'.

Grug – John Gregg, the UDA's former 'brigadier' in south-east Antrim. Shot dead in February 2003.

The Bacardi Brigadier – Jimbo Simpson, the UDA's former 'brigadier' in north Belfast.

Coco – Nickname given to John White, Adair's former spokesman, though used only occasionally (after Coco the Clown).

The only major character not to have a nickname is Jackie McDonald, the UDA's 'brigadier' in south Belfast and currently the most powerful figure on the organisation's ruling 'inner council'.

Prologue – An Audience with Johnny Adair

'SO YOU'RE HERE TO SEE OUR JOHNNY?' THERE IS A FRISSON OF EXCITEMENT in her voice as the prison warder utters her welcome. Prisoner A4544 has already been on the phone to find out if his visitor has arrived. 'He doesn't get many visits. All he does is clean the landing,' she says with a look of concern. 'But Johnny gets on with all of us. You couldn't ask for a better prisoner.'

Just after 3.30 p.m. on Friday, 11 July 2003, Northern Ireland's most notorious living terrorist strolls into the private booth that has been booked for the visit. The man known as 'Mad Dog' has a flask in one hand and a notebook and pen in the other. 'I brought these for you,' he says, putting the notebook on the table. 'They probably took everything off you when you came in. There's a number in there – speak to him, he'll tell you the truth about Johnny Adair.' On the first page of the notebook is a telephone number with the name 'Mr X' written next to it. 'Do you want some tea?' he asks as he unscrews his flask and pours away.

It has taken months to persuade Adair to agree to an interview. On 16 May, during the first of many telephone conversations from the jail, he said he wanted to write his autobiography and offered to do this with the authors. When told that this wasn't our plan, he asked for a slice of any profits from this book. 'What's in it for me? What am I going to get out of this?' he demanded. Three days later, he again asked for money. 'See, why should you be able to talk to the horse's mouth, and have all this, and have it for nothing? Can you not give me, you know, a couple of quid? I'm sitting in here with not a single "d" [penny] to my name so why should I help you?'

The minute Adair realised there was no money in it for him, his interest died. It was not until 8 July, after several letters to him in jail, that he got back in touch. He said it would put his mind at rest to let him know we were talking to 'the right people'. Referring to his enemies as 'gangsters' and 'silly cows', he bragged, 'Facts speak louder than words. They know what Johnny Adair sweated, what Johnny Adair came through, but they've poisoned people to hate me. I could show you the cards and the letters in this cell, all of them sent to me without names because they're too afraid to say they're supporting me. There have been hundreds of cards and I'm only in here four months.'

The Johnny Adair who walks into the visiting room at Maghaberry Prison is hard to reconcile with his public image as a ruthless terrorist and a mass murderer. Wearing a baggy white jumper and jeans, he is far more subdued than he has been on the phone. At 5 ft 3 in. tall and with his tattoos covered by his pullover, he almost looks harmless. He is courteous and polite, but not really interested. Every now and then his piercing blue eyes dart around the room and glance down at his watch. He looks tired. His life is considered to be in such great danger that he is kept in isolation in 'D' Wing of Mourne House, the women's accommodation block at the jail. He is on a landing by himself, in a cell with a built-in wardrobe, a television (which costs 50p a week to rent), a video, a desk, a chair, an armchair and a cordoned-off toilet and washbasin. He has his own kitchen and his own multi-gym. He is allowed out into the yard but has to be on his own.

In the past few months Adair has betrayed almost all his old friends, including members of the clique he grew up with and who became the core of his C Company on Belfast's Shankill Road. Most of his former colleagues despise him and believe he is an egotistical maniac. The only people who visit him are his daughter, Natalie, and occasionally his wife, Gina. He keeps amused by cracking jokes with prison staff. 'This man wants me to tell him all the military stuff we did,' he tells a warder as the interview ends. 'Has he paid you yet, Johnny?' asks the warder with a grin. 'How much are you going to get for this?'

'It's not just the military stuff, it's your early life we're interested in. It'll all be in the book – the band you were in, the riots . . .'

PROLOGUE

'Five-a-side football.'

'You played football, Johnny?'

'All the time.' He grins to the prison officer. 'With taigs' [Catholics'] heads.'

Another warder interjects. 'Johnny, there's some taigs through there,' she says, pointing to the main visiting area.

'Through there?' he asks, sensing he now has an audience. He performs an exaggerated swagger as he walks towards the hall, playing along with the game for a few more seconds before turning back.

Northern Ireland's most notorious terrorist is doing what he does best: being a caricature. Everything he does – whether it is playing the role of the mafia godfather, the sectarian bigot or even the loving father – he does to extremes. As he turns to go, he shakes hands and promises to be in touch. He has arranged for somebody else to meet us, a man who, like him, 'fought the war'. Although he has done little to help, he is desperate to maintain an input. He is worried that we have discovered his secret, a piece of information so sensitive that, until recently, even his closest friends did not talk about it. We have. And it is right at the heart of this book.

1. Made in Ulster

'The most shining example of a skinhead has to be Johnny. After shaving his head he sprayed Mr Sheen on his smooth-top and marched out into the sun. "I did it for a laugh but it actually worked. It made my head really shine," he said.' – *Interview with* Sunday News *(Belfast), January 1984*

MABEL ADAIR WAS GIDDY WITH EXCITEMENT. IT WAS FRIDAY, 25 OCTOBER 1963 and she had just found out that Belfast was about to receive a special visitor. On Monday, no matter how she felt, she would be wearing her best outfit and her smartest hat to mark the guest's arrival in Northern Ireland. On Tuesday, when the visitor was expected in Belfast, she would be up extra early and do her best to make it into town. It would almost certainly be raining but she was not going to let this opportunity pass her by. Queen Elizabeth the Queen Mother was coming to Belfast. She ran over the sentence again in her head and smiled with childlike delight. Every summer she followed the Orangemen as they paraded up and down the road, waving her flag proudly and displaying her favourite Union Jack socks. Nothing, she told herself, would stop her joining the tens of thousands outside the city hall to welcome their royal guest.

That was the plan, but as she stood in the living room and rubbed a damp cloth over a portrait of the Queen, she knew it was ambitious. A decent, strong woman with a solidness about her that was typical of many Belfast women, she leant against the wall and took a few deep breaths. The baby inside her was almost due. Two days later, on the eve of the Queen

Mother's visit, Mabel Adair gave birth to her seventh child at home in Fleming Street off the Shankill Road. John James Adair, or Johnny as he would become known, was born on Sunday, 27 October 1963. He was his mother's second and last son, though a third would follow later but die at birth. Of all her children Johnny would cause her the greatest pride but also the greatest heartbreak. Much as Mabel wanted to see the Queen Mother she could not, in truth, have picked a happier date for the birth of her son. It could only be a blessing, she thought, that his arrival came as Belfast was preparing to embrace a woman adored by Protestants and who symbolised everything their community stood for.

While the rest of the world was trembling under the shadow of the Cold War, the Northern Ireland into which Johnny Adair was born was enjoying an era of unprecedented peace and happiness. Although the threat of violence remained, the IRA's border campaign had fizzled out without support a year earlier. A vibrant music scene was taking off in Belfast, with jazz clubs and dance halls attracting both Catholics and Protestants. The biggest stories had nothing to do with politics or murder. On the same day that the Queen Mother opened Northern Ireland's new airport at Aldergrove on the shores of Lough Neagh, the *Belfast Telegraph* carried a story on its front page under the headline 'Charm of coloured child wins hearts'. It told of how six-year-old Manuel Godfrey Martin had been left £6,000 in the will of a Belfast woman and quoted one admirer as saying, 'He is a charming little fellow and very bright.' Its readers were clearly supposed to be astonished by the good fortune of this foreign rascal. On the same day, the nationalist *Irish News* ran a lengthy report under the title, 'The Catholic Nurse must be inspired by a high motive'. It began, '"To fulfil her vocation as a Catholic nurse, a girl must be unselfish and inspired by a high motive," said Rev. Father Sean Horgan, CSSR, Clonard, Belfast, when he spoke at the annual consecration ceremony of the Irish Guild of Catholic Nurses in the Mater Infirmorum Hospital yesterday.'

Northern Ireland was in its own little bubble and nowhere more so than on the Shankill Road in west Belfast. A poor neighbourhood but thriving with life and industry, it was enjoying the last few years of a golden era. Some 76,000 people were packed into the endless maze of streets stretching from the edge of the city centre to the foothills of the Black Mountain above Belfast. The majority lived in tiny two-up, two-down terraced houses that were up to 120 years old, constituting some of the worst public housing in the United Kingdom. But there was also an intense vibrancy. The Shankill was home to 86 pubs, one for almost every corner (there are just four today). Thousands worked in the Harland and Wolff shipyard three-quarters of a mile away and just as many were employed in the linen mills even closer to home. Within the space of one square mile there were 36 mills, where 9,000 people worked, and the famous Mackie's engineering factory, where 7,500 were employed. Most of the mills were on the Crumlin Road or the Catholic Falls Road. Sandwiched in between was the Shankill, Belfast's second busiest shopping street after Royal Avenue. According to Jackie Redpath, a community worker who has spent all his life in the area, 'It was a place that had this amazing amount of employment opportunities, where a lot of skilled tradesmen lived, where you could shop for everything you needed and with a population that was bigger than Ballymena or Bangor [two Protestant towns]. It had very strong and vibrant politics and was known commonly to people who lived there as the heart of the empire. That's what people called it. In the '60s the empire was still about and it was the sort of place that symbolised all that there was about Unionism and loyalism.'

It was not obvious at the time, but this age of prosperity and opportunity was about to end. The industrial era that had given birth to the Shankill more than a century earlier would shortly grind to a halt. By the end of the decade most of the mills were gone and the once-mighty shipyard, where the famous *Titanic* was built, had entered terminal decline. In 1966, on the 50th anniversary of the 1916 Easter Rising, sectarian riots broke out in Belfast and the newly re-formed Ulster Volunteer Force (UVF), Northern Ireland's first loyalist terrorist group, murdered three civilians. In west Belfast, where the differences between the Province's two communities were starkest, a battleground was opening up between working-class Catholics from the Falls and Protestants from the Shankill. For well over a century, trouble had sporadically flared on the faultline between the two districts, and in the late 1960s it returned with unprecedented fury. In an area where young school leavers had always been guaranteed jobs, the sudden arrival of an economic crisis made the Shankill jittery and insecure. 'Those first five years of the '60s were the end of the good old days – they were the last years of what the industrial revolution created,' said Redpath. By the end of the 1960s, large parts of the Shankill were being rebuilt and many families moved up the road to the new housing estates of Springmartin and Glencairn. The redevelopment caused massive disruption in the area, adding to the economic upheaval that was starting to tear it apart.

MAD DOG

Beneath the camaraderie of the Shankill, there was a rough sectarian sub-culture. One teacher who taught on the Shankill in the 1960s and 1970s remembers having to patiently explain that Catholics were people, just like Protestants. 'I remember a wee boy in my class, he was a very nice little boy with curly hair,' she said. 'We were talking about the importance of dogs having collars on their necks with their names on them and he said, "Miss, a taig [Catholic] dog came into our estate last night," and then went on to tell me about how some woman had risked life and limb to take this dog back because it had its name and address on its collar. And I said to the children, "Put down your pencils for a minute," and I tried to explain to them — I said, "These people you are speaking about, they just go to another church."' The curly-haired eight-year-old was Curtis Moorehead, who in time became a senior terrorist colleague of Johnny Adair. The teacher also remembers a five-year-old boy being caught smoking in the school toilets. The child was Lenny Murphy, who went on to become the leader of the infamous Shankill Butchers.

The Adair family lived in the heart of the lower Shankill in a small street of terraced council houses with outside toilets. Fleming Street was off the Old Lodge Road, which ran from St Peter's Hill at the bottom of the Shankill through to the Crumlin Road, the main artery into north Belfast. Their neighbours included the White family, one of whose nine children, John, would commit one of the most brutal double murders of the Troubles and eventually stand shoulder to shoulder with Johnny Adair as his political mouthpiece. Like Adair, John White was born and brought up in Fleming Street, though his future colleague, some 13 years his junior, knew him only vaguely as a child.

At home Mabel Adair ran a tight ship and her children were regularly smacked for misbehaving. Johnny, who was the youngest, lived in a family dominated by women. Of his five sisters, Margaret was the oldest and most sensible. Next came Mabel Jnr and Jeanie, who were easily led and prone to tantrums. The youngest were Etta and Lizzie, both of whom suffered from severe learning disabilities and were relentlessly teased by children in the street. From an early age Adair played the fool in front of his older sisters and they adored him for it. Adair's father, Jimmy, who worked in the timber yard in the docks, was constantly playing practical jokes and Johnny quickly became his sidekick. His brother, Archie, was quieter and more withdrawn. Two years older than Johnny, he would achieve notoriety in his own right when in 1992 he was found guilty of attempted murder after attacking a Catholic with a hatchet. He was sentenced to 12 years in prison but was released early, like his brother, under the terms of the 1998 Good Friday peace accord.

Adair's mother and father were simple people who sent all their children to Sunday School. 'Johnny's was not a loyalist household. His was just like any other house – they were an ordinary family and they were not sectarian,' said one childhood friend who moved away from the Shankill. Margaret, his older sister, recalls, 'To us, he [Adair] was just an ordinary kid growing up and knocking around. He wasn't a bad kid at all. The fact was that he was just like everyone else. He went to Sunday School, worked hard at school and would run about on the streets with his friends. He was no different from any other kid in our neighbourhood.'

In 1969, the year the Troubles erupted, Adair started at Hemsworth Primary School around the corner from his house. Known simply as the 'Hen House', by the late 1960s it had a reputation as a rough school. The young Johnny Adair did not stand out, taking little interest in either his studies or his classmates and preferring the company of his sisters and brother. He had one or two friends in the neighbourhood, and occasionally they would tour the streets on a rusty old butcher's bike, taking it in turns to pedal and to ride in the basket. His only real hobby was helping his father with the homing pigeons they kept in the small yard at the back of the house. His father, ironically, was for years a member of a pigeon club in the republican New Lodge area of Belfast. He was frequently invited to tea by some of his nationalist friends but felt embarrassed that he could never return the favour. 'I've got two boys who are bad bastards,' he told one member. 'Their mother made them like that.'

It was not until he started at secondary school in September 1975 that Adair fell in with a proper circle of friends. Within days of starting at Somerdale School on the Crumlin Road he had met the three individuals who would change his life: Sam 'Skelly' McCrory, Donald Hodgen and Jackie Thompson. The four caught the bus together every morning, taking them past the republican Ardoyne district up to Somerdale, whose pupils were almost exclusively Protestant. It was a school with notoriously violent pupils, and many of Adair's contemporaries, including a teenage Ken Barrett, went on to become leading terrorists or victims of the Troubles. As one of them explained, 'The four of us would have went up to school together and that in the mornings and you'd have always got fighting and that on the buses. You got stone throwing as we passed the Ardoyne shop fronts every day. The police used to have to sit there and the bus would be stoned coming down.' After class there would also often be fights with boys from the local Catholic secondary school, St Gabriel's, 200 yards up the road.

Of the four friends, Adair was by far the smallest, though his short red hair and raucous laugh made him stand out. He was the hyperactive one, always dancing around and trying to be the centre of attention. 'Big Donald', the oldest and quietest of the four, was already 12 when he started at Somerdale and a giant compared to the other schoolboys. Although he was not quite shaving, his voice had already broken, a fact that made him seem years older to Adair. Not far behind in size was 'Fat Jackie', who was just two weeks younger than Adair and fast becoming a chubby, well-built young man. His parents owned a sweet shop off the Shankill Road and he greedily ate everything he could lay his hands on. He already knew Skelly, having mucked about with him on the streets of the mid-Shankill. While Thompson lived in Snugville Street, Skelly's family were just around the corner in Jaffa Street. Soon the two would have an opportunity to get to know each other even better, as within weeks both were put in the same class of troublemakers where their behaviour was closely monitored. It did little good. Within a few years, Skelly, a tall, gangly boy, was causing so much trouble that he was sent to the Rathgael Young Offenders Centre in Bangor.

Back at Somerdale, Thompson and the others became increasingly bored with school and frequently skipped class. Instead of going to school they would travel out into the country on the buses, scraping together what money they had and sharing it around. By the time Adair and his friends were 15, 'riding the buses' had become a regular pastime, made more amusing by a few bottles of cider. Thanks to his size and appearance, the job of buying the drink invariably fell to Hodgen. 'Whenever there was any money we'd all ride the buses,' recalled one friend. 'We'd get on the buses with a load of drink, sit at the back and go to places like Millisle or Ballyhalbert out on the sea. You'd just sit there all day and wait for it to bring you home. If you were lucky, there'd also be a fight on the bus on the way back.'

Fighting was a way of life for a teenage boy on the Shankill and Adair would not hesitate to take on people bigger than himself. In the dog-eat-dog world in which he was growing up, even neighbours turned on each other to survive. William 'Winkie' Dodds made a habit of stealing from the young Johnny Adair as he went from door to door delivering the *Belfast Telegraph*, a part-time job he had taken on to earn some money. Dodds, who would later become one of Adair's closest allies, was 16. His unsuspecting victim was only 12 at the time. 'He was a paper boy and I used to wait and take the money off him,' he remembered with a laugh. 'You would have just ambushed him anywhere, just jumped out and grabbed him. It was more for a laugh than anything else.'

To toughen them up, Adair and his friends went boxing at a local youth club, while they got plenty of real-life practice on the streets. 'Johnny was streetwise – he wouldn't back down in a fight,' said one friend. 'We all had to learn how to fight. When you were with a crowd of teenage boys like that, you also had to learn how to fight amongst yourselves.'

In the late 1970s and early 1980s there were regular riots with neighbouring Catholics, particularly during the summer. In August 1980, at the age of 16, Adair was found guilty of disorderly behaviour by Belfast Juvenile Court and fined £10. It was his second juvenile conviction, the first coming more than a year earlier in May 1979, when the 15-year-old was given a 12-month probation order for attempted theft. To be a teenager with a criminal record was nothing remarkable among Adair's peers, most of whom embarked on a life of crime whilst still at school. Over the next few years Adair would clock up a lengthy string of convictions. In January 1981, he was bound over in the sum of £100 after being found guilty at Belfast Magistrates' Court of behaviour likely to cause a breach of the peace. On three further occasions that year he appeared before the same court and was ordered to pay fines of up to £50 after being convicted of obstructing the police, disorderly behaviour and assaulting a police officer. In April and July the following year he was again fined after being convicted of disorderly behaviour and breach of the peace.

Adair and his friends lived within 300 yards of each other and about 500 yards from the frequent street battles between Catholics and Protestants. By his mid-teens his family had moved to Century Street, just across from the Shankill in the Oldpark district of Belfast. Hodgen's family were in Albertville Drive, which ran parallel to Century Street, while Skelly and Jackie Thompson lived in the rabbit warren of streets on the other side of the Crumlin Road. By this time the four friends were starting to pass their time by hanging around on the corner of Century Street, where they soon became the nucleus of a bigger gang. More than a dozen of them would stand outside the entrance to the 'Buff's' Social Club, where warders from the nearby Crumlin Road Prison came at lunchtime for a quiet pint and a bite to eat. As well as Adair and his three best friends, the gang included Bobby Harrison, Jackie Thompson's young uncle, Mark Rosborough, Brian Watson and a guy called 'Chimp' from Sandy Row in south Belfast. The majority were from the surrounding streets of the lower Shankill and the Oldpark. William 'Winkie' Dodds and William 'Moe' Courtney also occasionally joined the crowd. In days when there was little by way of local entertainment, Adair and his gang revelled in the chaos they created. As well as taunting and fighting with police, they enjoyed nothing better than to ambush customers as they left the Buff's Club.

'John', one of Adair's closest friends during these years, remembers passing the summer evenings drinking outside the club: 'In the summer we would have got the carry-out and we'd have stood in the street for hours. There was an old lock-up next to the chemist at the corner of Century Street and we'd wait for the old hands to come out of the Buff's and we'd have just locked people up in there. There was one old hand we locked up for eight hours . . . About ten of us used to hang around there. Mark Rosborough would be up there now and again, and so would your man Chimp. Chimp was mad: he used to have tattoos on his face and eat pint glasses.'

The price for being released from the lock-up was normally a bottle of cider. According to Winkie Dodds' wife Maureen, who lived in the mid-Shankill and knew her future husband even then, the gang was constantly harassing passers-by. 'They used to hide behind the wall and wait for the wee men to come by and then lock them up and ask them for 50p. You could get a bottle of cider for 50p and a big, big bottle at that,' she recalled.

But it was not all fun and games outside the Buff's. On 14 September 1979, when Adair was just 15, a prison officer was shot dead as he and a colleague drove away from the club after lunch. He was barely 200 yards away from the Crumlin Road Prison, but as he clambered into his car an IRA active service unit was watching from across the street. George Foster, a 30-year-old with two children, was shot dead as he drove down Century Street. He was hit in the head while a colleague, one of three other prison officers in the car, was shot in both arms. Adair and his friends were standing yards away as the shooting took place. One of the crowd tried to steal a packet of cigarettes from the car but Adair shouted at him and punched him. 'I remember a car lying on its side in Century Street following an IRA attack,' recalled one old friend. 'Johnny saw another boy taking a packet of cigarettes, which was covered in splashes of blood, and he stopped him. I remember him going mad over that and telling him to have some respect.'

Whether Adair and his friends had any political thoughts at this time, IRA incursions into the middle of their neighbourhood were guaranteed to push them in one direction only. Five days later, Edward Jones, the assistant governor at the jail, was gunned down by the Provisionals as he waited at traffic lights at the junction of the Crumlin Road and Cliftonpark Avenue. He was murdered 50 yards from the Buff's and just 100 yards from the prison. Aged 60 and with 10 children, he had been awarded the British Empire Medal after serving with the Irish Guards during the Second World War. He had worked in the prison for 33 years. Three months later the IRA killed another prison officer at the end of Adair's street. On 17 December, William Wilson was shot in the back as he was walking into the Buff's Club. The 58-year-old was killed by a lone gunman who followed him up the pathway to the building and shot him on the front steps as he was going in for lunch.

By the time he was 16, Adair had left school and joined his father as a wood machinist in the Ulster Timber Company in Duncrue Street in Belfast docks. Although the work was menial it gave him enough money to buy drink and to finance his new hobby: music. With their dark suits, pork pie hats and shades, the ska band Madness caught the imagination of many British teenagers and Adair was no exception. In 1979, the 'nutty boys' from Camden in north London released their first two singles, 'The Prince' and 'One Step Beyond'. Adair and Skelly were hooked. Through their friend Brian Watson, who lived off Manor Street in the Oldpark, they started to listen to other ska bands including UB40, Bad Manners, The Specials and The Beat. But Adair's love of ska was only a warm-up to a style of music that was far more direct and aggressive. By 1980, the skinhead revival was in full swing. On street corners across Britain, shaven-headed young men and women, angry at rising unemployment and immigration, stood in packs drinking and sniffing glue. Their music, known as 'Oi!', was as blunt as their image. Among the bands Adair enjoyed and admired were The 4-Skins and Infa Riot (pronounced 'In For A Riot'), but the one he and Skelly listened to most was Skrewdriver. A neo-Nazi group that openly proclaimed its support for the National Front (NF), it was so right wing that its lead singer, Ian Stuart, made speeches between songs attacking immigration. A leading member of the Blackpool branch of the National Front, Stuart was even pictured on the cover of one album shaking hands with a Ku Klux Klan grand master in full ceremonial dress.

The anti-immigration outbursts meant next to nothing to Adair and his friends in Northern Ireland, where there were hardly any black faces. But for Protestants living under the shadow of the IRA, there was one message above all that hit home with a vengeance. 'It was the Britishness thing,' said one former skinhead. 'The first song I ever heard was "The Voice of Britain" by Skrewdriver. The Britishness, the whole red, white and blue thing, was easy to pick up on. It gave you a sense of pride, that you were a British skinhead, that you were proud to be a Protestant.' Like many other Shankill Protestants, Adair and his friends were swept up by the skinhead scene. As well as shaving their heads, they sniffed 'Evo Stik' glue from plastic bags and listened to Oi! music in a community centre on the lower Shankill estate. Called The Ultimate, it cost £1 to get in but you were allowed to bring your own drink. According to one skinhead who hung around with Adair and his friends: 'There used to be a disco called The Ultimate and they used to have skinhead dos in it. All the skinheads would have went there and we used to then go into the town and fight with the fenians [Catholics] outside Lord Hamill's [a chip shop on Wellington Place in central Belfast]. We all used to go to the YMCA after coming out of the chippie. You were guaranteed good craic because there would always be a fight coming out of it . . . You used to get fenian skinheads and you all knew each other's names. There was one called Art with a wooden leg – we used to love to see him trying to chase after us. There was another one called Ghostie; I don't know where he came from. There was one called Marty who used to set his two Rottweilers on you. Sometimes you'd get lucky, one would have broke free from the crowd and he would have got a big beating.'

Another old Shankill skinhead recalls: 'The Catholic skinheads would have held anti-National Front gigs. Sometimes the rival crowds would have crossed in the town and there was a good old digging match with the taigs. Everybody looked forward to that. If you'd have got one you'd have danced all over them. You have to remember at that time there was coffin after coffin going down the Shankill Road and that's what did it for a lot of these people.'

Like his friends, Adair was often getting into fights and to this day his head bears a number of scars that date back to these years. More often than not knives were produced and bottles thrown. On one particular night,

MADE IN ULSTER

Winkie Dodds recalls being with Adair when he was badly cut after a bottle came flying out of the night sky and landed on his head. Though he knew how to fight, he was small and less physically intimidating than Skelly and Donald Hodgen. As one former Shankill skinhead recalls, 'I can't really remember Johnny. I remember Skelly and big Donald more. They had the tattoos on their heads and all. Donald had a Union Jack on his head and used to have a red, white and blue mohican. On the other side of his head he had another tattoo that said, "Oi Skins!"' But although Adair was not the biggest or the strongest, his friends looked to him as their leader, largely because he was always daring them and egging them on. 'He would say and do crazy things,' said one old friend. 'You'd all be starting to walk home from the town and it would be Johnny who would suggest going up the Falls Road and cutting across rather than walking back up the Shankill. At that stage you would never have thought about walking up the Falls but because Johnny suggested it, you did it.'

As well as going into Belfast, the skinheads would travel to other loyalist towns and estates. Every Easter Monday, hundreds from across Northern Ireland converged on the Co. Antrim town of Portrush, while there were also regular skinhead discos in Rathcoole and Monkstown on the outskirts of north Belfast. Whenever they could, Adair and his friends still enjoyed travelling out to the coast.

Adair was often accompanied by his girlfriend, Gina Crossan, a slim, dark-haired girl from Manor Street. Three years younger than him, they started dating in 1980 when Gina was just 14 and would stay together on and off for the next two decades. Gina, too, was a skinhead, sporting just a tiny tuft of hair at the front of her shaved head. But by far Adair's best friend was Skelly. By now the pair were extremely close, and throughout their youth they would often hug and hold each other, provoking constant speculation about the nature of their friendship. To this day Skelly remains a complex personality. A thug and a bully, he also has a soft side and is openly gay. Even by his late teens the contradictions were glaringly obvious. One moment he was in the thick of a skinhead brawl and the next he was going to bingo, as he did every week, with a bisexual man who was later driven off the Shankill for allegedly molesting children.

Skelly could not bear anything bad to happen to his best friend and he blamed himself for an incident during one of their excursions. The pair were on a train coming back from a drunken day out in Bangor when they had an argument and Adair kicked the door shut. Before he had time to pull his hand away, the door slammed against one of his fingers and cut it clean off at the tip. As Adair screamed in agony, Skelly scooped it off the floor and put it in the top pocket of his denim jacket. The pair rushed to hospital, where Skelly rummaged around in his pocket and, like a best man producing a ring at a wedding, eventually pulled out his friend's fingertip. It was covered in blood and greasy black oil. Although the doctors tried, they were unable to reattach it. As a result, to this day Adair has a slightly deformed right index finger.

By 1980, Adair had to be careful with his fingers. He and Skelly had formed a skinhead band together with Brian 'Watsy' Watson, who lived around the corner from Adair, and Julian 'Tarzan' Carson, whose father ran a tattoo parlour on the Shankill. Although Adair likes to claim responsibility for founding and naming Offensive Weapon, in reality the idea came from Watson. The only talented one among them, Watson played the lead guitar and wrote most of Offensive Weapon's songs. He also taught Adair to play the bass guitar, on a distinctive-looking instrument that Johnny had sent away for from a catalogue. 'I'll always remember that guitar,' said one former skinhead. 'It was light brown with black strings. I thought it was a fucking cracker.' Until he parted with the band in 1983, Carson played the drums. He was a year and a half younger than Adair and looked like a baby. Although Adair would later claim that he was the band's lead singer, he only ever opened his mouth to back up Skelly, who shouted and spat into the microphone and delivered the band's incomprehensible lyrics with a growling rage. On stage, the four would hit, kick and spit at each other. Their dedicated followers were known as the 'Offensive Weapon White Warriors'. They were led by Donald Hodgen, the band's unofficial roadie, and a Skrewdriver bodyguard called Matty, who came across for the concerts. At the end of almost every gig, the pair would jump up onto the stage, punch and kick their friends and roll around on the floor.

'They were mad,' recalled one Shankill woman who went to several of the gigs. 'They were mustard, cat [rubbish]. You couldn't make out a word Skelly was singing, it was just like a blur. At the start it used to be OK but the more drink that got into them the more outrageous it became. They would stand up on the stage and do dancing and trying to sing. They would be kicking their legs and kicking the fuck out of each other on stage. And on the floor you'd be standing and kicking your legs out and hitting each other. You used to come out black and blue all over.'

Between 1981 and 1984, Offensive Weapon played around 20 concerts.

MADE IN ULSTER

The venues included the loyalist club in Romford Street off the Shankill, the Buff's Club, the White Cross Inn in North Street and the Times Bar in the loyalist Tigers Bay district. They practised at the Cairn Lodge youth club – where Adair also went boxing – the YMCA and a converted church. Several of their songs were borrowed from English bands, including 'Sorry' and 'Evil' by the 4-Skins. Skelly's rendition of the latter went down especially well:

> I like breaking arms and legs
> Snapping spines and wringing necks
> Now I'll knife you in the back
> Kick your bones until they crack
> [chorus] Evil, evil, evil, evil [x4]
> Jump up and down upon your head
> Kick you around 'til you're dead
> Fill your body full of lead
> See the roads turn to red
> [chorus]
> I don't like trendy cunts who pose
> Gonna punch you in the nose
> Stick my Marten in your crotch
> Don't like you, you're too much
> [chorus]

The band also played several Skrewdriver covers, including 'Sick Society', 'Shove the Dove' and 'Voice of Britain'. But by far the most popular Skrewdriver hit they played was 'Smash the IRA'. It tapped a raw nerve for Protestant skinheads, and when it was released in 1982 it was the first time any of them had heard a song that dealt so bluntly with the situation on their doorstep:

> On the streets of Ulster, the battle rages on
> British people fighting for their land
> Fought in two world wars for us, fought and died for Britain
> Gotta help them, support the Red Hand
> (chorus) Smash! Smash! The IRA!
> Smash! Smash! The IRA!
> Smash! Smash! The IRA!

> Remember the victims of their bombs
> Gotta change our policies and hang the IRA
> Let the Army deal with them their way
> Corrupt politicians and snivelling left-wing scum
> Are quite content to let them get away
> Come on, Ulster!

Brian Watson wrote several songs for Offensive Weapon including 'Gestapo RUC' and 'Made in Ulster', which boasted the simple chorus, 'Made in Ulster/Proud to be British/Made in Ulster/Sworn to fight'. The lyrics were strongly reminiscent of Skrewdriver, with attacks on both republicans and left-wingers:

> The IRA and communists
> Are walking hand in hand
> They're killing people in Ulster
> They're killing off our land

But no Offensive Weapon concert was complete without their popular song 'Bulldog', which provoked frenzied hysteria whenever it was played. The song shared its name with the magazine of the Young National Front. It was invariably preceded by Nazi salutes from the band and chants from the audience of 'Sieg Heil! Sieg Heil!' and 'National! National! National Front!' Again, the hate-filled lyrics were nothing if not blunt:

> We're the voice of the country
> We're the voice of the youth
> The Government's trying to ban us cause we're telling the truth
> Britain for the British is our main stand
> We've got to get the Commies out of our Fair Land.

Johnny backed up Skelly on the chorus, which called for an exclusively white society even though there were virtually no blacks in Northern Ireland:

> Bulldog – it's gonna have its say
> Bulldog – and it's here to stay
> Bulldog – we're gonna stand up and fight
> Bulldog – we've got to keep Britain white

MADE IN ULSTER

By 1983, the links between Protestant skinheads and the National Front were becoming increasingly close. A number of NF supporters came from England to attend Offensive Weapon concerts and seized the opportunity to hand out leaflets and newsletters. Some time in 1983 Adair attended a meeting at the Ormeau Road Library in south Belfast, which had been booked in the name of a local fishing club but was in reality just a cover for the NF. They were preparing for a big day that was intended to launch their campaign for support in Northern Ireland. That day came on Saturday, 3 September 1983, when Adair and his friends were among up to 300 who took part in the NF's first ever rally in Northern Ireland. Dubbed the 'gluesniffer's march' because it consisted almost entirely of skinheads, it set off from the loyalist Sandy Row district and proceeded through the city centre before stopping on the Shankill Road. It was denounced by Sinn Fein as an ultra-fascist and sectarian show of strength. Not surprisingly, Protestant skinheads did not echo this view. 'It was class. All you would have seen was Union Jack after Union Jack,' said one. 'We returned up the Shankill Road and we all piled into a club facing the Shankill leisure centre. The room was bunged, there was no windies [windows] in it. We went in there and they had three or four different speakers from London and outside they were selling the "Voice of Britain" by Skrewdriver. Everybody was just standing there listening to these people talking about niggers taking over our land, niggers taking our jobs and money, and niggers spreading all over Britain. They maybe would have mentioned the IRA once. We weren't interested in all that because we had nobody from an ethnic culture living next to us. There was all this stuff about blacks, lefties and Britain for the British.'

Adair himself never took the NF's anti-immigration views terribly seriously. Like other youths on the Shankill, he went along with the politics because of the NF's anti-IRA stance and because it was an exhilarating movement that swept up many from the same background and generation. As well as the Belfast march, he attended an NF rally in Coleraine the following year. Along with Skelly, Donald and four other Protestants from the Shankill and nearby Tigers Bay, he also spent a weekend in London, where they attended a National Front 'tea party' and met Ian Stuart of Skrewdriver. They stayed in Islington, in a flat owned by a former soldier. According to one of the group, whilst in London they beat up and mugged a black man as they caught the tube to Elephant & Castle, where they went drinking with another Nazi sympathiser.

But in truth Adair was an unlikely NF supporter, and throughout his life he has enjoyed reggae music and apparently had a fascination with black women. Although the Belfast rally attracted reasonable support, the conditions did not exist in Northern Ireland for an anti-immigration party to have any great success. As well as being almost exclusively white, the Province's main loyalist paramilitary groups, the Ulster Volunteer Force (UVF) and the Ulster Defence Association (UDA), viewed any pro-Nazi display as a direct attack on the United Kingdom. 'What you have to remember is that a lot of people in the paramilitaries would have had relatives who fought in the war,' said one skinhead. 'I remember one English bloke coming into a club and trying to sell the National Front magazine. He got a dig in the face and then he was shoved out.' As a result, the link between far-right groups in Britain and loyalist terrorists never took over, although informal connections remain up to the present day.

For Adair and Skelly, the most important thing was their music, and neither had anything to do with either the UVF or the UDA. Adair in particular was proud of being a member of the first skinhead band on the Shankill, and he believed they had started a new trend when another local band, Self Defence, came onto the scene in 1984 and professed it had been inspired by Offensive Weapon. By now Adair had even bought an old drum kit from Smithfield Market in Belfast and was torturing his family every evening. He was convinced that he had all the makings of a star and was delighted when the group was mentioned in an article in the *Belfast Telegraph* on 14 June 1983 as a leading local skinhead band. Although none of the band was mentioned by name, it was his first taste of being in the media. In January 1984, the now-defunct *Sunday News* devoted an entire story to Adair and Skelly under the headline, 'Headache! Hairy poser for skinheads'. The author was Stephen Grimason, who went on to become the BBC's Northern Ireland political editor and is now a spin doctor for the Stormont power-sharing assembly. It was possibly his finest moment. Talking of the woes of being a skinhead, Skelly described in detail how his naked scalp had burnt in the sun the previous summer and how he had made his condition worse by splashing aftershave all over it. 'I thought my head was going to come off. It was scalding hot and skin started coming off in big lumps. It left a big rash,' he said. Adair told the reporter that he wanted a harder head because he was getting in so many fights. 'In the past seven months I've been hit over the head with a hammer, a crowbar, a cider bottle and a hurley stick,' he disclosed. But by far the biggest revelation came when

Adair admitted spraying his head with furniture polish. 'The most shining example of a skinhead has to be Johnny,' concluded the article. 'After shaving his head he sprayed Mr Sheen on his smooth-top and marched out into the sun. "I did it for a laugh but it actually worked. It made my head really shine," he said.'

2. C8 and the Young Turks

'I remember Johnny telling us, "Your man stood at the top of the stairs and as I went up after him I sprayed him from top to bottom, started on the legs and then worked my way all the way up, just cut the fucker in half."' – Johnny Adair boasting about the murder of Gerard Slane, as recalled by one of his friends

'ANYONE WANT TO HELP US DO A BUS?' THE WORDS CAUGHT SOME OF Johnny Adair's friends by surprise as they stood drinking cider outside the Buff's Club on Century Street. Adair and Skelly had just returned from a meeting of the Ulster Defence Association's C8 team on the Shankill Road and the pair, egging each other on as usual, had volunteered to hijack a bus and set it alight. Their commander, Andrew 'Doodles' Calderwood, had made the instructions short but clear. 'We want the peelers [police] to know we can take them on,' he had told them. 'Just get the driver to park it up, let him off and torch it.' As always, most of Adair's friends had little else to do and the idea sounded far more entertaining than hanging about in the street. Nobody had any masks or weapons, but as there were so many of them they thought it wouldn't be necessary. Several were already drunk on the 50p bottles of cider they had been passing around. 'John', a childhood friend of Adair's, recalls: 'I remember we were all standing at the Century Street corner. They [Adair and Skelly] came up to us and were saying they had to hijack a bus – they would have just come back from a C8 meeting at 275a Shankill Road. Because we had nothing else to do we decided to go and hijack the bus with them. About 20 of us piled over to the bus stop facing the Buff's Club, the bus came up and we jumped on and said it was a hijack, but your man [the bus driver] just laughed at us. We told your man to drive across the road, but it just turned into a laugh rather than anything else and somebody poured the petrol over one of us rather than the bus.'

According to one of Adair's C8 superiors, the hijacking descended into a farce. 'They weren't successful in their operation, let's just say that,' jibed the C Coy veteran. 'They all got on the bus, the whole lot of Johnny's wee clique, but the funniest thing was they didn't have a lighter or a match between them. Not one of them had anything on them to set the bus on fire with. That's been a common joke on the Shankill over the years.'

Adair's first terrorist operation had ended in embarrassing failure, with police recovering the bus before serious damage could be done to it. The date was Wednesday, 15 August 1984 and the Shankill was entering several nights of ferocious rioting, the worst in a Protestant district for a decade. Earlier that day a scuffle had broken out in the Crumlin Road Courthouse between police and nearly 50 loyalist terrorists fingered on the evidence of the UVF supergrass, William 'Budgie' Allen. Relatives of several of the accused pelted police with bags of urine, and in the resulting mêlée eight RUC men and several defendants were injured. That night more than 500 loyalists took to the streets, setting two shops on fire as well as makeshift barriers they had erected. A steady stream of rioters tore up paving stones, smashed them into chunks and hurled them at police. Although most of the violence was orchestrated by the UVF, the UDA was also involved. Over the next four nights Protestant mobs torched several cars and threw petrol bombs, gasoline bombs and anything else they could lay their hands on. For the first time in ten years loyalists opened fire on the RUC, who responded with plastic bullets. The trouble started in the Shankill but quickly spread to Ballysillan in north Belfast and the east of the city. Agnes Ritchie, owner of a children's shop off the Shankill Road, did not sleep for two nights protecting her shop. 'We're right back to 1969,' she said. 'It's taken us so long to rebuild the place and now they're destroying it again.' Andy Tyrie, the UDA's supreme commander, warned, 'We've been trying to damp things down, but there's a lot of bitterness and frustration.'

In an interview with one of the authors, Adair confessed that the hijacking was his first operation as a young UDA volunteer. Although Adair was still a skinhead, the movement was dying a death and Offensive Weapon had come to the end of its natural life. He had swapped one gang for another, joining the UDA several months earlier after it drew up a list of nearly 20 people, all of whom it considered to be a nuisance in the area. Not surprisingly, the majority belonged to Adair's extended circle of friends and the gang who hung around outside the Buff's. Word had reached the UDA that they had been attacking police officers, locking up old men and breaking into new houses in the Oldpark. They were told in no uncertain terms to join up or take a bullet in the leg. Most were well known as rioters, and by 1984 Adair had a criminal record that was typical of many youths from his area. Since 1979 he had been before the courts an average of three times a year. He had not mellowed as he left his teenage years behind him. On 16 May 1983, he appeared before Belfast Magistrates' Court and was fined £30 for disorderly behaviour, one of many such convictions during this period. On 1 July, the same court found him guilty of criminal damage and ordered him to pay a fine of £50 and the same again in compensation. His quick temper and refusal to back down were repeatedly landing him in trouble.

At the end of October 1983, Adair and Skelly went to London for a skinhead concert and became involved in a bad fight. On 2 November, Camberwell Magistrates' Court in south London ordered Adair to pay £100 compensation for assault occasioning actual bodily harm. Back in Belfast, it was not long before he was arrested again. On 2 May 1984, he was fined £25 by Belfast Magistrates' Court for riotous behaviour, while on 27 September he was convicted of disorderly behaviour and forced to pay £50.

It was little surprise that Adair and his friends were attracting the attention of their local paramilitaries. But although they were regularly breaking the law, there was nothing to suggest that any of them would go on to do anything more sinister than rioting. 'We were all rioting,' said one childhood friend who later moved away from the Shankill. 'The Johnny Adair I knew is not the Johnny Adair that emerged later. I can honestly put my hand on my heart and say that, although he was occasionally slightly crazy, he was not a psychopath. Where that came from I don't know, but it must have been something that happened in his early 20s.'

Neither Adair nor his friends had previously even toyed with the idea of joining the UDA or the UVF, the two main loyalist paramilitary groups. Although the UDA, which was formed in 1971 as a network of vigilante groups and at one point had more than 40,000 members, was born on the Shankill and continued to have a strong power base in the area, in the first years of the 1980s most youths of Adair's generation regarded it as little more than an overgrown working men's club. It had little appeal to him and his friends, who had no respect at all for its authority. The organisation had far more to gain by recruiting them than they did by joining. For the UDA there was an element of opportunism: it saw them as a source of extra money (each volunteer had to pay £1 a week in dues), but also needed fit young men to put on the streets and to rob banks. The UDA was able to openly recruit new members: to the disgust of nationalists, it was technically legal though its killing arm, the Ulster Freedom Fighters, was not. 'Back when we were standing at Century Street corner none of us was in anything, but because we were doing a bit of arsing about the UDA were called to sort us out and they gave people no choice but to join,' explained 'John'.

Over a period of several months in 1984, the UDA swore in a healthy new intake of volunteers, including Adair, Skelly, Donald Hodgen, Jackie Thompson and Bobby Harrison, Thompson's uncle. Adair was sworn in on a Friday night in an upstairs room at the Langley Street Social Club, the C Coy bar off Tennent Street. Four masked men stood in front of a table draped in a UDA flag, on top of which was a copy of the Bible and a 9mm pistol. Although Adair claims he does not know who led the ceremony, the hooded figures included Andrew 'Doodles' Calderwood and Sam 'Hinty' Hinton, who between them ran C8. Slowly and deliberately, the UDA's solemn oath was read to Adair and slowly and deliberately he repeated it:

> I, Johnny Adair, am a Protestant by birth and, being convinced of a fiendish plot by republican paramilitaries to destroy my heritage, do swear to defend my comrades and my country, by any and all means, against the Provisional IRA, INLA, and any other offshoot of republicanism which may be of similar intent. I further swear that I will never divulge any information about my comrades to anyone and I am fully aware that the penalty for such an act of treason is death. I willingly take this oath on the Holy Bible witnessed by my peers.

He finished the oath, like all new recruits, by repeating the UDA's Latin motto, '*Quis Separabit*', meaning 'Who Will Come Between Us?'

Adair and his friends went into C8, one of 18 'teams' of between 30 and 60 men which divided C Coy into manageable units based loosely on geography. 'They all wanted to join C8 – it was the most militant and the most popular because it was all headers in it,' said one C8 veteran. Between them the teams covered more than 50 streets stretching from Brown Square at the bottom of the Shankill to Tennent Street half a mile up the road. This was the territory of the UDA's 2nd Battalion C Coy, though in 1984 it was also looking to extend north-east into the Oldpark. Technically the Oldpark was under the control of the UDA's north Belfast brigade but they had repeatedly failed to get volunteers down during riots with nationalists, largely because they had to cross republican areas to do this. By the start of 1984, large parts of the Oldpark were being rebuilt and many Protestant families moved into the neighbourhood from the Shankill, providing the ideal opportunity for C Coy to take over. C8 took most of the new recruits from the area, though there were also several who joined C9.

Like most volunteers in the 1980s, Adair did relatively little to begin with. He paid his dues and attended C8 meetings, but was otherwise busy with the arrival of his first child, Jonathan, who was born on 23 August 1984, just days after the riots ended. He also had a new home to tend to. In the middle of 1984, Adair and Gina Crossan, his girlfriend, moved into 10 Beechnut Place, one of a new development of council houses off the Oldpark Road. It was a tight-knit community and just around the corner from his parents in Century Street. Adair's new neighbours included Ian Truesdale, a young C9 member two years older than himself who had followed his two older brothers into the UDA. Truesdale's house, at 113 Manor Street, backed onto Adair's. 'The back of my house was the back of his house,' he recalled. 'He used to run in and out of my house and I'd run in and out of his.' At this time Adair was still working at the Ulster Timber Company in Duncrue Street in the docks area. 'He was getting a house, having kids, working and leading an ordinary life,' said Truesdale. 'He was going to the meetings and all but he didn't just join the UDA and go straight into being a gunman. You have to work your way up. He'd have gone to the meetings, started to know who was who, sat back and done his homework before saying, "I want a piece of the action."'

Adair himself is vague about his early UDA career and his memory of these years has been badly damaged by years of glue sniffing. He says he tried to join the Ulster Defence Regiment (UDR), Northern Ireland's locally recruited Army regiment, but was turned down after attending several recruitment meetings on the Malone Road in south Belfast. 'I tried to join the UDR to do something legitimate to protect our country from the IRA, but because of a few minor criminal convictions they wouldn't let me in – things like breach of the peace, rioting,' he told one of the authors. 'They [the Army] must have realised. They probably realised I had criminal convictions or was on the periphery of the paramilitaries. I regretted it [not being able to join]. I would have been an extra pair of hands to stop republicans from destroying the country.' The claim, like many others he makes, must be taken with a large pinch of salt. Adair is shrewd enough to realise that the story helps to paint him as a victim of his circumstances. Like others of his generation, Adair held strong views about the IRA and Britain's failure to defend Northern Ireland's Protestant majority, but he did not become a paramilitary because of his political beliefs. He joined the UDA because he had no choice, drifting into it with his friends and giving little thought to the future. It was only once he realised that he was good at organising those around him that he became ambitious to do more. There was no single turning point, though many events affected him. As Adair himself put it, 'It was every day – every day when I was waking up and hearing UDR and police being murdered on a daily basis and towns and villages blown to smithereens. Every day was a turning point, every single day.'

During Adair's first two years as a UDA foot soldier, the most he was involved in was shooting at police, taking part in punishment beatings, robbery and arson. In 1986, he was also given the role of being a look-out for Tucker Lyttle, the UDA's west Belfast brigadier. According to 'John', 'Tucker was getting a couple of death threats and Johnny sort of got the job of watching out – he was given a couple of pounds a week to watch Tucker's motor and watch for Tucker coming out of the house.'

But for most of the 1980s Adair's bread and butter was still rioting, and there was plenty to keep him busy. On 15 November 1985, Margaret Thatcher and Garret FitzGerald, the Irish Prime Minister, signed the Anglo-Irish Agreement at Hillsborough Castle outside Belfast. For the first time, Dublin was given a direct say in the internal administration of Northern Ireland and a 'secretariat' for Irish government officials was established at Maryfield, Co. Down. Among Unionists, the agreement went down like a lead balloon. Never one to mince his words, the Rev. Ian Paisley called on God to strike down Mrs Thatcher. 'We pray this night that thou wouldst deal with the Prime Minister of our country,' he told his congregation. 'We remember that the Apostle Paul handed over the enemies of truth to the Devil that they might learn not to blaspheme. O God, in wrath take vengeance upon this wicked, treacherous lying woman. Take vengeance upon her, oh Lord, and grant that we shall see a demonstration of thy power.'

Britain had committed the ultimate betrayal. On 20 November, Tom

C8 AND THE YOUNG TURKS

King, the Secretary of State for Northern Ireland, was attacked by a crowd of loyalists as he visited Belfast City Hall. His attackers included George Seawright, a firebrand loyalist councillor from the top of the Shankill who had been expelled from Paisley's Democratic Unionist Party (DUP) a year earlier after saying the council should buy an incinerator to burn Catholics.

On 23 November, Adair was among more than 100,000 people who attended a huge 'Ulster Says No' rally outside the City Hall. William 'Moe' Courtney, who attended the rally with Adair, recalled how he and other loyalists felt at the time. 'The atmosphere was very twitchy. I thought we were on the rocky road to Dublin, to be quite honest with you. I actually thought we already had one foot there. There was a large, large crowd that day and I think everybody in Northern Ireland – well, on the Unionist side – felt the same.'

Over the next few months Adair and his friends were in the thick of rioting as civil unrest swept loyalist areas. On 3 March, nearly 50 policemen were hurt during a Unionist 'Day of Action' that brought much of the Province to a halt. In April, the riots worsened after 20-year-old Keith White became the first and only Protestant to be killed by a plastic bullet, fired after trouble flared at an Apprentice Boys march in Portadown. C8 was heavily involved in the Shankill area, where the violence simmered throughout the year. It peaked with the first anniversary of the agreement in November, when Alan McCormick, a 29-year-old Protestant, was killed after being struck by a police Land-Rover during rioting at the top of the Crumlin Road. On at least one occasion, Adair and Skelly, wearing masks this time, opened fire on a police patrol as it came up the Shankill Road. According to an eyewitness, who knew both men, they burst out of an entry on the lower Shankill and assumed a textbook firing position, Adair crouching on the ground and Skelly standing behind him. They yelled at the crowd to move and opened fire. The bullets bounced harmlessly off the armoured Land-Rovers but they had made their point. 'We opened up on the peelers a couple of times,' said 'John', who was not involved in that attack but was with Adair on similar occasions. 'There was a few shooting incidents in and around that particular time. There was that many, to be honest, that it's hard to remember.'

Adair and his friends were fast gaining a reputation for their desire to get stuck in. Not long after the signing of the Anglo-Irish Agreement, a C8 team, including Adair, Skelly, Donald Hodgen and Jackie Thompson, crept into a local factory and set fire to a fleet of vans. The company, Pork

Produce on the Hillview Road, had been employing too many Catholics for their liking. 'It was mostly all taigs that worked in it so we decided to burn the vans. We went in one night and there must have been about a dozen torched,' recalled 'John'. It was typical of the operations Adair was involved in at that time, but for him and his friends it did not go far enough.

Following the Anglo-Irish Agreement there was a massive intake of new recruits into the UDA's ranks and nowhere more so than in west Belfast. According to Moe Courtney, C Coy alone nearly doubled in size between the end of 1985 and 1987, from around 1,000 to 1,700 members. A and B companies – the other two divisions in west Belfast, representing the upper and mid-Shankill areas respectively – enjoyed a similar influx of new volunteers. While the vast majority took no part in active military operations – carried out under the cover name of the Ulster Freedom Fighters (UFF) – many foot soldiers were calling for a more proactive terrorist campaign against republicans and nationalists. Since the early 1980s, the UFF had been virtually non-existent, particularly in west Belfast, where the level of military operations was kept to a minimum by Tommy 'Tucker' Lyttle, the UDA brigadier who was also a paid Special Branch informer. But the Anglo-Irish Agreement was to change all that. 'I noticed an awful lot more activity starting within our own ranks – preparing for assassinations, preparations, a bit of training and more recruiting,' said Courtney. 'The training at that stage got more serious. We went off on training days outside Belfast – Co. Derry, in that direction.'

The exact location was a farm in Magilligan Point in Co. Derry, on the edge of the Atlantic Ocean and about two hours' drive from Belfast. The training camp was run by Ken Kerr, a former Royal Marine and UDA member who later became a leading figure in the Ulster Democratic Party (UDP), the UDA's political wing. It was not used for weapons instruction but rather for teaching a series of basic military and survival skills, initiative tests and fitness training. Above all, it was intended for young volunteers who had been singled out as 'officer material' by the UDA's hierarchy and selected to join a special outfit called the Ulster Defence Force (UDF). The brainchild of John McMichael, the UDA's second-in-command and head of the UFF, it was initially formed in 1983 and was already well established by the time of the Anglo-Irish Agreement. Its teachers included Brian Nelson, a former British soldier, who taught volunteers how to map-read and operate radio equipment, and Sam 'Hinty' Hinton, who taught them drill. The volunteers were normally brought down on a Friday, spending three nights camping out before going home the next Monday. In the words of one UDA 'brigadier', 'The UDF was meant to be like Sandhurst or something. The idea was that the people in it would have no criminal record and a squeaky-clean image, but the training camp became more of a physical thing than anything else.' It was no easy ride, as one former instructor recalled: 'Ken Kerr was a terrible man. He used to put jam around a tree that you had to climb as part of the assault course and it would attract all the wasps and bees. There used to be all sorts of challenges. One guy had to get dropped in Dublin with 15p and he had to find his way home. Up at the camp you used to get £1 to survive for three days. You were in a team of four and you had to decide what to do – what to buy with your money and all that.'

As it seemed increasingly clear to loyalists that the Government was preparing to hand control of Northern Ireland to Dublin, the UDF also began studying 'Doomsday' scenarios. The idea was to create a private army ready to defend Ulster in her hour of crisis. Maps were drawn up showing military bases, airports and other strategic installations such as radio stations and important commercial centres, but the Doomsday plans were never put into effect. The UDF was doomed from the start because there was nothing for its members to progress onto once they had completed their silver and gold 'wings'. It was also compromised by the large number of volunteers with criminal records who took part in the training, undermining its core principle. Among those who blagged their way onto the course by lying about their brushes with the law were Johnny Adair and several of his friends. 'Johnny got his silver wings before he was kicked out – Big Donald [Hodgen] and Skelly did as well,' said one C Coy veteran who was a frequent visitor to the camp. 'At one time just about everyone was getting up for a weekend.'

Many young UDA militants were now convinced that the time had come for more than just training. While John McMichael had long felt that it was probably necessary to take Northern Ireland to the brink of civil war before a compromise could be agreed between her two communities, the leadership in west Belfast was not so happy about a resurgence in UFF activity. It tried to ignore the militants – the 'Young Turks' as they became known – but could not do so forever. Moe Courtney believes that the Anglo-Irish Agreement was a turning point for the UFF. 'That's when I believe that the UFF stood up and said to themselves, "Right, let's be counted here, let's go for it." As I say, there was a recruiting drive – guns didn't seem to be a problem, men didn't seem to be a problem and the intelligence didn't seem to be a problem. It was just how we managed it that was the problem.'

The inevitable finally happened on 26 August 1986, when Paddy McAllister, a 47-year-old Catholic with four children, was shot dead as he watched television in his home off the Falls Road in nationalist west Belfast. He worked as a black taxi driver, an occupation that marked him out as a republican sympathiser in the eyes of loyalists. In the aftermath of the murder, Andy Tyrie, the UDA's supreme commander, described it as 'totally justified'. It was an ominous warning that loyalists, who had never been particularly discriminate in their targeting, would have few qualms about shooting members of the nationalist community who were viewed by most people as innocent Catholics. The UFF had already killed one person that year, a Protestant woman in north Belfast, but the McAllister murder was different: it was C Coy's first 'hit' in nearly five years. The last it had carried out was in November 1981, when Artie Bettice, one of its own, was shot dead in the Shankill home he rented from Ian Truesdale's brother, Freddie. The UDA had suspected him of being an RUC informer.

By the time Paddy McAllister was shot dead in 1986, Johnny Adair was just starting to take part in C Coy murder bids. In the summer of 1985, William 'Winkie' Dodds had been released from jail after serving six years for robbing a post office. The 27-year-old Oldpark man started running C8 and shortly became C Coy's military commander. To police he was known as 'the Big Evil' but to his friends he was 'Stinky Winkie'. A quiet, thick-set man with a pistol tattooed on his left forearm, Dodds was a dedicated sectarian killer. One of his oldest friends was Moe Courtney, a young C8 man three months older than Adair who had been in the UDA since the age of 15. A petty thief, Courtney had been threatened and beaten by his own organisation for breaking into houses on the Shankill but calmed down once Dodds came out of jail. With his stocky build, square face and no front teeth, Courtney looked like a Chicago gangster. 'Even back then I don't think he had teeth,' said Dodds' wife, Maureen. 'Moe hasn't had teeth for as long as I can remember, and then he'd have [false] teeth but he'd go out and get drunk and lose them.'

Dodds took Courtney under his wing but he was also keen to bring on Adair and his friends, most of whom he knew from growing up in the Oldpark. It was Winkie who showed Adair how to use and fire a gun.

C8 AND THE YOUNG TURKS

According to 'John', a C8 member who was close to Adair in the 1980s, there was little formal weapons instruction and it was a question of learning as you went along. Winkie was the main source of help, though occasionally there were others. 'We never really got any formal weapons training. I think once we were shown how to use a gun in The Ultimate [a community centre in the lower Shankill]. We weren't actually stripping anything, there was just somebody who brought down an old .22 handgun and we fired a load of shots. I think it was a Walter PPK.'

In 1986, 'John' went out on his first murder bid accompanied by Adair: 'It was Johnny, me and Bobby Harrison. What happened was we were let down because somebody else was meant to go on it with them and they asked me to go. It was up the Oldpark. Somebody supplied information on a republican and we went out with a shotgun and a Magnum and we rapped the door and your man came out but he slammed the door shut. There was a wee windie down the door and he was shot through the windie but he didn't die or anything. I had the shotgun, Johnny had the Magnum and Bobby was driving the car. Bobby went to drive off without Johnny in the motor. I put the shotgun to his head and told him to fucking stop. He was panicking. Johnny would have been left in the street otherwise. It was the last time Bobby went out on a job with us.'

'John' believes the operation took place not long after Adair had come out of hospital, where he had spent weeks recovering after being badly injured in a fight. Adair was in intensive care for several days after he was stabbed by a Protestant from Mountview Street off the Oldpark Road. As Winkie Dodds recalled, 'It was kids fighting or something and Johnny played the hard man and tried to sort it out. Him and Skelly went to the guy's house with a replica gun and he just bounced out and stuck a knife in him, straight in his back.' Skelly, who was with Adair, was also stabbed. According to Adair's sister Jeanie, her brother was in a terrible state. The timing could not have been worse, with Gina, his girlfriend, pregnant with the couple's second child, Natalie. 'The blood was pumping out of him, it was everywhere,' Jeanie said. 'He somehow made it back to the house and just collapsed in the street outside. Gina was wiping up the blood but the police later told her she shouldn't have done, that she was interfering with the scene of a crime.' Adair lost his spleen and punctured a lung. 'All the family were called to see him – we thought that was it, he was about to die.' Adair pulled through, though he was weak for several months and has never worked since.

It was a difficult time for him. In February 1985, his old friend, Mark Rosborough, had been found dead on a rubbish tip after being savagely beaten by three UVF men. It was Rosborough's belated comeuppance, having left the brother of one of his attackers with brain damage after a beating six years earlier. The 21-year-old suffered an excruciating end. After his face was smashed in, a gun was produced and he was shot in the back of the head. Amazingly, he was still alive. He was choked with a belt, which snapped, and then a length of wire, but he still refused to die. It was not until his assailants placed a mat over his head and stood on it for 15 minutes that he finally died. He was so badly disfigured that he had to be identified by his tattoos.

In 1986, Adair lost another friend, this time through his own doing. Maurice Drumgoole was one of several passengers in a car Adair was driving when it crashed just outside Belfast. Adair had no licence and was also drunk. They were on their way to Ballyclare when the car veered off the road just beyond the famous Horseshoe Bend in north Belfast. 'John', who was supposed to be going with them that night but stayed on the Shankill, said, 'The car hit the bank and went onto the roof. They all got out and Maurice Drumgoole was alright but then he just collapsed and died.' According to another old friend, 'What killed Maurice Drumgoole was the fact that they all landed on him when the car tipped. The weight of it broke his neck. He got up and he walked over and sat on the footpath, but then he just keeled over. It affected Johnny very badly. After that he thought he was indebted to the Drumgoole family.' On 19 November 1986, Adair appeared at Antrim Magistrates' Court and was convicted of reckless driving, driving whilst under the influence of drink and without insurance or a licence. He was sentenced to six months' imprisonment, banned from driving for three years and fined £150. After losing an appeal, he was jailed at Crumlin Road Prison in Belfast in February 1987.

When he came out in June, Adair vowed to devote himself to his girlfriend and their two young children and to keep a low profile. It was fine in theory, but in reality it was never going to happen. The lure of his friends was always too great to resist, and as usual Adair had to be the centre of attention. Within weeks, under the guidance of Winkie Dodds, he was going out on regular murder attempts. According to 'John', 'Whenever we started coming through there was no real attacks against republicans. Winkie Dodds was in jail for robbing a post office but when he got out of jail he started doing a bit of operating and he was running C8. We were in bed with him and we started doing a bit of operating and you gradually build into it.'

Dodds and Courtney took Adair out on several occasions but without success. He and his friends, all in their mid-20s and keen to prove themselves, were now racing each other for their first kill. They did not have to wait long. On 9 September 1987, two UFF gunmen shot dead Patrick Hamill, an English Catholic, at his home off the Falls Road in nationalist west Belfast. According to police intelligence, the killers included a C8 volunteer who was one of Adair's oldest friends. Aged 29, Hamill was shot in the middle of his forehead as his wife nursed their 11-month-old baby girl, Catherine, while her 3-year-old sister played on the floor. Within hours of Hamill's murder, a Protestant lorry driver, 38-year-old Harry Sloan, was shot dead in retaliation by the IRA.

Next up was Sam 'Skelly' McCrory. At 7.30 a.m. on 9 October, wearing a balaclava and a blue boiler suit, he shot dead a Catholic pensioner at his home in the nationalist Ballymurphy estate. The murder of Francisco Notarantonio became one of the most controversial of the Troubles. Almost immediately there were allegations of collusion between loyalists and the security forces, while years later it was claimed that Notarantonio had been set up to stop the UFF from targeting another Catholic of Italian descent, an IRA double agent known by the codename 'Stakeknife'. The 66-year-old was shot in the chest and back as he got out of bed, his wife still dozing beside him. A retired black taxi driver, Notarantonio had been a member of the IRA during the 1940s and had been interned in the 1970s. He had 11 children. The murder was ordered by Winkie Dodds, who picked Notarantonio's name off a security forces' photomontage sheet supplied by Brian Nelson, the UDA's head of intelligence in west Belfast who was also an Army informer. Notarantonio was nicknamed 'the Ice Cream Man' because he was Italian. 'Davy', a Shankill gunman from this era, admitted, 'We were told he was an ex-republican. He was a republican, there's no two ways about it.' He insisted that Notarantonio was always the person they intended to kill, not Stakeknife. Even though Notarantonio was no longer active in the IRA, to C Coy he was a legitimate target.

By late 1987, C Coy operations were being mounted with increasing frequency. In the same month that Notarantonio was shot dead, a C Coy team attempted to murder the IRA's Danny McCann, who was killed by the SAS in Gibraltar the following March. According to one of those involved, the operation came 'very, very close . . . We actually jumped a front windie of his mother's house and the Danny boy actually got over the wall. He escaped by the skin of his teeth. That was just before Gibraltar.' He added: 'The ASU [active service unit] had him tied down to a butcher's shop, his father's butcher's shop where he worked on the Falls Road, and on a number of occasions they went to do him but getting away from there with police activity and all in the area was near enough impossible. He was actually targeted at the butcher's. The intelligence was there on him that he worked in the butcher's, but the people that was actually watching the butcher's says, "Too dodgy here, we'll tail him home." He was tailed home and that's when the operation was put into place. He was actually in the house and the UFF came knocking on his door. They went straight through the windie after him, but I gather there was a bit of confusion in the house and Danny was able to get away. His mother and father was actually in the house.'

Over the next few months C Coy members were involved in several murders and attempted murders. In January 1988, the UFF shot dead Jack Kielty, 44, whose son, Patrick, would go on to become a successful comedian. His death was ordered by C Coy's Jimmy Craig, who was suing Central Television after its programme, *The Cook Report*, accused him of racketeering. Kielty, who worked in a building firm in Dundrum, Co. Down, was to be the main witness in the television company's defence. According to 'Davy', the hit team included volunteers from B Coy and C Coy. 'It was actually B Coy that did it, carried out on behalf of west Belfast, but there would have been somebody from C Coy in the ASU.'

Four months later the Winkie Dodds squad were at it again. On 10 May 1988, Terence McDaid was sitting in his home in north Belfast with his wife, his mother and father when two gunmen burst in and shot him several times in the head and back. The 29-year-old bricklayer and his wife had just put their two daughters to bed when the killers arrived. It was just after 10 p.m. 'We were in the house with Terry's mother and father, who always came round on a Tuesday night,' McDaid's widow, Maura, told a newspaper in October 1991.

> Tracy and Patricia had their juice and their biscuits and we had our tea. I said to them, 'Say night-night to Daddy and Nanny and Granda and get to bed because you've to get up for school in the morning.' I put them in their bunks. I normally say their prayers with them but that night I didn't. I said, 'Say a quick Hail Mary and go to sleep quickly, I'm away down.' Soon after I went downstairs

and sat down there was this horrendous thundering noise, it was a terrible noise. Terry and I just sat and stared at one another. At that the living-room door flew back to the wall. Two men were standing at the door, they were completely clothed, there was no flesh to be seen. They ran in and kept shooting around the room. It was deafening. I screamed at them to get out, get out. I shouted, 'There's nobody here, there's nobody here, go away, go away, stop it, stop it, stop it.'

Maura hit one of the attackers with the hose of a vacuum cleaner, but she could do nothing to stop them killing her husband. He was shot seven times in the head and back, his youngest daughter running downstairs just in time to see her father dying on the floor. The 1992 trial of Brian Nelson heard that Winkie Dodds approached Nelson a week before the murder and asked for republican targets. Nelson gave him the name of Declan McDaid and supplied him with a photograph. But the killers were sent to the wrong address, where they found a man who looked almost identical to Declan McDaid but was in fact his younger brother. When Nelson remonstrated with Dodds, he was told the dead man 'looked like the picture'. 'We got the wrong fella,' said Winkie. 'I didn't know that. I mean, the boys went in to see this fella that looks like him . . . what are they supposed to do, go up and ask his name?'

Another murder that featured heavily in Nelson's trial was that of Gerard Slane. In the early hours of 23 September 1988, the 27-year-old was gunned down at his home off the Falls Road. At around 4 a.m. Slane's wife, Teresa, heard noises outside the house and got up to see what it was. She later recalled: 'John had just bought a new car and there was a British Army foot patrol at the front of the house radioing through his new registration, the way they always do. So I came back to bed and told Gerard what I'd saw and we went back to sleep. That was about four in the morning. The next thing I remember is waking up with this commotion going on, with Gerard running up the stairs shouting, "Teresa, it's the Orangemen." Then they opened fire on him.'

She said that her husband had probably heard the sound of breaking glass and had gone downstairs to investigate. Halfway down the stairs he was met by four armed intruders. 'Five of them came that night. One of them sat on the bonnet of the car with a rifle, while the other four sledgehammered their way into the house and came up the stairs. After

Gerard shouted at me, all I heard were these popping noises and I saw flashes and then I heard a thud. I got up and rushed down the stairs to see if Gerard had been shot, but when I got onto the landing they turned the light off downstairs, and when I turned it on Gerard was lying there and I knew he was dead. His hand was raised, then it just went limp and fell. I ran outside screaming, cutting my feet on the glass in the hall from where they had smashed their way in and the first thing I saw was the sledgehammer they had used to break their way into the house.'

Most of Slane's face was blown off and one bullet had ripped off his nose. His next-door neighbour heard the shots and looked out of the window to see Slane's 'little boy, his son, in his pyjamas, and in such distress and grief that he was jumping up and down in the front garden, lacerating his feet on the broken glass from the front door where the killers had smashed their way in'. Slane had received a two-year prison sentence in September 1985 after a rifle was found in the outside lavatory at his house. But the judge suspended the sentence, believing his protests that somebody else had stashed the weapon. Despite denials from his family, his killers claimed that he had driven the getaway car used in the murder of C Coy's Billy Quee two weeks earlier. The 32-year-old UDA man was shot dead by gunmen from the breakaway Irish People's Liberation Organisation (IPLO) as he stood outside his shop on the Oldpark Road. The UDA's magazine, *Ulster*, claimed that Slane had been murdered in revenge. 'This individual will never again rob a wife of her husband and her children a father,' it trumpeted.

The UDA had obtained a photo of Slane from Nelson, and two eyewitnesses to Quee's murder – one of whom was Norman Truesdale – identified Slane as the getaway driver. In January 1992, Nelson made a statement admitting that he had handed the picture to Jim Spence, B Coy's commander. According to Nelson, Spence told him, 'I'll soon deal with him. We can't have these bastards getting away with this.' He later added, 'It was a gift. You wouldn't fucking believe it. The same day you give me the card, I sent two young bucks down to have a look at the house. They came rushing back and they were very excited, saying, "Fuck me, he's standing outside his door where you said his house was."'

In later years, Johnny Adair recounted in graphic detail how he had stood at the bottom of Gerard Slane's stairs and peppered him with gunfire. One friend said, 'I remember Johnny telling us, "Your man stood at the top of the stairs and as I went up after him I sprayed him from top to bottom, started on the legs and then worked my way all the way up, just cut the fucker in half."' It was typical of Adair's bragging, which was usually intended to instil in his audience a mixture of fear and admiration. As the friend recalled, 'He would turn to us and say, "Well, do you think you could do that, could you?"'

In fact, the boast was a total lie. Adair was not even at the scene of the murder, though he sat and listened with an expression of childlike awe as one of the killers talked him through the gory details. 'What did he look like?' Adair asked. 'Where did the blood go? Did he say anything? Did you look in his eyes?' Two of his oldest friends had already been 'blooded' but not him, and that hurt his ego. He saw no reason for facts to spoil the image, which he sought to promote at every opportunity, that C Coy's Johnny Adair was a ruthless killer. Possibly by way of consolation, talking about his alleged participation in murders, and observing the reaction this produced, became one of his great pleasures. Years later he even made the claim that he had once been knifed by a group of Catholics and inflicted a gruesome revenge along with Donald Hodgen and Skelly. After tracing four of his attackers to a flat where they were playing poker, Adair and his friends tied them to their chairs, doused them in petrol and set them alight. They were burned alive, screaming in agony as they died in unbearable pain. The story, told a decade later to Jackie 'Legs' Robinson, Adair's girlfriend for most of the 1990s, was packed with a wealth of detail, including what Adair and his friends had been wearing (boiler suits) and how they had found their enemies. In reality, the entire episode came straight from Johnny Adair's imagination. He was a lively storyteller, but he often took it too far. Even in his own mind there was only the thinnest of lines dividing fact from fantasy, and on occasions there was no line at all.

3. Who Shot Pat Finucane?

'I think, er, the UFF made it quite clear that day, they didn't shoot dead a solicitor. They shot dead Pat Finucane, the IRA man.' – 'Davy', a UFF gunman, who confessed to the murder in an interview with one of the authors

'DAVY' WILL NEVER FORGET THE MOMENT HE ARRIVED AT PATRICK FINUCANE'S house to shoot him dead. As he stepped out of the hijacked taxi he was astonished to see that the front door of the house was wide open. It suddenly seemed that killing the solicitor, who for months had been a priority target for C Coy, would be much easier than he and his colleagues had imagined. A 25-year-old from the Shankill, 'Davy' had been through thick and thin with the UDA since joining as a teenager in 1978, but he believed that this would be the moment that would make him. Two weeks earlier, two west Belfast hitmen had set off with their weapons but had been forced to turn back because of police activity in the north of the city. This time it looked like they were going to have better luck. Alongside 'Davy' was another west Belfast gunman and Ken Barrett, a B Coy volunteer with a growing reputation as an eager assassin who would shoot just about anybody if he was given a gun and pointed in the right direction. Tonight Barrett was the driver.

It was 7.25 p.m. on Sunday, 12 February 1989. The police were nowhere to be seen, a fact that would later be cited as evidence of dirty tricks by the Finucane family who claimed that only an hour earlier roadblocks had been in place close to the house. According to 'Davy', he and his fellow assassin, armed and masked, made off down the driveway towards the front door. They walked straight into the vestibule where they kicked open an inner door and charged up the hallway. Fourteen shots rang out as Barrett waited outside in a red Ford Sierra. It had been stolen earlier that evening from a Protestant taxi driver in the Forthriver estate in west Belfast. The driver, William Reid, told police that the three men who hijacked his car had seemed nervous and panicky. While this may have been the case for two of them, the third, as always in these situations, was just being hyper. According to 'Davy', it was Johnny Adair. He had performed the role many times as he advanced through the ranks of C Coy in the late 1980s. He had stolen the car used by the killers of Terry McDaid, the 29-year-old Catholic shot dead by the UFF in May 1988. In March 1990 he would hijack the taxi used in the murder of Eamon Quinn, a Catholic gunned down by the UFF as he worked on his car outside his house.

Those murders were quickly forgotten by the wider public, but the killing of Pat Finucane was not. Almost immediately, allegations were made of collusion between the security forces and the UDA, raising the prospect that the British state had wanted the solicitor dead and even helped to set up the murder. For the UDA, Finucane's death remains one of its most celebrated moments. It was the first assassination of a lawyer in Northern Ireland and as such set a new low in the conflict – or high, as far as the UDA was concerned. Adair, jealous of the role 'Davy' had played in such an infamous murder, would later dismiss it using his standard phrase, 'Sure, you don't get medals for ones like that.' He was hopelessly wrong. To most loyalists the murder was a chilling execution, carried out with a clinical cold-bloodedness that showed what the UFF was capable of if it put its mind to it. Finucane was shot dead when he least expected it, as he sat in the comfort of his home eating Sunday dinner with his wife and three children. At least one of the shots fired into his head was from a range of just 15 inches. The other 13 bullets, fired from two separate guns, struck him in the head, neck and torso. He died on his kitchen floor still clutching a fork in his right hand, leading loyalists to give him the sick nickname 'Fork Finucane'.

At 38, Finucane, a Catholic whose family had been burnt out of the Falls Road when the Troubles erupted in 1969, was one of the most high-profile lawyers in Belfast. His large detached house in Fortwilliam Drive off the Antrim Road was testimony to his professional success. His career had been built around the republican movement's decision to abandon its traditional approach of not recognising the British legal system, and he was one of several lawyers who persuaded republicans to fight their cases in the courts and to challenge Britain's record on human rights. To the outside world Finucane was the solicitor for well-known IRA men such as Bobby Sands, the hunger striker, and Patrick McGeown. At the height of the Troubles it was hardly surprising if many Protestants believed that there was a thin line at best between a solicitor who represented IRA members and the IRA itself. Militant loyalists needed little encouragement to suspect the worst, and their suspicions were heightened by the fact that three of Finucane's brothers – John, who died in a car crash in 1972, Dermot and Seamus – were known to have joined the Provisionals.

The UDA made no distinction between Finucane and his brothers, and the day after the shooting it admitted responsibility for 'the execution of Pat Finucane the PIRA [Provisional IRA] officer, not the solicitor'. But despite its claims, the relationship between Pat Finucane and the IRA remains unclear to this day. One person who knew the lawyer better than most is Kevin Sheehy, a Catholic from Glengormley, outside Belfast, and a former Detective Superintendent in the RUC. He spent several summers with the teenage Finucane working at a canning factory in England, and forged a close friendship with him at Trinity College, Dublin, where the pair were both students and lived in the same house. Sheehy believes that the solicitor played an advisory role to the republican movement, though he doubts he was ever a fully fledged IRA member.

After leaving Trinity, Sheehy still kept in touch with his old friend, even though their careers took them in sharply different directions. He recalled, 'I didn't see so much of him except three or four times a year, when we'd get an invite to Geraldine and Pat's house for dinner. Inevitably after dinner the topic of conversation turned to politics and the women used to complain. Pat and I had different points of view. I was very much a unionist committed to the police and committed to the established order. Pat was a republican, committed to the end of British involvement in Ireland. Some of the discussions became heated and the women used to come into the room to complain about raised voices and noise, but they were never bitter discussions and there was never any possibility of coming to blows. In the end we always agreed to differ. During discussions with Pat, I always put the issue of IRA violence to him. As far as I was concerned, Pat Finucane was an intellectual republican who believed in the theory of republicanism and I think if that is your belief then inevitably armed struggle becomes the basis of your thought. Pat had a full appreciation that to be a republican meant you had to give credit and understanding, and at least tacit support, to a violent, orchestrated campaign. I also know that Pat, through his legal work, saw himself as defending IRA prisoners in court and so on and I think that he saw that as his major contribution to it.' Sheehy added, 'I believe he played an advisory role to the republican leadership. They would take advice on how to reply to documents and so forth. I believe Pat, along with other legal experts, was giving advice on the preparation of republican responses to Government positions. Like Gerry Adams, he knew that if the republican movement were to be credible it had to be in a position to respond intelligently.'

After an investigation spanning 14 years, Sir John Stevens, the Metropolitan Police Commissioner, concluded in April 2003 that there was collusion between the UDA and the security forces in the murder of Pat Finucane. His findings, contained in a 3,000-page report, are based on the roles allegedly played by two pivotal figures: Brian Nelson, the UDA's intelligence officer in west Belfast and an agent for the Army's top-secret Force Research Unit, and Billy Stobie, a UDA quartermaster and a £20-a-week informer for the RUC's Special Branch. In addition to supplying a photograph of Finucane, Nelson is widely reported to have driven the killers into north Belfast to show them where the solicitor lived. Stobie, who was shot dead by his former UDA colleagues in December 2001, said that he had supplied both weapons for the murder, a 9mm Browning pistol and a revolver. Although Stobie did not know who the target was, he claimed he alerted his Special Branch handlers to an imminent murder attempt and told them the UDA was about to whack a 'top Provie'.

Despite the longest criminal investigation in British history, the identity of Finucane's murderers remains hotly disputed. In the immediate aftermath of the attack, Special Branch believed that the killers were Johnny Adair, who was now second-in-command of C8, Winkie Dodds and A Coy's Matthew Kincaid. Within weeks, however, CID officers had reached their own conclusions. The police inquiry team identified three completely different men who to this day remain the prime suspects in the murder. They believed the main shooter was Barrett, while the 'back-up gunman' was a young C Coy volunteer whose brother later became an active hit man under Johnny Adair. The driver, they believed, was a young man, known simply as Richie, from the Rathcoole estate on the outskirts of Belfast.

Senior UDA figures, however, tell a very different story. They insist, almost without exception, that the man who 'put down' Pat Finucane was 'Davy'. Either the UDA has orchestrated an unusually sophisticated black propaganda campaign or its members are telling the truth. In an interview for this book, 'Davy' admitted being one of the gunmen and boasted that it was the best 'hit' of his career. He is a C Coy veteran in his early 40s who always dreamed of joining the British Army. Although he has been arrested several times over the Finucane murder, he has never been charged. Until now he has never spoken about his part in the murder and the only people who have questioned him about this are police officers.

'Davy' nodded his head and grinned when asked by one of the authors whether he was the murderer of Pat Finucane. He disclosed that the second gunman was a young west Belfast volunteer who now lives in the Four Winds area in the south of the city; again, this claim is corroborated by his colleagues. 'Davy' may simply be bragging, but if his basic confession is true it raises questions about the part played by B Coy's Ken Barrett, who in a secretly filmed interview with the BBC's *Panorama* admitted being one of the gunmen. 'Davy' claims that Barrett was the driver. He said the same team of volunteers – with one or two changes – was responsible for several murders, including that of Paddy McAllister in August 1986, Terry McDaid in May 1988, Gerard Slane in September 1988, and Eamon Quinn in March 1990. By February 1989 they were experienced assassins. This is an edited version of the interview, which took place in Belfast in May 2003:

Where was that Finucane operation actually put together?
Well, it was in west Belfast. Pat Finucane was actually supposed to die two weeks before it, believe it or believe it not. And the ASU just couldn't get in and out the way it did.
Was it a reconnaissance run?
Well, let's say it was a dummy run, it was two weeks before it. But he was actually supposed to get shot dead two weeks before it and certain things just couldn't allow it to happen. So them guns was actually there, in the same place, for over two weeks, without anybody knowing they were there. So for Billy Stobie to turn around and say he told them [his police handlers] that Sunday morning that he handed over guns, the big one was going down, is the biggest load of shit.
Were they on the Shankill estate?
No, they were somewhere safe.

MAD DOG

Outside of Belfast?

No, inside Belfast.

Two weeks before Finucane was shot dead was there too much police around?

Well, there was a bit of activity around the Woodvale, round about Ballysillan. So they couldn't get moving.

But guns did go up?

They did, oh aye. Yes.

Did Johnny Adair have any involvement in it at all?

He was on the periphery of it.

Hijacking?

Hijacking, yes.

Did he organise the hijacking?

He lifted the car, yes.

And would he have done that on his own?

No, no, there was a few people up with him. The taxi sign and all had to be taken off the car, you know.

And all this about Brian Nelson a few weeks beforehand taking you up there, showing you up there?

He never showed any of us it, I can assure you of that.

So how did that all come out?

I don't know.

What was Nelson's involvement?

Nelson supplied one photo. And the photo came out of An Pho-crap magazine [a reference to *An Phoblacht*, the republican newspaper – 'Davy' is talking about a photo in which Finucane is standing next to one of his clients]. No intelligence on him, no address on him, no nothing. That's, er, I think it was your man, what do you call him, the Army corporals, he was walking down the street and it shows you a picture of him, I can just see it now . . . He was acquitted of the Army corporals.

It's Patrick . . .

Patrick McGeown, that's him.

So that was the photo?

That was the photo Brian Nelson supplied.

It's amazing in a way that a photo was needed to be supplied because a lot of you must have known what he looked like from the courts anyway. How was the address found?

Through our own intelligence ASU.

WHO SHOT PAT FINUCANE?

From west Belfast overall or C Coy?

From west Belfast.

Did they follow him?

He was followed on a number of occasions.

See, it's not a terribly difficult thing to do, is it?

No.

Where did you go immediately after the murder? Where would you have gone to clean down?

Oh, we'd have been all split up.

And then did you meet back at a bar?

Well, the next day we'd have met up. We wouldn't have met up that night.

One of the bars around here or Heather Street or somewhere?

Well, it could have been UDA headquarters or somebody's house, you know. More likely the Shankill Road graveyard.

The next day you met at the Shankill Road graveyard?

More than likely, yes.

And Tucker Lyttle's involvement in it? Did he have any involvement in picking the target?

Tucker Lyttle knew nothing about it until that night, you take it from me, until he was dead and all.

So who initially suggested the target?

Well, initially C Coy wanted to kill Pat Finucane and it was turned down, the request was turned down from upstairs.

That was always the way, wasn't it, back then? And who in C Coy? Was that Winkie [Dodds]?

That would have been Winkie, yes.

Winkie was military commander back then?

Mm-hmm.

And what did Winkie and what did you at that time — who did you at that time think Pat Finucane was?

Oh I knew who he was, I knew who he was. It was me who was doing a wee bit of work on him, you know.

What did your enquiries establish about him?

He was an IRA man.

Doing what? Finances? Intelligence?

Everything for the IRA. He was the brains behind the IRA, he was the brains.

Did you . . . I mean . . .

Well, let's put it this way. He was going to strange places at strange times of the night, where he shouldn't have been, i.e. clubs on the Falls Road, barred places.

Were you part of that intelligence ASU that was following him at that time?

I was, yes.

Were you head of that intelligence ASU?

I was.

How long were you following him for?

I followed him, it must have been, I would say for about seven or eight weeks.

On and off?

On and off, yes. Not every day now.

And where would you pick him up from? The courts?

Courts, or else his office or else his home.

And did you see him with a lot of IRA men at that time?

Well, I've seen him with strange people, yes, that's what I done. Identified him with strangers.

Was there anything more damning than that, than the company he kept, in terms of intelligence you had on him?

Well, he kept company with IRA men, make no mistake about it. And that's after hours, like, no mistake about that.

Do you personally think that was the best hit you were ever involved in?

Mm-hmm.

Just because of the person you believe you had killed or the way the operation went so smoothly?

I think it was a combination of both . . . But for me the point is, as I said to you before, every murder is quite unique, you know what I mean, in their own rights.

Later in the interview 'Davy' recalled the moment when he and his UFF colleague entered Finucane's house. He said the front door was 'lying open', but there was a 'wee mortice lock' on an inner door, which had to be forced open. The gunman's account of the front door being open tallies with that of Geraldine Finucane, the dead solicitor's widow, who was shot in the ankle during the attack on her husband. Although reports of the murder frequently refer to the front door having been smashed open with a sledgehammer, this was not the case. Mrs Finucane confirmed, 'The front door was open but the vestibule door was closed'. Asked about the sledgehammer, 'Davy' recounted:

> Well, to be quite honest with you, there was no sledgehammer used.
> *How did you get in?*
> Well, the front door was lying open.
> *You just walked straight in?*
> Well, no, on the other door there was just a wee mortice lock, inside the hall.
> *And when you got to the kitchen, Finucane was trying to shut the door on you?*
> Finucane was trying to shut the door. He was shot through the glass panel in the door.
> *Did the sledgehammer come out at any stage?*
> No.
> *Was it you who coined the name 'Fork Finucane'?*
> Well, what I'm led to believe is that in the interviews when people was arrested, they put down a couple of photos of Pat lying there. And apparently he had a fork in his hand, and that's where that came from.

Although 'Davy' says he never had a conversation with a policeman or soldier about Finucane, it can no longer be doubted that there was collusion in the murder. Finucane's family believe to this day that there was a high-level conspiracy to set him up. Less than a month before he was killed, on January 17, 1989, Douglas Hogg, a junior Home Office minister, told the House of Commons that 'there are in the Province a number of solicitors who are unduly sympathetic to the cause of the IRA'. His comments were based on a private briefing from Sir John Hermon, then RUC Chief Constable, and two senior officers. Mrs Finucane later said that her husband had received threatening phone calls, while some of his clients had been told by police that he would be removed from the scene. At about the same time, young loyalists were emerging from Castlereagh holding centre in east Belfast saying that police had urged them to target Finucane. In a BBC *Panorama* documentary broadcast in June 2002, Ken Barrett said that they would 'come out and said to us what they [police] said about Finucane; they say this and they say that. And they must have said it, because kids wouldn't have come out and say, "they said it about Finucane," because why would [kids] mention Finucane. You understand what I mean? Finucane wouldn't have been a name in their heads.'

In the same interview Barrett made the sensational claim that he had shot dead Finucane, an admission initially made in a taped conversation with Detective Sergeant Johnston 'Jonty' Brown in October 1991. The tape on which the confession was recorded subsequently went missing. It was a disturbing postscript to the story, but by no means the only one. In 1995, the Forensic Laboratory in Northern Ireland inexplicably transferred the Browning pistol used in the murder to the Army, which replaced the barrel and slide of the pistol, destroying potentially vital forensic evidence. In another worrying development, Barrett himself was later recruited as a Special Branch agent. While Jonty Brown had wanted to prosecute Barrett after his confession, Special Branch decided to use the information to convince him to become an informer. He told *Panorama* that Jim Spence, commander of B Coy and one of the 'young Turks' around Adair who would shortly seize control of the UDA in west Belfast, had initially suggested killing the lawyer. Barrett said that Spence arranged for him to meet a Special Branch officer with whom Spence was in regular contact, and the officer claimed that Finucane organised the IRA's finances. According to Barrett, the policeman said that Finucane was a 'thorn in everybody's side' and would 'have to go'.

According to police, the driving force behind the murder was A and B companies. However, C Coy was also looking to kill him, and one team in particular – C8. The team, in which Adair, Sam 'Skelly' McCrory, Donald Hodgen and Jackie Thompson were the rising stars, was actively plotting Finucane's death. 'C8 wanted to go for Finucane, but they [upstairs] wouldn't let us,' revealed 'John', one of Adair's closest friends. He said that C Coy had planned to kill Finucane outside the Crumlin Road Courthouse in north Belfast. 'We had planned to do him at the court. We were going to shoot him as he was getting in the motor but they wouldn't let us do it. We had him under surveillance at the time. He was doing one of the big trials. Once we mentioned it [to the UDA leadership] there seemed to be roadblocks up and around the court every day. We were either going to do him there or as he was getting out of the car to go to his office.'

Throughout the 1980s, Tommy 'Tucker' Lyttle, another Special Branch informer, had been regularly blocking operations put forward by C Coy and the rest of west Belfast, although by 1989 he was facing mounting resistance. Lyttle's lack of involvement in UFF military operations in the late 1980s raises serious questions about the true extent of collusion in the Finucane murder. In reality, the detail of murder attempts was dealt with by Eric McKee, Lyttle's second-in-command and military commander in west Belfast, though it was Lyttle who set the tone for how much activity took place and had the final decision on what happened. The real reason the Finucane murder went ahead was because Lyttle was losing his influence. Accounts from west Belfast UDA figures at this time suggest that he had repeatedly sought to block an attempt on Finucane's life, but by 1989 a new generation of young UDA men was coming of age and they were no longer prepared to take no for an answer.

'It was frustrating,' said 'Davy' of the resistance from Lyttle and the west Belfast leadership. 'They were quite happy enough with one [killing] a year, maybe two a year and everything's OK, let the war go on. But the people down the stairs was getting more and more frustrated. They were becoming more military. Guns didn't seem to be a problem; all equipment didn't seem to be a problem. The men didn't seem to be a problem either, but here we had people up the stairs dictating to the ones down the stairs, you know?' Asked what kind of operations the new militants were looking to mount, he said, 'Murders, attempted murders, bombings. We'd have wanted to do everything. We were all young, we had no fear, we'd have done anything, you know.' The resistance from their superiors was so great that, as Adair and his friends in C8 started to take part in regular operations, Winkie Dodds was asked questions about what they were doing. Whenever they fired a weapon, his volunteers destroyed their clothes to remove forensic evidence, a normal precaution but one that provoked suspicion further up the hierarchy. According to 'John', 'We were burning our clothes a lot and they were only giving us £20 each for new clothes. Eric McKee started pulling Winkie and said, "I hope these ones aren't doing it for the money," which disheartened us a fair bit.'

The leadership of the UDA had a more sophisticated plan at that time. While Tucker Lyttle was unofficially keeping the number of killings to a minimum, John McMichael, the UDA's deputy leader and its chief tactician, was steering the organisation towards establishing a foothold in politics. His paper, 'Common Sense', published in January 1987, argued for a power-sharing executive and became the UDA's primary political platform for many years. McMichael was the closest thing the UDA had to a ruthless strategist in the republican mould: he realised that, although the violence might have to get worse before it could go away, in order to make long-term progress it was necessary to go down the political route. In December 1987, however, McMichael was blown up in a car bomb planted by a team including Sean Savage, one of three IRA volunteers killed by the SAS in Gibraltar the following year. As the team was driving away from McMichael's house, Savage looked back and noticed that the bomb had dropped off the bottom of the car. The team went back and rectified their mistake, sealing McMichael's fate. His loss was a crushing blow to the UDA, removing from the organisation its most charismatic figure and the person most able to give it a coherent vision. As head of its military wing, the UFF, he had won the respect of many young hotheads, including a young Johnny Adair. According to Adair, McMichael was the UDA's only military leader in the early 1980s. 'In the early '80s, the UFF weren't in existence except John McMichael and a small unit in south Belfast who were doing the odd murder, one or two a year, but good ones – republicans,' he told the authors. As 'Davy' put it, 'I think John had a vision both politically and militarily. I admired him – I always looked up to him. John was one of the ones that you could have took to the side and had a yarn with him and ask him where we were going and he'd have told you, he'd have told you straight.'

In March 1988, as internal differences mounted, Andy Tyrie, the UDA's supreme commander, resigned after finding a bomb under his car. At about the same time, many ordinary members were becoming increasingly disillusioned with the organisation in west Belfast, where corruption had steadily taken hold throughout the late 1980s. Many volunteers believed that, with McMichael dead, the UDA was drifting without direction or purpose. In October 1988, a C Coy gunman was involved in the murder of Jimmy Craig, a leading west Belfast UDA man and one of Northern Ireland's most notorious racketeers, who was executed by his colleagues after an internal investigation found that he had colluded with republicans to line his pocket and set up for murder other UDA figures, including McMichael, and the UVF's William 'Frenchy' Marchant.

Rumours were also inevitably flying about Lyttle, a man in his 50s, who had angered many members because of his chumminess with the local UVF commander, John 'Bunter' Graham, and his apparent willingness to take a back seat. Ordinary UDA members started to ask themselves why he appeared so relaxed about potential IRA threats to his life. They also wondered how he was able to mingle every week with nationalists as he

A teenage Johnny Adair, wearing one of his favourite cardigans, in a typically affectionate pose with Sam 'Skelly' McCrory, his closest friend.

'Are you looking at me?' A tough guy in the making.

With friends, including his girlfriend, Gina Crossan (directly behind him), outside Belfast City Hall. Even at 18, Adair was always the centre of attention.

Belfast's answer to Lennon and McCartney. Adair plays pulsating bass to Skelly's indecipherable skinhead rants during rehearsals at the YMCA in central Belfast. Roadie Donald Hodgen is seated between his friends.

Offensive Weapon – Adair, Skelly and drummer Julian 'Tarzan' Carson – acknowledge the rapturous applause at a gig on the Shankill in 1982. Brian Watson, lead guitarist and the band's songwriter, is out of the picture.

Close as always, Adair and Skelly
share a seat.

Enjoying a drink with William
'Winkie' Dodds, Adair's C8
commander, in the late 1980s.

Left to right: Skelly, Gina and Adair share a joke
at a dinner in Langley Street Social Club.

The cream of C Coy check in for a few days at Castlereagh Holding Centre. Left to right: Johnny Adair, Sam 'Skelly' McCrory, 'Fat Jackie' Thompson, Donald Hodgen, William 'Moe' Courtney, William 'Winkie' Dodds, Tommy Potts and John 'Paddy' Patterson.

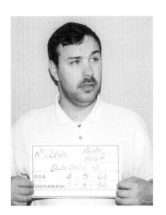

From left to right: James 'Sham' Millar and his brother, Herbie Millar, Stephen 'Dick' Dempsey, Alan McClean, Jacqueline Newell, Ian Truesdale, Andrew Green and Norman Green Snr.

Jackie 'Legs' Robinson, Adair's former girlfriend and fiancée.

Detective Sergeant Johnston 'Jonty' Brown.

The devastation of the Shankill bomb, which killed nine Protestants and the IRA's Thomas Begley in October 1993.

C Coy's victims included 18-year-old Gerard O'Hara (above) and Noel Cardwell (right), 26, who had a mental age of 12.

Adair's arch enemies and repeated C Coy targets: the IRA's Eddie Copeland (above) and Brian Gillen (right).

Gina Crossan on her way to become Gina Adair on 21 February 1997. She hated the photographs so much that she refused to look at them.

Lining up before the wedding inside the Maze Prison. Left to right: Adair's pals Jim Spence, Derek 'Snow' Hamilton, Donald Hodgen, Winkie Dodds and Skelly's boyfriend, Harry Cowan.

indulged his favourite hobby – racing greyhounds – at a track in north Belfast, where he had his own table in a private members' lounge. In the words of one UDA man who went on to become a gunman for C Coy, 'The old leadership was just totally corrupt. They were having dealings with republicans and they didn't want to take on the Provos in case it came to their own door.'

By autumn 1989 the net was closing in on Tucker Lyttle's cosy regime in west Belfast. In September, John Stevens, then Deputy Chief Constable of the Cambridgeshire police, was called in by Hugh Annesley, who had succeeded Sir John Hermon as head of the RUC, to investigate allegations of collusion between the security forces and loyalist terrorists. The trigger was not Patrick Finucane's murder but the killing of Loughlin Maginn, a 28-year-old Catholic shot dead by UFF gunmen in Rathfriland, Co. Down, the previous month. In a desperate attempt to prove the credibility of its targeting, the UFF claimed police had told them Maginn was in the IRA. To back up their claims the UFF distributed police intelligence files to the media, and by the end of September had released suspect lists and photomontages covering some 250 individuals.

On 16 January 1990, Lyttle was accused at Belfast Magistrates' Court of withholding information that could have prevented an act of terrorism. He was released on bail but re-arrested three weeks later and charged with attempting to pervert the course of justice. This time the charge was more sinister. Among the papers seized by the Stevens inquiry team was a letter written by Lyttle to potential witnesses in a trial into alleged UDA racketeering. 'Do you want to spend the rest of your lives looking over your shoulders?' he wrote, adding that they were assured a place at the top of a loyalist 'hit list' if they gave their evidence. He was also linked in court to another threat. Brian Nelson, himself arrested in January, was considering taking the stand to implicate dozens of his former UDA colleagues, and in an attempt to make him see sense his sister was sent a bag of bullets. Although there was no direct evidence that Lyttle was behind this, the court was told that if anybody could enforce a threat against Nelson or his family, it was him. The following year he was sentenced to seven years for making threats to kill.

But it was not just Lyttle for whom the decade started badly. At the start of 1990 Tucker's second-in-command, Eric McKee, was charged with possessing police intelligence documents. Among others imprisoned were the leading west Belfast UDA figures Jim Spence of B Coy, Matt Kincaid of

MAD DOG

A Coy and Winkie Dodds, C Coy's commander. In March, the fallout widened when the UDA's 'brigadier' in east Belfast, Billy Elliott, and Joe English, its leader in south-east Antrim, were charged with possession of confidential security files. Also in jail was Sammy Duddy, editor of the UDA magazine *Ulster*, though he was later acquitted.

By the time he completed his investigation in May 1990, John Stevens had charged 59 people, the majority of them loyalist paramilitaries. Although the first Stevens report was not as explosive as many had expected – low-grade police and Army intelligence had been passed to loyalists, but Stevens stressed that the abuse was 'not widespread or institutionalised' – the inquiry had decimated the UDA. So long as Nelson and Lyttle had been in place, the security forces were able to rein in the more hardline elements of the organisation in west Belfast. With both men in jail, however, Adair and the young militants around him, most of whom did not have a political thought in their heads, were free to seize the initiative. In the end the Stevens I inquiry, though a necessary response to anger from Dublin and nationalists in Northern Ireland, removed any restraining influence the security forces had over the UDA in its Shankill Road heartland.

Four years later, during a period of detention in Castlereagh holding centre in east Belfast, Adair was asked by police what he thought of the first Stevens inquiry. According to police notes of the conversation, 'He said he [Stevens] had done a good job, had got rid of all the shite. All Tucker Lyttle and his crowd worried about was money. In Lyttle's time there would have been one hit, about fifty robberies and a bit of extortion. Now there was a lot more hits and maybe one robbery.'

Despite their efforts to recruit him, the Special Branch would soon learn just how difficult it was to try to control Johnny Adair. Between 1990 and his imprisonment in May 1994, Adair masterminded a wave of terror in west Belfast that claimed the lives of up to 40 Catholics. His influence extended right across the Province as fellow commanders in the UDA and the UVF came under pressure to emulate his attacks and young loyalists looked up to him as their idol. The upsurge in violence was horrendous. By 1992, the UDA and the UVF were out-killing the IRA for the first time since 1975, claiming the lives of 36 people compared to the Provisionals' 34. In 1993, the contrast was even greater. The loyalists claimed 47 victims, 31 of whom were killed by the UDA, compared to 36 by the IRA. The Adair era was about to begin.

4. Dream Team

'We had to sit and wait for two hours while he was delivering and we just got fed up and said, "He'll fucking do" [the other delivery boy].' – *'John', one of the killers of Francis Crawford*

'They were the cream of the fucking crop' – *Johnny Adair*

JACKIE THOMPSON WAS SO CLOSE TO HIS VICTIM THAT HE COULD FEEL THE heat from the bright orange sparks flying off his head and smell his hair burning. Despite being 22 st., 'Fat Jackie' had beaten his colleague to their target. Out of breath and sweating heavily, he stopped shooting and waddled back to the car, where he stood watching his friend, James 'Sham' Millar. It was his turn now, his chance to get 'blooded'. Millar clasped his left hand tightly against the side of his pistol and slowly squeezed the trigger with his right index finger. It was now or never, he muttered to himself. As he looked down at the dying man he dispatched a final bullet into his body. He had been given a faulty weapon, which was missing a small catch that held the magazine in place, and it had to be clasped tightly to stop it falling out. It was not what you wanted on your first kill, but at least he wasn't driving. 'He's down, let's fucking go,' said Thompson as Millar stepped into the maroon Ford Orion that had been hijacked earlier from the Shankill. 'Go, go, go!'

By the time John Judge's wife returned home shortly after 11 p.m. on Tuesday, 31 July 1990, her 34-year-old husband was dead and her three children fatherless. Two days later the Ulster Freedom Fighters admitted responsibility for the murder, which was deemed so unimportant that it merited just a paragraph in most London newspapers.

The hit team had set out for the attack from the Mayo Street Social Club just across the 'peaceline' dividing the Catholic Falls Road from the Protestant Shankill. Thompson and Millar did the shooting while Sam 'Skelly' McCrory was the driver. The real star, however, went by the nickname of 'J.C.'. She was a 9mm automatic pistol named after the fatal shots she had fired into Jimmy Craig in 1988, since when she had become one of C Coy's best-loved weapons. Tonight J.C. had found success with Thompson, who always had a good time when she was in his hand. 'Occasionally she used to jam and you used to have to hit her forward,' recalled one gunman. 'But once she went she went sweet.'

All in their mid-20s, Thompson, Skelly and Millar (another burly man, weighing 16 st.) were young, unemployed and keen to murder. One of Judge's assassins, 'John', who has never been convicted in connection with the killing, laughed and joked as he talked about it with the authors. 'There was a dispute over that one, over who was driving, who was shooting. We were near enough going to shoot each other over it,' he said, adding, 'People wanted me to drive. I was fucking pissed off with driving.' The team had been given Judge's name and address by a UVF contact in south Belfast and told that he was a leading IRA man. Although they had no idea what he looked like, as they drove past before the attack they saw a crowd talking and drinking beer outside the house and identified their target as the person who appeared to be in charge. 'There was no photo but we knew the house and all,' said 'John'. 'He [Judge] seemed to be the organiser of the party.' Although a number of people had been standing outside the house, they all disappeared as fast as they could when they saw two gunmen get out of the car and by the time the gunmen started firing Judge was the only one around. 'They ran down the street, just scattered everywhere,' said another member of the hit team. 'By the time the car was turned round there was no cunt left in the place.' Recalling the moment Judge was shot, the assassin confided, 'Judge tried to run. He was in mid-flight. One arm was up and one leg was up. It was good night, Irene.'

In a statement two days later, the UFF said that Judge, who had been celebrating his son's fifth birthday with friends and relatives, was a 'known IRA bomber' who had been murdered to avenge the killing of Ian Gow, the Conservative MP and close ally of Margaret Thatcher, who had been blown up by the Provos at his home in Sussex the day before. The claim was total rubbish, and rejected as such by both Sinn Fein and the RUC. At the dead man's funeral on the Falls Road, Bishop Cahal Daly described it as a 'despicable lie'.

In reality, neither Thompson nor Millar, who to this day has the simple message 'Fuck Taigs [Catholics]' tattooed on the back of his neck, cared who they had killed. Asked whether he regretted killing innocent civilians, 'John' said, 'Shit happens. I've never missed a night's sleep over it, nor has anybody else I know over it. Maybe when you missed the cunt. The way we looked at it was that they [the IRA] were blowing people up seven days a week whether they got the right one or the wrong one – they didn't give a fuck.' Like Adair, both would later become corrupted by drugs and money, Millar even earning the nickname 'Boss Hogg' after the rich scamster in *The Dukes of Hazzard*, the hit American television series. For the moment, though, killing gave them the buzz they craved and any old Catholic would do. Between Judge's murder and July 1992, the pair, along with Skelly, Donald Hodgen and several others, formed the core of a self-styled 'Dream Team' that would redefine C Coy under the leadership of Johnny Adair.

Their callous disregard for their victims was partly the result of growing up on the Shankill, where many people had been brutalised by life in the ghetto, including Adair. As 'Davy', a senior C Coy figure and a former friend of Adair, put it: 'Johnny's famous saying was, "Anybody in a leather coat is a fenian." See, if you'd have drove up the Falls Road and somebody had been in a leather coat, you'd say, "He's a Provie." If it was the black square-toed Oxfords [shoes] they were wearing, you'd all say, "He's definitely a republican, he's definitely a republican."'

Before Judge's murder, the young militants of C Coy had been heading out on operations for months but without much success. Adair in particular was having a run of bad luck. To his irritation, he also found himself having to give way to more experienced gunmen such as B Coy's Ken Barrett and Moe Courtney.

Just before 10.45 a.m. on Sunday, 11 March 1990, a light-blue Opel Ascona with Skelly at the wheel pulled into a small street in the shadow of a 30-foot-high fence separating the Falls from the Shankill. Skelly and his passengers were looking for an Easter Rising commemoration that was meant to be taking place at a local IRA memorial. Along with Skelly were Jackie Thompson, Ken Barrett and another B Coy volunteer. Half an hour earlier they had spotted two men cleaning an IRA commemorative plaque, but now they were nowhere to be seen. As Skelly drove the car round the block they noticed a man eyeing them suspiciously. Eamon Quinn, a 32-year-old Catholic, had been working quietly on his car outside his home when he saw a vehicle full of strangers pull into the street. Quinn watched the car turn slowly round the bend but was surprised when, just a few minutes later, it reappeared. Again Skelly and his passengers saw him watching them. Whoever he was, he would do. As one of the hit team put it, 'The original target wasn't there so we paid him [Quinn] a visit on the way back.' Before Quinn could even consider a course of action, Thompson had wound down his window and fired a silver .38 Special, hitting him once in the head. Barrett quickly jumped out and shot him several more times in the head and stomach, finishing him off from close range as he lay on the ground.

It was Thompson's first kill, and although Johnny Adair had hijacked the murder car along with B Coy's Jim Spence, he was secretly jealous of his friend. 'He had been out plenty but he'd never actually had a victory, as I would say,' revealed 'John'. By now Adair was so keen for his own success that he was frequently going out in the early hours of the morning to scout addresses in republican areas. On one occasion, at 1.45 a.m. on 28 April 1990, he and Jackie Thompson were stopped by a police constable in Silvio Street off the Shankill. While Thompson kept quiet, Adair boasted to the police officer that he was a notorious gunman.

By the summer Adair was becoming desperate to prove himself. On Thursday, 7 June, Adair, Skelly, Thompson and Sham Millar came tantalisingly close when they attempted to murder Sean Keenan, a former Sinn Fein councillor who worked in the party's publicity department, at his home in Andersonstown in the heart of republican west Belfast. Shortly before midnight the C Coy unit parked their car on the hard shoulder of the M1 motorway overlooking Keenan's house in Riverdale Park South. While one of the group stayed with the vehicle, a red Cavalier hijacked from the Shankill earlier that evening, three of them crept up on Keenan's house as he sat in his living room watching television.

According to one of the team, 'We stopped on the motorway and climbed down the bank and over his back wall. He was sitting in the living room but he had a drop bar on his back door. As he tried to run up the stairs he was shot . . . in the arse.' The account differs only slightly from the version carried in *An Phoblacht*, the republican weekly newspaper. 'The assailants attempted to break down the door four times, unaware that it was reinforced,' it reported. 'Keenan, who was sitting underneath the living room window, dived across the floor to try to get out of the room when the venetian blind fell down off the back door. Eight pistol shots were then fired, one hitting Keenan in the left buttock as he lay crouched beside the living room door.' According to eyewitnesses quoted by *An Phoblacht*, the three men – one carrying a hand gun and a sledgehammer, the second a machine pistol and the third what appeared to be an assault rifle – acted with 'military precision', covering each other as they made their way to and from the house.

Throughout the spring and summer of 1990 Adair and his small clique were out repeatedly trying to assassinate people they suspected of being republicans. The Dream Team made a point of giving their targets nicknames. Edward McKinney, who lived in Atlantic Avenue in north Belfast, was dubbed 'the Sugarman' after the McKinney's sugar company, while another was called 'Whistler' because he whistled constantly. The 'Fat Man' was an IRA suspect living in the New Lodge area of north Belfast. 'We went for him three times in the one day, me, Skelly, and Sham as driver,' said one of those involved. Adair hijacked the car and the previous night went with another C Coy man to view the target's house in Hillman Street. Said his companion, 'We got stopped [by police] in the street, me and Johnny, about 12.30 the night before. The peelers then tipped him off [the target].' The following morning a number of workmen were busy installing new security measures at the property, but the Fat Man was nowhere to be seen. Again, the Dream Team's only victim was somebody shot in the buttock. 'He [the Fat Man] was there outside the house the next morning but by the time we got the stuff he was away. That happened twice. The last time his car was there and we thought he was in. We kicked the front windie in and bounced into the house. We hit one of the workmen in the arse and then the whole street came out and attacked the motor. I don't know how we got away, but we're still here today, aren't we?' On another occasion Adair and another C Coy gunman travelled into east Belfast to murder Joe O'Donnell, a Sinn Fein activist from the Short Strand, but he was not at home when they called.

Jackie Thompson and Sham Millar were both arrested following the murder of John Judge, and Thompson was forced to appear in a police identification parade. Although neither was charged with the killing, on 9 August 1990 Adair, Thompson, Skelly and Tommy Irvine, a B Coy man who had recently been made 'brigadier' of the UDA in west Belfast, were charged with three murder attempts, that of Sean Keenan on 7 June, Edward McKinney on 8 May and John McGuinness on 5 July. In addition,

Adair was accused of possessing firearms and ammunition with intent to endanger life, while he and Skelly were also charged with making a threat to kill Katherine Spruce, a woman with whom Adair had been having a stormy affair. Asked to explain in court what the evidence was against Adair and his co-defendants, a police officer told the court, 'The evidence is the word of a civilian witness'. The witness was Spruce.

A small, blonde girl with a half-decent figure improved by short skirts and tight tops, Spruce quickly caught Adair's eye. By coincidence, she was living in the very same house in Alloa Street, off the Oldpark Road, that Adair's mother, Mabel, later moved into. 'He took a shine to her because she wore these skimpy skirts and a lot of lipstick,' remembered 'John', who was constantly in Adair's company. At a time when Adair's relationship with Gina Crossan was on the rocks and he was living on his own in a flat in Glencairn, at the top of the Shankill, there was nothing to stop him playing around. But there was also another reason Adair was attracted to her. Spruce boasted that she was also seeing Martin 'Rook' O'Prey, a leading member of the Irish People's Liberation Organisation, a republican splinter group, who would be shot dead the following year by the UVF. The thrill, as always with Adair, was impossible to resist. 'That was part of the kick for Johnny, you know what I mean?' said 'Davy'. 'As a matter of fact, I remember one time she tied him up and she handcuffed him to the bed and told him she was going to get Rook for him. And wee Johnny started panicking and she went out of the house for a couple of hours, and Johnny was just handcuffed to that bed, waiting for her.'

Although Adair's relationship with Spruce lasted only a few months, at one stage his new girlfriend moved her belongings into Adair's flat. Adair took huge pleasure in showing her off to his mates. 'She was a nut, a complete and utter fucking nut, just Johnny's type right down to a tee,' said 'Davy'. 'I'd see them driving about, up and down the road, Johnny driving and her with nothing on her. I'm serious, not a stitch on her. Up and down the Shankill, up and down the Crumlin Road, up and down the Oldpark. He would have had his clothes on but he would have stopped, he'd have beeped his horn at you, "Look at this fucking header here." Johnny would have done anything for a thrill, anything at all.'

For Adair and his clique it was a time of wild parties, not just on the Shankill but in loyalist areas across Belfast. At a time when Adair – the 'Wee Man' to his friends – was fast acquiring a reputation among loyalists, he would strut about in one of his favourite waistcoats, making it plain that he was a man on the way up. 'There were lots of parties, lots of them,' recalled one old colleague, who said Adair never had to try too hard to find a woman. 'Johnny would have poked a black eye, let's put it that way. He was always getting his clothes off at house parties and wandering around buck naked.' But while Adair's flat was the scene of late-night drinking binges, it was also a place of round-the-clock plotting, with a steady stream of UDA men through his door. While Spruce overheard some of this planning, Adair almost certainly volunteered a great deal more, probably to wind her up, and during an argument one day she threatened to go to the police. 'I think somebody actually tried to throw her out of the window,' said 'Davy'. However, according to 'John' it was just her belongings that left the flat by this route, including an ornamental marble elephant. 'We didn't throw her out, we threw her ornaments out, a big marble elephant and her clothes. We couldn't be bothered to carry them downstairs so we just fucked them out of the window.' Shortly afterwards, Spruce went to the police, claiming that Adair and Skelly had threatened to kill her. She revealed a wealth of detail about the man who was starting to pop up with increasing regularity in Special Branch reports. In addition to the four men arrested, she also implicated Sham Millar, who went into hiding before he could be lifted. Her disclosures included the claim, repeated in later years, of Adair's uncontrollable excitement on returning from murder bids. As one former colleague close to Adair recalled, 'The police said to her, "How did you know Johnny had done anything?" And she said it was because he always wet the bed. She made that famous statement. He always wet the bed, that's what she said.'

Adair himself refers to Kathy Spruce as 'the supergrass'. 'At that time the police was constantly lifting me, Thompson and McCrory,' Adair recalled. 'They just used her as a weapon to get at us because they had nothing else . . . She was a lunatic who fell in love with me and because I didn't want her she went to the police and told them that I threatened her.' On 12 December, after four months on remand in Crumlin Road Prison, the charges against Adair and his three colleagues were suddenly dropped. The case, based on a single witness, had never stood much of a chance. 'The whole case was fraught with difficulties. It had been brought by a team who didn't know how to seek corroboration, didn't know how to present the case and had no knowledge of Adair's unit,' said Johnston Brown, the detective sergeant who would later help to nail the loyalist terror chief. To a lesser charge – that of spraying the slogan 'Up the Leak Regiment' and

'Ha Ha We Have Got Your Photos' on the side of the Ulster Bank on the Shankill Road in February of that year – Adair pleaded guilty and received a 12-month conditional discharge. A police patrol had spotted him painting the graffiti, and although Adair sprinted off he was chased and discovered hiding in a hut. Given the situation that had faced him on 9 August, it was a happy result. Over the next three and a half years there would be too many occasions when the RUC would wish they had found something more damning on Adair.

The Spruce case, though not front-page news, marked Adair's first real outing in the press as an up-and-coming terrorist. By early 1990 he had replaced Winkie Dodds, who was now in jail, as the most influential figure in C Coy thanks to his eagerness and the group of young friends who naturally looked to him as their leader. Throughout the year a series of meetings took place in west Belfast and further afield as the UDA was forced to reshuffle its personnel following the fall-out from the Stevens inquiry. Ian Truesdale, at the time an up-and-coming member of C9 in the Oldpark, remembered, 'There was a big west Belfast brigade meeting where all the talk was about emphasising new blood in the UFF. They just said they wanted to get rid of the old brigade and bring in new blood, that a younger role model was needed to serve and protect the community against "pan-nationalists/Sinn Fein" – those were the exact words used.' According to Truesdale, among those who stood up and spoke about the need for reform were B Coy's Jim Spence, a 29-year-old from the Woodvale who was already a close friend of Adair and, over the next decade, would become one of the few people able to restrain his C Coy colleague.

However, the injection of new blood did not take place overnight. According to one UDA veteran, who was central to the transformation in west Belfast, 'There was no one big night of the long knives. What you had was a series of meetings in west Belfast and the rest of the Province, and the meetings in west Belfast had a dynamo effect across the rest of the UDA. There were meetings in people's houses, elsewhere in Belfast and way out in the country.' Colin Crawford, a sociologist who has studied the UDA for 20 years, agrees. 'In 1989 and 1990, the process was really very erratic and the remilitarisation took time. There were one or two important meetings but that was part of a general movement, all of which was secret and covert. Their whole ethos was about the cult of the individual. In terms of operations, it often came down to a group of men who knew each other very well, operating without strategic command.'

DREAM TEAM

By 1990 there was already a strong cult developing around Adair and it would not be long before he had the chance to exploit this. The chain of events that transformed the UDA in west Belfast began in earnest at the start of the year with the arrests of Tommy 'Tucker' Lyttle, his military commander Eric McKee, and Winkie Dodds, C Coy's commander. Lyttle was replaced as brigadier by B Coy's Tommy Irvine, an arrangement far more to the liking of Adair and his cohorts. 'We went to Tommy Irvine and said, "We want to do this," and he gave us a free rein,' said 'John'. 'Before that it all had to be okayed through Eric McKee and Tucker Lyttle. He [Irvine] was a brilliant man because he said, "You do what you want." We just went at it full time then.'

The role of military commander went to Jim Spence, though within weeks he himself was arrested in connection with the Stevens inquiry and replaced by another B Coy figure, Ken Barrett. Adair plugged the final hole, succeeding Dodds as C Coy commander. The changes came just in time to head off a looming split in the organisation. The UDA veteran recalled: 'In the old-style UDA you had all these ranks and lots of self-appointed brigadiers and stuff. We actually wanted to get away from that because it was the biggest load of nonsense. They [the old guard] were more interested in their magazine than anything else, but we were getting more and more frustrated. "Kill or be killed" – those were the words coming through. The danger was that the good people we had would break away and set up their own grouping. The IRA was going from strength to strength but more of our young men were saying, "What is this about here? We didn't join to sell magazines and stand minding doors." The plan to set up a separate grouping wasn't at the stage where it was openly being canvassed, but people would have met people from other areas and been talking and saying they were fed up. It was just informal, there was no strategy as such, but that was the talk.'

Shortly after his appointment, Adair and his fellow commanders from across Northern Ireland met at a secret location in Co. Antrim, where the decision was taken that each brigade area would kill at least one target a month. 'There were things discussed at that time which were far more serious than people being put into posts,' said the UDA veteran, referring to a number of similar meetings at which stepping up the UFF's violent campaign was the key topic of discussion.

But although the remilitarisation was now well and truly underway, in August the process suffered a setback when Irvine and Adair were arrested on

Kathy Spruce's evidence. To the disgust of Adair and his friends, the new brigadier was Billy Kennedy, an old-style UDA man and Tucker Lyttle's brother-in-law. 'What happened was Tucker Lyttle put his brother-in-law in charge, Billy Kennedy. Tucker sent word out from jail for Billy to take over but the whole arrangement didn't go down well. It was like a mafia thing, just getting Billy to hold the reins while he was in prison,' said a senior UDA figure. For Adair, the situation was particularly frustrating as C Coy was still under the thumb of its finance and welfare officers, specifically Sammy Verner, his son, Sam Verner Jnr, and Tommy 'Tucker' Ewing. Like Billy Kennedy they were old-style UDA men and wanted nothing to do with anything military. The Verners were viewed by Adair and his colleagues as too preoccupied with money and the running of the Langley Street Social Club, C Coy's bar off the Shankill Road, where team meetings and training sessions were held and, unbeknownst to the Verners, guns kept in a storeroom. 'All the operators used to sit in Langley Street Social Club on a Wednesday night to have a wind-down and pick the next target,' said 'John'. 'We would have kept gear in a room in the back and tested it in the club.'

Among the C Coy militants, the Verners commanded little respect and were seen as an unwanted hangover from the Tucker Lyttle era. They had no involvement at all with the UFF. According to one C Coy hitman, the Verners strongly disapproved when they discovered that guns had been hidden in the club. 'We used to leave weapons in the store room all the time. There was one time I had a row with the two Verners about a gun that had been left in the club. They tried to disassemble it and couldn't. They didn't even realise it was a fucking replica.' While Adair was in prison the Verners provoked controversy by attempting to cut back on the £12-a-week welfare paid out to UDA prisoners and their families. 'On one occasion when Johnny was in prison he asked for a pair of jeans and a pair of trainers. The trainers he got were a size seven and a size eight. The jeans had to have about eight inches cut off them,' said 'John'. Adair tried to laugh, but it was not the way he expected to be treated.

Following his release from prison in December, Adair decided to confront the Verners. Several dozen people were assembled in the upstairs room at the Langley Street Social Club when the showdown finally occurred. Most of the C Coy team commanders had turned up, as always every Friday night, to pay their weekly dues or 'totes'. They knew what was about to happen: cautious not to move too fast, Adair had sounded them out beforehand. According to one person present that night, after everyone had turned up, Adair and his two oldest friends, Skelly and Donald Hodgen, walked into the room and quickly shut the door behind them. However, exactly what happened next remains the subject of confusion and the situation is not helped by the fact that no written record was kept of the meeting. 'Adair liked to say afterwards that he came in, guns blazing, that he forced the Verners to stand down there and then,' said one west Belfast UDA man. 'Some people say the guns were just shown, that they weren't fired, others that there were shots. But the Verners wanted to leave anyway, they had had enough, they wanted out.'

However, one eyewitness insists that shots were fired. 'The staff were in the middle of the floor. When they [Adair, Skelly and Hodgen] came in the doors were closed. Two people had firearms. The first was cocked and fired into the ceiling and Sammy Verner ordered to stand down. The second was cocked and fired into the ceiling and Sammy Verner Jnr ordered to stand down.' Another C Coy member, who was in prison at the time but was told about the meeting shortly afterwards, said, 'Johnny, Skelly and Donald just seized control at a weekly meeting upstairs at the club. They were the ones who fired the shots in the ceiling. It had been going on for too long, they were fed up with the way things were run. Johnny told the brigade staff that their time was up. They were so weak and corrupt that they ran away without a shot being fired.'

The myth surrounding Johnny Adair has probably left history with a slightly exaggerated version of events that night, but the result is not in dispute: the old guard, many of whom had never fired a single shot in their lives, had been ousted.

In truth, the writing had been on the wall for the Verners since October, when Jim Spence was freed from jail and took over the reins as brigadier in west Belfast. At around the same time, Ken Barrett, who had shown little interest in his role as military commander, was stood down, paving the way for Adair to assume this position on his release.

Spence's appointment was not the only piece of good news for Adair as he sat in prison. On 16 October 1990, a C Coy team gave their military commander a much-needed morale booster. Dermot McGuinness, a 41-year-old Catholic with three children, was shot dead as he walked back from the off-licence on the Oldpark Road where his wife worked. She said afterwards, 'We had a good chat and a bit of a laugh as we always did. He told me to watch myself and be careful walking home because it was a dangerous area, and waved goodbye.' As McGuinness stood at the corner of Rosapenna

MAD DOG

Street clutching a bottle of wine, a maroon Ford Sierra pulled up and a man with a handgun stepped out and shot him from close range. In its statement of responsibility the UFF branded the dead man a well-known republican and a member of the IPLO, but the claim was scathingly dismissed by his family. It was an easy kill, less than five minutes' drive from the Shankill and on one of Belfast's most violent sectarian faultlines. Over the next three years Rosapenna Street – which saw so many murders and attacks that it was dubbed 'Roselawn Street' after the Belfast cemetery – would become a particular favourite for Adair's killing teams. However, on this occasion there was an additional reason for the murder: to take the heat off Adair and his three colleagues in jail. 'That was done to get us out,' recalled one of the four in prison. Plainly, the slaying – and any Catholic would have done – had been ordered by Adair from inside. If the murders continued while the UFF leaders were in jail, it would undermine the police's belief that they were largely responsible for the carnage.

With Adair, Skelly and Thompson out of jail, the Dream Team resumed their activities with redoubled ferocity, although they continued to be dogged by bad luck as most of their operations ended in either failure or fiasco, without so much as a grazed buttock to boast about. To their C Coy comrades, however, they were heroes. 'Jackie would have been well there within an ASU; he would have been a good operator. Like Skelly and ******* [one of Adair's closest friends] he was a gunman, and they all commanded a lot of respect,' said 'Davy'. While Thompson could also handle a car, his main skill was his shooting. 'Because of Jackie's and Skelly's height the two were great as front gunmen,' recalled one volunteer who went out on operations with them.

Six weeks after their release from prison, the Dream Team finally claimed another victim. On 27 January 1991, Sean Rafferty, a 44-year-old Catholic, was gunned down as he cooked Sunday dinner in the kitchen of his house in Rosapenna Court off the Oldpark Road. He was killed in front of his screaming children after two masked gunmen burst into his house and shot him dead, dispatching the final bullets from point-blank range as he lay helpless on the floor. 'He was doing the dishes and your woman, his daughter, chased the gunman up the street,' remembered one of the killers with a snigger. The UFF said that Rafferty, who was a close neighbour of Dermot McGuinness, had been 'deeply involved with the Provisional IRA in north Belfast' but the claim was nonsense. The shocking reality was that Adair had ordered the murder as a dare during a drinking session in a

Shankill bar. It was typical of his style of leadership, and the speed with which the attack was put together would become a hallmark of the way he operated. His sheer unpredictability meant the police were frequently unable to anticipate C Coy's actions. In a reference to Rafferty's murder, Special Branch later reported:

> One shocking example of Adair's capacity for ruthlessness was made known to Special Branch following a sectarian murder in north Belfast. It emerged that the 'C' Company team were present on a Sunday evening in a Shankill Road club with the intention of engaging in a session of drinking. Upon the arrival of the first round of drinks the mood of the party was jovial when one of the assembled dozen or so members shouted "Let's bang a taig" (slang for let's shoot a Catholic). Although this comment was intended in jest, Adair picked up on the suggestion and within five minutes had detailed every member of the team to play a specific role in the murder attempt which had now become a reality. Incredibly, fifteen minutes later the operation was underway and it was only then that the team realised that they hadn't actually discussed a target. At this point it was decided to drive into a local Catholic area and shoot the first male person they encountered. Approximately twenty-five minutes after the first suggestion, the entire team had returned to the club and resumed their drinking, the celebration of the murder being led by Adair.

Throughout 1991 Adair gradually became bolder in the targeting and planning of operations but, to the frustration of police, less and less predictable. On 12 April, his red Ford Orion was stopped by police in Berlin Street off the Shankill Road. Asked where he was going, Adair turned to Jackie Thompson, who was in the passenger seat, before replying with a wry smile that the pair were on their way to visit the IPLO's Martin 'Rook' O'Prey. At 12.40 a.m. on 14 April 1991, he was sighted by a police patrol wearing body armour as he drove into the republican Ardoyne area of north Belfast. In May, he was spotted again in Ardoyne and, on another occasion, near the Falls Road, while for the rest of the year the RUC continued to record his regular sightings in republican districts of north and west Belfast. They also kept a careful note of the company he kept, which showed his closeness to just a handful of individuals. In April alone, Adair and Thompson were spotted together 20 times, while in May he was sighted on 67 separate occasions with Skelly. He was also frequently seen with the new west Belfast brigadier Jim Spence, Ken Barrett, William 'Moe' Courtney and Sham Millar.

Another brave blow for Ulster was struck on Saturday, 31 August 1991, when Francis Crawford, a 57-year-old Catholic who had just come out of hospital after a heart bypass operation, was shot dead in north Belfast. He had been working as a fast-food delivery driver for a Chinese takeaway for just two days when his company took a call for an order at an address off the city's Antrim Road. As the father of five arrived with the delivery he was shot from a range of less than 18 inches by masked gunmen who were waiting in a hijacked taxi. It was the Dream Team. In its statement of responsibility, the UFF alleged that the dead man had been using his job to collect information for the IRA, a claim that was rubbished by the RUC. According to 'John', his killers knew the wrong delivery man had turned up at the house but went ahead with the shooting anyway. He explained to one of the authors, 'We had to sit and wait for two hours while he was delivering and we just got fed up and said, "He'll fucking do" [the other delivery boy].'

Four days later C Coy claimed another scalp, but this time, to Adair's great delight, the killers were from a new active service unit – his efforts to build a larger, more ruthless fighting force were proving successful. Seamus Sullivan, a council refuse disposal worker, was gunned down in a depot off the Springfield Road in nationalist west Belfast on 3 September. The 24-year-old, a son of Jim Sullivan, a prominent Belfast republican since the 1950s and a former member of the old IRA, was shot six times as two gunmen, one from C8 and the other from C13, opened fire on the bin-lorry he was riding in. He crawled into the back of the lorry in an attempt to escape but was shot in the body and then killed with a fatal shot to the head. Later that month, on 28 September, Lawrence Murchan, a 63-year-old Catholic, was shot dead by the UFF as he burned rubbish near his shop off the Falls Road. To sow a measure of confusion in the minds of the security forces, a group called the Loyalist Retaliation and Defence Group claimed the murder,but in reality it was C Coy.

By late 1991, sectarian tensions in Belfast were boiling over. On 7 October, two people were injured after the IPLO, which had become increasingly indiscriminate since Rook O'Prey was killed by the UVF in August, opened fire on a bar in loyalist south Belfast. Three days later two gunmen from the same organisation walked into the Diamond Jubilee Bar on the Shankill Road and shot dead a 42-year-old Protestant, Harry Ward, apparently mistaking him for John 'Bunter' Graham, the UVF commander. Hours later, a Catholic taxi driver, Hugh Magee, was murdered in retaliation by C Coy. He was shot at the wheel of his cab as he pulled out of Rosapenna Street in the Oldpark area. The killers were told by Adair to shoot the first black taxi driver they came across. His wife said he had feared for his life following the shooting earlier that evening, adding, 'I knew something would happen to him some day. Just being in a black taxi was enough to make him a target [loyalists believed black taxis in nationalist west Belfast were run by the IRA].' In a sobering assessment of the rise in violence, a senior police officer commented, 'No effort is being spared, in both overt and covert operations, to try and end this awful nightmare. People are living in dread and we are doing all that is humanly possible.'

On 13 November, the IRA joined the fray with a ferocious assault on loyalists that left four people dead. After shooting dead a UDA veteran, Billy Kingsberry, and his step-son at their home, the Provisionals smashed their way into a flat owned by Joe Bratty, the leading south Belfast UDA figure, but he was not in. At 7.30 p.m., an hour after the first murders, two brothers, Stephen and Kenneth Lynn, were shot dead while renovating a bungalow in north Belfast. They had no paramilitary links whatsoever, though at their inquest the court was told that the house they were working on had until recently been owned by a prominent UVF member. Shortly afterwards a fourth attack was carried out, this time off the Shankill Road just yards from Adair's front door in Hazelfield Street, to where he had recently moved. An IRA booby-trap bomb exploded under a black Ford Orion owned by Gerry Drumgoole, who lost a leg. Adair, who was friendly with Drumgoole, was incensed by the attack on his neighbour, who would frequently look after his children and invite them in for jam sandwiches. The two were often seen together. 'Johnny broke his heart over that,' revealed one close friend. 'That car bomb was meant for him because they would have driven about together.'

Despite near-saturation of Belfast with police and Army patrols, the violence continued to worsen. During a bloody weekend near the end of December, two Protestant civilians, Thomas Gorman, 55, and Barry Watson, 25, were shot dead in the Donegall Arms in south Belfast. A pair of IPLO gunmen, brandishing a revolver and a sawn-off shotgun, kicked open the bar door and sprayed the pub with bullets, yelling, 'Orange bastards'. The UDA responded by killing two Catholics within the next 24 hours, William Johnston and Aidan Wallace. C Coy carried out the first attack, murdering Johnston, a 28-year-old Catholic, in the loyalist south-west of the city. He was shot dead just before midnight when two UFF gunmen burst into his home off the Donegall Road, where he had moved just a few weeks earlier to live with his Protestant girlfriend. Known as Liam, the Irish form of his Christian name, he had started referring to himself as Billy to disguise his background. Most nights he slept fully clothed to enable a quick escape. 'You are a liar, you are LIAM Johnston,' his girlfriend heard one of the gunmen shouting after rushing up the stairs and into the bedroom. He shot him once, then put the muzzle of the gun into his mouth and fired again. On the way out the killer paused to tell her, 'You better go up there, your boyfriend is dead.'

By the end of 1991, Belfast was on the verge of all-out sectarian warfare, thanks in no small part to a remilitarisation of the Shankill Road UDA. In recognition of the role he had played in the carnage of the past two years, Adair was given a special gift at a UDA awards ceremony that Christmas. The plaque, which took pride of place on Adair's mantelpiece, was noted with interest during a police search of his home two years later. It made no mention of the murders he had helped to carry out but then it hardly needed to. 'Presented to John Adair in appreciation of your sterling work – 1991,' said the simple inscription. Nobody reading it could doubt what type of 'work' it referred to.

5. 'Legs'

'Johnny would say to me, "I don't want to die, Jack, I really don't want to die." I believe he still doesn't.' – *Jackie 'Legs' Robinson*

THE NATIONAL ANTHEM WAS PLAYING IN THE BAR IN SOUTH BELFAST WHEN Johnny Adair decided to make his move. For half an hour he had been telling his friends that the blonde in the pink-and-black dress would be his that night, but now, with the club about to close, he could wait no longer. His friends sniggered as they watched his loins take command of his brain. 'All of a sudden this face came from nowhere and he was pulling my friend, saying, "What's her name? What's her name? Tell her I want her, tell her I want her." He was trying to grab my attention, but I was too embarrassed because I was out with a whole crowd of them. And it was "Coke", he was the commander of the estate, he says to him, "Oi, mate, the Queen's playing, do you mind?" And Johnny looked straight up but the minute the Queen stopped he was back in there. "What's her name? What's her name?" But I got up and left him standing.'

It was February 1991 and the first encounter between Johnny Adair and Jackie Robinson was a bruising setback for the loyalist's ego. Jackie was trying to rebuild her life after moving back to Belfast from Birmingham following the collapse of her marriage. She'd never heard the name Johnny Adair and the excited little man who kept tugging at her friend's sleeve did nothing to impress her. She could barely stand the sight of him, let alone imagine that they would one day be engaged to be married and stay together, on and off, for nine turbulent years.

'The best bit about it was I used to say, "He's a wee fat bastard." He used to do my head in. I used to say to my mate, "I hope that little fat bastard doesn't come near me tonight."' Although Adair thought he looked distinctive in his expensive waistcoats and baseball caps, he was small and podgy and bore little resemblance to the muscle-bulging hardman he would become after years of body-building in jail. 'Johnny was a right chubby wee man. He was like a wee rolly, a wee barrel,' recalls Jackie with a laugh.

Every weekend, Adair and his friends would turn up at Jackie's favourite bar, the Taughmonagh Social Club, where a disco drew a large crowd on a Sunday night and occasionally the UDA held events and dinners. For weeks he kept pestering Jackie but with the same result – abject humiliation for Adair in front of the entire bar.

'I knew everybody would be talking about me the minute I walked in the club because it was a fascination with them, everybody was watching to see what he was doing,' says Jackie. 'I'd have gone to the bottom of the hall and he'd have come flying down after me, begging like a child. He just kept begging me to go out with him, "Please, please, please will you go out with me? I want you, I want you."' But after nearly two months of turning him down, Jackie experienced a moment that would change her life completely. 'It was one night we were leaving, probably about six or seven weeks later. I got into the car and as I turned round he [Adair] was banging on the window and he went, "Get the window down, get the window down." And here's me, "Oh my God, here he goes." So I put the window down and all of a sudden as I turned and looked at him I saw a different person. That was when it clicked with me. I'd never looked at him properly before because I was embarrassed by the way he used to behave.'

The next time she saw Adair, again at the club in Taughmonagh, Jackie was still embarrassed but decided to talk to him: 'There was an LPA [Loyalist Prisoners' Aid] do and I'd had quite a bit to drink. And as usual, bang, he was down, and he'd had quite a few himself. And he was down and just to get rid of him I said, "Are you married?" and he said, "No." And I said, "Do you live with a girl? I want the truth." And he says, "Yeah, I do." And I said, "Have you any kids?" And he went, "Yeah, I've got three." Everyone was just sitting there glued. And I asked how old they were. And he says, "Look, please, I just want to go with you." So I says, "All right then, come on." So he handed me the car keys. So we went out, I drove his car and we went up to Lady Dixon's Park and it was tipping down with rain and I shouldn't actually have been driving because I'd had a few to drink. And as

I pulled in and I turned round he was pushing the car seat back. And I went, "What are you doing?" And he had his thing in his hand. And I couldn't believe it, me. And he says to me, "From the first time I seen you I said I was going to screw you." And I just whacked him and I said, "No, I don't think so, I'm no slut." And he went, "What?" And I just started the engine and drove off. So when we got back into the car park I lifted the keys and threw them at him.'

The very next week Adair, dressed as usual in his trademark waistcoat and wearing a baseball cap back to front, was sitting at the bar talking to Winkie Dodds when Jackie walked into the club. 'I walked in and he was sitting with Winkie. He was a bit sheepish-looking because I think he was embarrassed about the week before. And I was actually meant to be meeting somebody that night, I was meeting a fella that night. And when I saw him sitting there I didn't want to go because I had started to find myself attracted to him. I was sitting with my friend and the next thing he got up and put two Carlsberg Specials down and I said, "God, I don't want to go and meet this fella," but I left my friend and I went. But I had said to her, "Give him my number," so that's how he got the number. And it was a couple of weeks after that that he phoned and that's when things started taking off.'

By May 1991, Johnny Adair and Jackie Robinson were seeing each other two or three times a week. Adair, who liked to think of himself as a womaniser, had been dating two other girls when he met Jackie, one from the Shankill and the other from south Belfast, but had dropped them both. He was also seeing less and less of Gina, his long-term partner, who had just given birth to their third child, Chloe. Gina had confessed to him on his release from jail the previous December that she had slept with 28 men while he was in prison for the Kathy Spruce charges, and Adair had not forgiven her.

By the time Adair met Jackie he was thoroughly fed up with Gina and was eager to throw himself into a new relationship. But he was not quite ready to be completely monogamous. The one woman Adair was not prepared to give up, though he did not mention her to Jackie, was a policeman's wife he was sleeping with. At least once a week Adair and Jackie Thompson travelled to the affluent seaside town of Holywood just outside Belfast. There they would have a drink or two in the Railway Tavern before meeting up with the woman. She never had a clue who Adair and Thompson were. As far as she was concerned, they were amusing new friends who were keeping her entertained while her husband was drying out in a clinic for alcoholics. After meeting her in the bar one night, Adair plied her with drinks and went back to her house. As he ripped off her clothes, he noticed a pistol under the table next to the bed. With his jeans around his ankles he was suddenly torn between his libido and his personal safety. He chose his libido. After finishing his business, he asked his breathless companion what the gun was for. Laughing, she told him her husband was an RUC man. It was what Adair had suspected. Lonely and vulnerable, she was the perfect prey. Adair went back to see her regularly in the summer of 1991. He gradually won her trust and used her to gather information on CID officers, many of whom lived in Holywood or had relatives in the area. On 17 June, he bragged to Johnston Brown, the detective sergeant who was busy befriending Adair and plotting his downfall, that he had obtained the addresses of several police officers and their relatives, including Brown's mother and brother. The boast was a clear attempt to unsettle Brown. It also came at a time when Adair was seriously contemplating murdering a policeman because of the daily harassment he claimed he was receiving from the security forces. Brown duly noted his concerns and passed them on to his superiors, but he never discovered the name of the woman Adair was seeing or that of her husband.

Although he still wanted to kill a policeman, within a few months Adair had drifted away from his Holywood mistress. He was becoming increasingly involved with Jackie Robinson. In Jackie, a good-humoured, lively 34-year-old, he had found somebody totally different. 'When he was with his mates he was very bubbly and always had to be the centre of attention, but when he was with me he was the complete opposite,' said Jackie. 'That's when I found out the real person that he was, because the two of us would have sat and talked away for hours, just about stupid things. Johnny likes affection and he wasn't getting it anywhere else.'

In Jackie's company, the ruthless terrorist became a little boy, prone to self-doubt and fits of emotion. 'No matter how hard any man is, they've still got feelings deep inside. They might not show them to those around them but there's always somebody that they'll open up to and I happened to be the one,' says Jackie. 'Johnny would have cried very easily, but I think the thing was that he could cry in front of me and he knew I wouldn't judge him on it. He would never have cried in front of his men, it was only me. Johnny was a very emotional person. He would have said to me, more than once, "You know me, you know that I've got a heart." He was obsessed with people realising he had a heart. "But you know what I'm like, Jackie, you know I've got a heart. I'm not a bad person, I'm not a bad person.'"

During the day Adair would plan attacks and send his men out to commit murders, but whenever he had a spare moment he would drive to Jackie's home in south Belfast to visit the girl he had started to nickname 'Legs'. He was so smitten that his C Coy henchmen, despairing of ever seeing him again, were frequently forced to turn up at Jackie's house and carry him out of her bed. Recalls Jackie: 'A car would have pulled up with a whole crowd of them. "Where's the wee man?" they would say, and they used to push past me, march up the stairs and say to Johnny, "Right, out." They would just take him out of bed and take him home.'

Although Jackie knew her new boyfriend was a member of the UDA, it was a while before she realised exactly who he was. 'I'd been seeing him a few weeks and a friend of my daughter's came into the house and said, "God, you'll never guess who you've been seeing." And I said, "Who?" and he went, "Mad Dog Adair." And I said, "Who's he?" and he says, "Commander on the Shankill." So I asked him [Adair] a couple of days later. We were talking and I said, "Are you commander on the Shankill?" And he thought it was hilarious. He made a big laugh and a joke out of it because he called everybody. I was sitting on the stairs and he went, "Oi, she wants to know if I'm commander on the Shankill," and the whole place went up in an uproar, they all cracked up laughing.'

By the time Jackie asked that question her boyfriend was more than just an ordinary UDA commander: he was fast gaining a reputation as the most ruthless and devious of them all. But Adair was also highly insecure. Some time in 1991, Jackie held a party at her house in south Belfast, which was attended by a number of loyalists, including Billy Wright, the mid-Ulster UVF commander who would later found the dissident Loyalist Volunteer Force.

'Billy Wright was sitting there in the living room but I didn't know who he was,' says Jackie. 'We had gone into the kitchen and I'd had the walls knocked down and sliding doors stuck in so you could see into the living room. He was sitting there on a roll of carpet with his head down. I happened to look at him because I thought he was not bad looking. About 15 minutes later Johnny calls in with Big Donald and Paddy Patterson [another C Coy volunteer], and Johnny stayed in the kitchen and didn't go into the living room at all. The next morning a carload of them pulled up and Johnny came flying in and said, "What the fuck did you have King Rat in here for?" He said he was a bastard. He always hated Billy and Billy hated Johnny with a passion. Anybody that took a bit of limelight off Johnny he didn't like. Billy was already there [as an established loyalist] and Johnny would probably have seen that as a threat, also the fact that he was UVF too.'

As his reputation grew in loyalist circles, Jackie gained a unique insight into the different sides of Adair's personality – the terrorist, the party animal, the family man and the lover. There were times when the different facets of his character collided, with some of the wildest parties coming hot on the heels of some of C Coy's most appalling murders. More than anything else, the Adair era of the early 1990s was defined by the lifestyle he and his friends started to lead, killing by day and partying by night. According to 'John', the hitmen themselves normally started with a low-key celebration. More often than not, the unlikely location was the scenic country park at Crawfordsburn, Co. Down. On the eastern shores of Belfast Lough, Crawfordsburn sits in the heart of Northern Ireland's sophisticated 'Gold Coast', home to luxury yachts, lawn tennis clubs and many of the Province's leading policemen, judges and civil servants. 'You'd have went and dropped the car, somebody would take the stuff away and then you'd go down to Crawfordsburn and have a carry-out and let things cool down for an hour or two,' explained 'John'.

Although the killers were often keen to lie low in case they made themselves obvious to the police, Adair and his friends would frequently celebrate for days at a time, according to Jackie. Although he never told her what he had been doing, she always knew if he had been involved in a murder because he would become even more hyper than usual. 'Sometimes Johnny would have phoned me and said, "Right, meet me down at the Kimberley," or Rangers Club or whatever bar they were going to. And then half an hour later they'd have put the news on and it [a murder] was on the news and they'd all be screaming and shouting and yo-hoing, so you knew. The west Belfast ones were the most excitable ones after a killing. They always made it known, they would have come into a bar ranting and raving so that everybody else knew they'd done it . . . How I always knew Johnny was up to something was he would disappear for a couple of days so he was doing his homework, that's the way I looked at it, he was setting something up. And then when the whole initial bang went off it was just a complete mad drinking session for about three or four days. That's how they worked.'

Jackie recalled, 'A couple of times we would have been talking and Johnny would have said, "I've always been military, I've been military from when I was no age and I worked my way up, I worked my way up the ladder." But he knew I wasn't stupid because he used to say, "You're not a bit daft; I don't have to tell you anything." And he said to me one day, "You know, Jackie, I would never send anybody out to do something that I wouldn't do myself." He said, "You get these bastards, they'd sit there and send these wee boys out to do it and they end up in jail and these uns are reaping the benefits.'"

By the early 1990s, Adair had two trademarks that set him apart from other loyalists. One was his selection of waistcoats, be they woollen, leather, multi-coloured or plain. The other was excess. By 1991, Johnny Adair was doing everything to excess – he and his friends were killing more Catholics than anybody else in the UDA, they were taking more drugs and they were spending more money. Said Jackie, 'He used to come into my house and try and throw me hundreds and I wouldn't take it. He would come in and say to me, "How do you manage? You've got a lovely home, your kids are well dressed – how do you do it?"' Even at this stage Adair was like a feudal chieftain, showering gifts and money over his most loyal subjects. For a murder his men were normally paid £100 plus the money to replace their clothes, which were burnt to destroy forensic evidence. But for his favourites the rewards were often greater. According to one former associate, 'If somebody was coming round selling jewellery or something, he would maybe say, "What about that chain? That would look good on you. What about it?"'

After one argument with Jackie, Adair rushed round to her house to apologise. She recalled, 'Within ten minutes – he came from nowhere – the car pulled up and he ran upstairs. And he says to me, and I could see he was really nervous, "Look, Jackie, I'm really sorry." And he says, "Do you want a gold necklace or do you want a bracelet? What do you want?" But to me he was trying to buy me because he had upset me and I said, "I don't want it, I don't want anything." "No, let me buy you something, please let me buy you something." But I used to joke with him; I used to say he had a job lot in Ratners jewellers because he had bought all his other girls gold chains. So the next night I was sitting and I saw the headlights pulling up and the door opened and he came bouncing in – "All because the lady loves Milk Tray". And he put this massive big box of Milk Tray down and a box with a chain in it.'

As well as jewellery, Adair was also generous when it came to drugs.

MAD DOG

From around 1990, as he started to make a name for himself, he and his friends were regularly taking Ecstasy at house parties in Belfast, some of which would go on for days. Bizarrely, for somebody so naturally hyperactive, the drugs would calm him down. 'Johnny would have sat with his head down half the night,' recalled Jackie. 'I didn't realise at first and I used to think he was just quiet when he was out, but more and more as time went on I realised. We were sitting in a bar one night and he lifted this thing out of his pocket and handed it to one of the guys, because he was very generous that way with his Es, he would have given them out. And I says, "What's that?" And he went, "None of your business." And he said, "Why, do you want one?" And I said, "What is it?" And he went, "Why, do you want it?" And I looked at him and I felt sick because I could see he was pushing me to take it and I thought, "What do I do here?" and I said no, and he said, "You're not fucking getting it anyway, you stay off them," and put it in his top pocket.'

As the Ecstasy scene took off across Britain, Adair and his friends, who by this time were starting to deal the drug on the Shankill, revelled in the chaos it created. At a house party in Taughmonagh one night, where UVF and UDA members mingled happily, Adair's friends played a series of sick jokes on a wealthy middle-aged woman who had returned with them from a pub in Bangor, Co. Down, where they had been drinking. The woman explained that her daughter, whose boyfriend was among those at the party, had been taking Es and said she wanted to see what the drug was like. She was clearly out of her depth and from an entirely different world. Having parked her brand-new Mercedes in the drive, she was initially too scared to enter the house. Once inside, however, Adair's friends relieved her of her mink coat and persuaded her to spend £60 on two E-tabs. According to an eyewitness, half an hour after taking both tabs, she was screaming wildly as she ran through the house, a carving knife in one hand, giving chase to a UVF man. Another leading UVF figure then persuaded her that her daughter's boyfriend was a serial killer who shot people in the head before leaving their bodies in wheelie bins. After being dumped in a bedroom, the woman charged downstairs and knocked herself out and was only brought round when her head was flushed down the toilet. By this time Adair's friends had not only let the tyres down on her Mercedes, they had also cut off the sleeves of her mink coat and were wearing them as hats. One of them had even taken a shit in the pocket. Before she left they relieved her of another £60 for two aspirin. It was an appalling ordeal.

'LEGS'

Another night, at a party in the Shankill home of Paddy Patterson, a senior C Coy member, Adair's friends dropped acid tabs in Jackie's drink before she left. 'By the time I got home I was looking at the wallpaper and it was dancing all over the place and bright lights were coming from under the door. And then the phone went and it was them. I said, "What have you done?" And they said, "Spiked your drink with four acids."' During another wild evening the wife of a south Belfast loyalist became jealous when a local woman started coming on to her husband. She sprayed the woman's hair with hairspray and set fire to it, seemingly as a joke. That same night Adair, never one to be outdone in the joke stakes, threw petrol over somebody's legs and set him alight before tossing a bucket of water over him. On another occasion, this time in a shebeen – an illegal drinking den – that had been set up on the lower Shankill estate, Adair told Raymond Elder, a south Belfast UDA gunman, to wind up a man known as 'Jackie Mad Dog' by yelling pro-UVF slogans. Said Jackie Robinson, 'Johnny was getting Raymie [Elder] to wind him up and they were shouting "Up the UVF" and Johnny was saying, "For fuck's sake, Jackie, listen to him, go and shoot him." And Paddy [Patterson] went to get a weapon and Raymie's face was a picture because he wasn't sure whether it was live bullets in it or not. Raymie was still screaming "Up the UVF" and Jackie Mad Dog was red with temper, he shot the gun but he just banged the bullets into the ceiling. Johnny was killing himself.'

When the four-day parties finally came to an end, it was back to the daily grindstone of being a notorious terrorist, a role which carried many perks but also came with the ever-present fear of being killed by the IRA and the pressure of being under constant surveillance by police. Jackie, who would later be arrested and interrogated because of her relationship with Adair, remembers the continual harassment whenever she was with him: 'They used to torture us. They used to sit and beep the horn all night outside the window and flash the lights. I'd have got into my car and I'd have only gone two streets and there's me pulled in. They pulled me in all the time, searching the car and asking for my driving licence, my insurance.' Whenever he was with friends Adair never lost an opportunity to brag about who he was to the security forces, but when Jackie was around he barely said a word. She feared, correctly as it turned out, that Adair would one day talk himself into prison. If she was near, Adair did his best to keep his mouth shut. 'Johnny got in the car one day and by the time he had turned round he was surrounded, they were waiting outside. I used to watch him when the police had stopped him and he used to stand with his head down and with his hands in his pockets, not a word sometimes. Not a word came out of him and they searched his car, they made him take his shoes off and he would have just stood there.'

By the end of 1991, Adair was still keen to attack the police and teach them a lesson. The only person holding him back was Jim Spence, his brigadier, who was becoming increasingly alarmed by the behaviour of his military commander. By late 1991, Spence was privately complaining that Adair was wielding too much power and that C Coy was becoming financially autonomous. His secret wish was for the police to shut down the Langley Street Social Club, the C Coy bar and its main source of money – by sheer coincidence the club was raided and put out of business. Far more worrying, however, was Adair's reckless desire to go after the security forces. The fact that a loyalist would even consider targeting the police astounded Spence, who knew the repercussions would be immense. But for Adair it was not just a question of police occasionally flashing their headlights into the house when he was in bed with Jackie or Gina. He claimed the harassment was often sinister. He complained that officers had told him they had passed his address and photo to the IRA, warning that he was going to get a bullet in the head. On several occasions, he claimed, they also suggested that he check under his car, a clear reference to the possibility of a booby-trap bomb.

Fortunately for Spence, he was able to talk sense to his friend and persuade him that murdering a police officer would land them all in jail. He reminded him that the forces of law and order were on their side. Even Adair knew that the fact that they were constantly on his back gave him a certain degree of protection. As Jackie put it, 'He was conscious that at the same time they were his life support and I think he was glad for that. Even though people didn't understand, he knew that while they were around him he was safe in more ways than one.'

The security forces also had other uses. Much has been said and written about collusion between the security forces and loyalist terrorists. In 2000, detectives from Sir John Stevens's third inquiry into collusion interviewed Adair after identifying his fingerprints on leaked photomontages of republican suspects dating back to the late 1980s, raising the prospect that he could have been imprisoned before C Coy embarked on its brutal killing spree. At a time when Adair was frequently going out on murder bids and searching for any intelligence he could get his hands on, it was only to be expected that he would be poring over documents brought in by Brian

Nelson. As he became a loyalist icon in the early 1990s, he continued to receive not just occasional help from the security forces but, among some at least, adulation.

Jackie, who was in a better position than most to observe this, remembers: 'A lot of the British soldiers had a lot of respect for Johnny, they really did. There was one in particular who used to come up, Andy, and I often wonder what happened to him. He was a nice bloke, a young bloke. And every time I got stopped and he was there, he used to say, "Look, Jackie, I'm sorry." And he used to say, "What about him? What about the wee man? Tell him I said hello." He used to say, "You tell Johnny, keep it up, all the respect of the day to him."' According to Jackie, Andy, who was from England, met with Adair on a number of occasions. 'They would have met up secretly, but this is what puzzled me because Johnny had all this surveillance around him so at the end of the day everybody knew what was going on.' However, although some members of the security forces helped Adair and many more may have been prepared to turn a blind eye to collusion, there is absolutely no evidence to suggest that Adair was benefiting from a formal arrangement or a policy decided high up the chain of command. Many British squaddies, sickened that they were still being killed on the streets of Belfast, felt the same hatred for the IRA as loyalists but also a solidarity with their fellow working class. As a result, many would have been vaguely sympathetic to the loyalist cause, though only a tiny minority would have considered helping the likes of Adair.

By 1992, however, Adair clearly had several sources of information. According to Johnston Brown, he claimed to receive a regular stream of intelligence from the security forces. 'He said he would get these unmarked envelopes through the letter box listing names and addresses and the car registration numbers of leading republicans. He said it had been going on for two or three months,' recalled Brown, who believed Adair was telling him the truth. At least two other senior UFF men in west Belfast were also receiving anonymous letters full of targeting information – Jackie Thompson and Jim Spence. Adair's claim did not surprise Brown, who had seen with his own eyes the help Adair received from members of the community sympathetic to his cause. 'He would be sitting at his house and all of a sudden one of his men would come up and say, "There's someone here for you, Johnny." It would be a businessman – suit, shirt and tie – with maybe five or ten grand in cash, saying, "You're doing a good job, keep Ulster right." But it would be as quick as that, he wouldn't even want to leave his name.'

Another source of information was a man from east Belfast who worked as a civilian for the Police Authority of Northern Ireland and installed security systems at police stations across the Province. Although it is not clear when he started to pass intelligence to Adair, in February 1994 he was arrested and charged with collecting information of use to terrorists. He also admitted stealing CCTV equipment from a police workshop – for which Paul Orr, Adair's finance and welfare officer, paid £1,100 – and installing it at the terrorist's home. The man's locker was searched and a slip of paper with Adair's home telephone number recovered along with the registration number of a car belonging to a leading republican in Derry. Adair later claimed that his mole had also provided him with montages of republican suspects. 'It wouldn't have been that difficult for him once he had access to police stations to get his hands on all sorts of things,' said one police officer familiar with the case. 'If he found himself alone, he could easily have taken a montage down from a noticeboard in a private section of a police station. Once you're there [inside police stations], you're there, you're regarded as part of the family.'

By the start of 1994, Adair had another valuable source of intelligence and once again he was local. Between January and April, Derek Adgey, a Belfast Protestant and a Royal Marine, passed details of republican suspects, including Sinn Fein councillor Alex Maskey and the IRA's Brian Gillen, to the UFF after walking into a loyalist bar and speaking to Winkie Dodds. Adgey, from a well-to-do family in south Belfast, had flipped after his unit came under attack during a tour in the city. According to one police officer who worked on the case, 'His unit got biffed, once with a coffee jar bomb and once with a rocket. Adgey just threw the head up and he went, "Right, I'm going to sort this out." The first time he got home leave he went down the Shankill looking for Johnny but Johnny wouldn't see him. Who he actually met was Winkie, and so he started to feed them all sorts of stuff through a drop address in the lower Shankill. I felt so sorry for that lad because he was from a superb family; his parents were devastated. He just got fed up because his mates were being hurt.'

At Adgey's trial in October 1995 the court was told that he supplied information by telephone and by letters posted from England to the home of Jacqueline Newell, a Shankill woman and his former girlfriend. Newell provided the perfect conduit into C Coy through her then boyfriend, Stevie McKeag, one of Adair's top gunmen. A mother of two, the 28-year-old admitted acting as a go-between for the Royal Marine and the UFF, but was freed when her two-year jail term was suspended. Adgey, who told police that he had wanted the UFF to 'scare off' or 'bump off' suspected IRA men, was jailed for four years after confessing to ten counts of soliciting murder and twelve of recording and collecting information. Although nobody was killed on the basis of his information, he justified handing over intelligence on the grounds that he 'hated the Provos and would rather they were killed than innocent Catholics'.

Although the arrangement between Adair and Adgey was short-lived, the Royal Marine clearly held the loyalist in high regard. According to one old associate of Adair, Adgey was eventually allowed to meet the terrorist. He said, 'I knew Del, I've met him a few times. He would have been around Johnny, you would have seen him with him.' It was proof that, although there was never orchestrated collusion between the security forces and Adair, among fringe elements of the police and Army the terror chief inspired a degree of respect and even admiration. Some of them believed Adair's war was just and necessary. As Jackie put it, 'You see, when the Provies hit one of the British Army, they [C Coy] were out there because they were British and they felt they were defending the British. If something had happened to one of the soldiers they'd have been out there, they'd have been doing something.'

6. Top Gun

'You can put Stevie down for about 14 hits . . . The main operator through all of this was [Stevie] McKeag. He set the standard.' – *'Pete'*, *a C Coy gunman*

JACKIE THOMPSON HAD A BAD FEELING. HE ALWAYS SLEPT LIKE A BABY THE night before an operation, but on 17 July 1992 he had lain awake for hours with a giant knot in the pit of his stomach. As he clambered into the car the next morning, the feeling, more intense than anything he had ever experienced, was still with him. His mouth was dry and his heart was racing. He was convinced that something was about to go terribly wrong.

'Skelly, I think we should maybe wait,' he said as he leaned past Tommy Potts to talk to Sam McCrory, the front-seat passenger.

'Fuck's sake, this is Gillen, we can't turn back,' came the reply as Matthew 'Muff' McCormick, another west Belfast volunteer, put the blue Cavalier into first gear and started to follow another vehicle driven by a local UDA man, Andrew Watson.

As they drove through the deserted streets of the loyalist Taughmonagh estate in south Belfast, Thompson told himself that his concerns were probably groundless. He had been on dozens of operations since 1990 and he had never yet been caught in the act. But at the back of his mind there were a couple of doubts nagging away. It was the first time C Coy had planned a hit together with another UDA brigade area, a fact that in itself made him apprehensive. He was also worried about the route they were planning to take. For Thompson, who had started off as a driver before becoming a gunman, there was one point in particular where he knew they were vulnerable. There was a blind spot at the railway bridge on Finaghy Road North. No matter how you approached it, it was impossible to know what was on the other side.

Thompson took a few deep breaths and steadied his nerves. It would be crazy, he muttered to himself, to abandon the operation at such a late stage. When Johnny had come to him the previous afternoon, the plan had seemed too good to be true: here was an opportunity to kill Brian Gillen, the IRA's Belfast commander, Martin Lynch, another senior Provisional, and two female republicans in one go. It would be an almighty blow to the IRA, and one that would make them heroes back on the Shankill.

As the two cars drove along Diamond Gardens on the way out of Taughmonagh, Thompson began to relax. It was roughly a mile to Andersonstown in nationalist west Belfast, where their targets were staying, and they would be in and out within 20 minutes. As the convoy turned onto Finaghy Road North, Thompson strained his eyes but could see no sign of trouble. Just to be sure, he told McCormick to take his foot off the accelerator as they approached the bridge. 'Take it easy here, Muff. Go as slow as you can,' he said.

It was too late. Shortly after 7 a.m. on Saturday, 18 July 1992, three of C Coy's most efficient operators were removed from the streets after driving straight into a police ambush beyond the brow of the bridge at Finaghy railway station. It was the exact spot Thompson had been worried about. Watson hit the checkpoint first, stopping and casually chatting to police in an attempt to pass himself off as an ordinary citizen. Then came the murder car. McCormick, who was doing about 20 mph, slammed on the brakes and threw the vehicle into reverse.

With the car still going backwards, McCormick flung open the door and jumped out but was shot in the leg as he ran off. Minus its driver, the car rolled down the hill and crashed into a lamppost. 'Lucky enough we were going dead slow,' said one of the team. 'We just bundled out and tried to run, but as soon as we hit the top [of the bridge] there was a peeler in front of us whacking into the car with rounds. To me it looked like there were four or five of the peelers who then opened up. There was an undercover soldier in the car behind us. He started shooting at us through his windie when we got out to run. The peelers were shooting at us but they actually ended up hitting the soldier. He got hit in the shoulder, so he did.' As the others bounced out, soldiers and police swarmed around them, pinning them to the road and the railings at the side of the bridge. 'If we'd have stayed in the car, we'd have been dead,' said the C Coy man. 'You just threw yourself on the ground – to be honest I thought we were going to be carried off the bridge.'

His view is borne out by another member of the team, who claims police and soldiers opened fire without proper warning, letting off several shots followed by two sustained bursts of gunfire. Had it not been for a jogger passing at that moment, he believes they would probably have been shot dead. 'That jogger saved our lives. They were trying to wipe us out – this was going to be our Loughgall,' he said in a reference to the SAS massacre of eight elite IRA men in May 1987. 'The police evidence was total rubbish on how they intercepted us. They told the court there was a man in the front of the [second] car with what appeared to be a rifle, but that was a lie. All the guns were on the floor in the back. They were under our feet.'

The attack had been set in motion less than 24 hours earlier under circumstances that say much about Johnny Adair's relationship with the security forces. According to one of the murder gang, details of where Gillen, Lynch and their two female colleagues were staying were supplied to Adair by a solider at a checkpoint in west Belfast on 17 July, the day before the operation. Adair was in the car with Thompson and Skelly when he was pulled over. 'You'd wonder about it being a set-up because it was actually a British soldier who had dropped us the information,' said one of the murder gang. 'We were up having a wee look around, just scouting about, and the soldier stopped us at a routine P check [a police 'personality' checkpoint]. One of them just whispered such and such and gave an address, said they'd be staying there all week. That was where we got a lot of information from, at ordinary P checks. They would just come over and whisper to you – blah, blah, blah, and "such and such", a couple of names and where we could find them.'

Adair decided there was no time to lose. He immediately started planning the operation and studied the routes in and out. Later that afternoon he briefed all four members of the hit team. For Thompson and Skelly, both dedicated killers, it would be just another murder. But for Potts, an intelligent, brawny 23-year-old who would be back-up gunman, it was his first big operation. Ever since joining C Coy in 1986, the Shankill man, whose family had a history of involvement with the UVF, had been desperate for a piece of the action. As usual, Adair's method was to send out inexperienced volunteers with seasoned operators. Like Potts,

McCormick, the fourth member of the team, was also young and untested. He was 25. 'Muff had been out once before with the WDA [Woodvale Defence Association – B Coy] but that was it. We were stuck for a driver that day,' explained another member of the team.

That evening the four were driven to Taughmonagh, where Alec Kerr, the UDA's brigadier in south Belfast, provided a flat for them to crash in. A member of the C9 Oldpark team brought the weapons – a sub-machine gun, a rifle and a pistol – across from the Shankill. He was one of Adair's closest friends but he had also been cultivated for a special skill. His boss had long ago noticed his ability to move guns and not get caught, on one occasion even taking an AK-47 into south Belfast in a pram. This time the job was more straightforward. He drove the weapons to a car park in south Belfast where they were entrusted to Andrew Watson, who looked after them overnight before taking them to the flat the next morning. After an early rise, Skelly, Thompson and Potts went over the operation one last time: the idea was to burst in while the occupants were still sleeping and overwhelm them with massive firepower. While Skelly and Thompson smashed down the outside door with a sledgehammer and went in from the front, Potts would cover the rear of the house in case they tried to escape through the back.

At least that was the plan. As Belfast started to stir, the security forces delivered a crippling blow to C Coy. They were arrested half a mile short of their destination of Riverdale Park North, a street that would make international headlines 11 years later as the address of a man alleged to be the Army's top spy inside the IRA, codenamed 'Stakeknife'. Unbeknownst to C Coy, the Dream Team had been under constant watch by the RUC's E4A undercover surveillance unit, and by 7 a.m. that morning the route into Andersonstown was swarming with undercover police and soldiers. 'Operation Hastings' had been planned since at least the start of the month, clearly on the basis of excellent intelligence. To this day those involved insist they were betrayed by one of their colleagues, possibly a senior UDA figure in south Belfast.

Adair could not believe it when he heard the news. It was the first time he had put together an operation with the help of another area, and he too suspected an informer. The following day he suspended all west Belfast military operations while a special C Coy team carried out an investigation into how police had found out about the attack. 'The thing that made Johnny so concerned was that it was a pure set-up and the police were going to wipe them out. They just lifted their guns and started firing,' said one C8 veteran. The loss was devastating. Nine months later, the killing careers of Skelly, Thompson and Potts were halted indefinitely when they were each jailed for 16 years after pleading guilty to conspiracy to murder. McCormick was given 14 years after the judge ruled that he had no terrorist record. In February 1995, Watson finally gave up trying to pretend that his presence on the road that morning had been totally innocent and pleaded guilty to conspiracy to murder and possessing firearms. He was jailed for ten years.

The ambush was also a blow to Adair's plans to target the IRA's senior commanders. By 1992, killing Brian Gillen had become a personal obsession for Adair, who hated him almost as much as he hated Eddie Copeland, the IRA's commander in Ardoyne. Whenever he had time to stop and chat to police or soldiers, Adair made a point of mentioning the names of leading republicans. Often this included Gillen. Sometimes, mainly because he could not help showing off, he would even throw in an address. According to police records, between 1991 and 1994 Adair was constantly asking officers for information. On one occasion, after being stopped on the Shankill, he told a sergeant, 'I know more than you,' and gave two addresses in nationalist west Belfast where he believed Gillen to be hiding. Asked who lived there, Adair replied, 'You know who lives there,' adding, 'What about Gillen?' Another time he was stopped by an Army patrol on the Andersonstown Road. 'I'm protecting the public of Great Britain. I'm looking for that man Gillen,' he said, before remarking that he preferred an AK-47 rifle to an SA-80. Adair claimed Gillen was so afraid of him that he was refusing to go out. 'Don't be fooled by my size, it takes balls,' he boasted. At another military checkpoint he asked for information about Gillen's 'new address' and said that he wished to kill him personally. Incredibly, although Adair was making a direct threat against another individual, no action was taken to arrest him.

Sometimes Adair's intelligence was worryingly accurate thanks to occasional help from the security forces and his own excursions into nationalist ghettos, often wearing a Celtic football jersey and with a cardboard cut-out of a Celtic player dangling from his back windscreen. But while some of his information was from excellent sources, there were many occasions when this was far from the case. Early in 1992 a Catholic woman from north Belfast called in to the UDA's offices on the Shankill Road and asked to see Adair. Over the course of several meetings she claimed that one of her neighbours was in the IRA and provided information on when he would be at home. At first Adair was not sure whether to trust her but played her along because he wanted to use her for sex. According to 'John': 'Some wired-up woman called into the old offices and asked to see Johnny. She said, "I'm blah, blah, blah," so Johnny went along to see her and she blabbed this out. But Johnny wanted a blowjob off her and she's giving him a blowjob in the car park of Belfast Zoo one day when she tells him all about this bloke, her neighbour. It was a fall-out and she was looking for revenge.'

The person she had fallen out with was Paddy Clarke, a 52-year-old Catholic taxi driver with four children. Just after 7 p.m. on Sunday, 2 February, a lone C Coy gunman kicked open the door to his house on Rosemount Gardens off the Antrim Road and strode into the living room where he was watching television. The gunman, a C8 volunteer and one of Adair's closest friends, looked enormous as he stood in front of Clarke, dressed in black from head to toe and wearing a motorcycle helmet. As Clarke shouted at his wife and five-year-old child to 'get down on the floor', he was shot four times in the head and body. Seeing his victim crash to the ground, the gunman turned and walked calmly out. His accomplice was waiting outside, on a hijacked motorbike that had broken down as they pulled up to the house and had had to be pushed the final few yards. After getting the bike going again, the killers drove to Ballysillan in north Belfast where it was disposed of by C Coy's Sammy McKay, who was later jailed for seven years for his part in helping the murder gang.

It was not long before C Coy struck again. Around 7.30 p.m. on Thursday, 12 March 1992, Liam McCartan, a 32-year-old Catholic, was shot dead on the doorstep of his home in Ardoyne in north Belfast. The unemployed social worker had been given £3 by his mother to buy a few cans of beer and was about to head out to a local shop. He was answering a knock at the door when the gunmen struck, shooting him five times in the head, groin and arm. In its admission of responsibility the UFF said the dead man was a member of the IPLO, although this was strongly denied by a local priest and the IPLO itself. In an interview with one of the authors, one of those involved in the operation highlighted the weakness of the UFF's intelligence on this occasion. He flatly contradicted his organisation's original statement by claiming that McCartan had been a member of the IRA's 3rd battalion. The UFF man said his task had been to collect two brothers shortly after the shooting. Both brothers were involved in the murder and were starting to become active C Coy operators. 'I picked him [one of the gunmen] and his brother up an hour after the killing from a house where they had cleaned up and got the residue off. Then two days later I went back and removed the gun,' he said.

The Clarke and McCartan murders were by no means the only examples of dodgy intelligence. At 9.20 a.m. on Monday, 28 April, Philomena Hanna was gunned down shortly after she turned up at the chemist's shop she worked in off the Falls Road. A UFF gunman, his face masked by a balaclava and motorcycle helmet, strode into the Springfield Pharmacy and shot her six times in the head and body while his accomplice waited outside on a red Suzuki motorbike. The final shots were fired from point-blank range as the gunman leant over his victim as she lay on the ground, the unmistakeable sign of a killer with frightening composure. Hanna, who had two daughters, aged six and one, was viewed on both sides of the nearby peaceline as a good Samaritan who never hesitated, despite considerable personal risk, to deliver prescriptions and oxygen to the homes of elderly Protestants too sick to reach her shop. Father Gerry Reynolds, the family's priest, said after the murder, 'I will never forget her little girl saying to me, "My mammy won't be there now for my first communion."'

The UFF claimed it had killed an IRA member and the sister of a Sinn Fein press officer but both allegations, which the loyalists said were based on 'high-grade intelligence', were denied. A detective at the inquest said, 'If that was high-grade intelligence I wouldn't like to see their low-grade intelligence.' In the eyes of the world the murder was an act of naked sectarianism, and Hanna had been singled out for the simple reason that her pharmacy was so close to the peaceline and easy to reach. For C Coy, though, no murder was too callous, and Adair and his friends had two reasons to celebrate that night. Their 'high-grade intelligence' had been an unsubstantiated piece of gossip linking Hanna to the car bomb attack on Gerry Drumgoole the previous November. 'Hanna got the blame for putting the car bomb under Gerry Drumgoole's car,' disclosed an old friend of Adair. 'Intelligence through our sources said she walked up and down the street with a pram past Gerry's house. Apparently she set it up or put it under the car.'

But there was also a bigger cause for celebration. The gunman was a new kid on the block who had only joined the UDA weeks earlier. His name was Stevie McKeag. 'That was Stevie's first – he was happy enough after that all right,' recalled 'James', one of McKeag's closest friends. He laughed when asked about Hanna's murder. 'That was about five in the head, right in the front of her fucking face.'

MAD DOG

McKeag, a balding, ginger-haired man with cold blue eyes, had lived an unusually full life for somebody in his early 20s. By the time he joined C Coy he had spent several years as a born-again Christian and had just split up with his wife, Alison, the mother of his two children. Although he no longer went to church, he still believed in God and considered himself a religious man. 'He always had a belief, definitely,' said Tracey Coulter, who was his girlfriend for more than six years. 'He didn't regularly read the Bible but he knew his commandments and all.' McKeag was good humoured and well liked on the Shankill, where he had lived all his life. Above all he was noted for his extravagant hobbies, which included collecting gadgets, mixing dance music and an interest in exotic animals. In addition to his Rottweiler, 'Butch', he was at one time the proud owner of a snake, a scorpion, an iguana, several tropical fish and a parrot called Nancy that never stopped singing the theme tune to *Laurel and Hardy*. When he announced that he planned to buy a monkey, however, Tracey's patience finally ran out. 'He was going to get a monkey but I had to put my foot down,' she recalled.

Even before he shot dead Philomena Hanna, McKeag was known for his coolness under pressure. He was the Shankill Road's very own Indiana Jones. According to friends, he was so unflappable that he even helped to deliver one of his two sons at a petrol station as he tried to get his wife to hospital, a story they repeat to this day. He rarely talked about politics but whenever he did expressed strong views. 'Pete', a fellow C Coy gunman and a close friend, described him as quietly passionate about defending his community. 'Stevie felt a huge responsibility to the people in the Shankill. It wasn't that he wanted to go out and murder people but he thought that the only way it was going to stop was by taking it to the IRA's door.'

The murder of Philomena Hanna set something off in Stevie McKeag. Over the next 18 months he waged an almost single-handed murder campaign that would write him into loyalist mythology but also provoke more than a tinge of envy in Johnny Adair. He saw himself as a solider and prided himself on his killing. McKeag's trademarks were the back-to-front baseball cap he wore on every operation and a thick gold necklace with a pistol-shaped pendant, specially made by a jeweller in Belfast. He quickly filled the gap left by the arrests of Thompson and Skelly, becoming C Coy's most efficient assassin and the best of a new breed of Shankill militants. 'Around 1992 there were now two ASUs,' said 'John'. 'Once the Dream Team got it going there were others who wanted to do a bit. You'd have maybe used them in the past lifting cars or something. It was just getting too much so we had to spread it out a bit. Every fucking day you had a new face but you always had somebody from before going out with them.'

In early 1992, McKeag became desperate to get involved. On 17 January, eight Protestant workmen, who had been carrying out repairs on an Army base in Co. Tyrone, were blown apart when an IRA landmine exploded under their minibus at the Teebane crossroads between Omagh and Cookstown. It was a brutal attack on ordinary Protestants, but loyalists did not have to wait long to see nationalists suffer. On 4 February, they celebrated when a policeman, Constable Allen Moore, distraught over the death of a colleague in a domestic dispute, walked into Sinn Fein's offices on the Falls Road and shot dead three party members before turning his gun on himself.

The following day five Catholics were killed, including a 15-year-old boy, when two gunmen walked into a crowded betting shop on the Ormeau Road in south Belfast and sprayed customers with automatic rifles. The UFF said the attack was carried out in retaliation for Teebane. The mastermind behind it was Adair. According to 'Davy', who was close to him at this time, Adair put pressure on the organisation in south Belfast to carry it out through his friendship with local UFF leaders Joe Bratty and Raymond Elder. He also helped his colleagues in south Belfast by providing one of the gunmen.

The attack created a bond between the three commanders, and when the murder charges against Elder were dropped in November of that year, Adair organised a special celebration party in Scotland and presented him with a gold ring with the initials 'UFF' cut into it. The view that Adair was ultimately responsible is echoed by Special Branch, which in a report in 1993 suggested he was the driving force behind the massacre. In a section marked, 'Personality/Attitude', focused specifically on his leadership, the report states:

> Throughout Adair's reign, the hallmark of his activity has been his unpredictability and willingness to attack innocent RC [Roman Catholic] targets. It is with Adair's sanction that his murder teams have regularly targeted PIRA/SF members in a given area for assassination, but on being unable to locate these targets, attacked innocent members of the RC community, rather than leave without a 'kill'. Moreover, examples of sheer sectarian murder abound, such

as the Murray's Bookmakers murders [in November 1992], or the
Sean Graham Bookmakers murders and numerous other examples.

Around the same time as the bookies bloodbath, McKeag joined the C13
team on the Shankill, whose members included two brothers, both of whom
had already distinguished themselves as eager gunmen. Although
inexperienced, his enthusiasm marked him out. 'If there was something
happening and you were eager enough and you've been saying, "Fuck, I
want to try something here," that's how you got on an operation,' said
'John'.

In the words of Ian Truesdale, one of Adair's oldest friends, 'He idolised
Johnny. He would have stood in front of Johnny and took two or three
bullets in the head.' He even dressed like his boss, phoning Jackie Robinson,
Adair's girlfriend, on numerous occasions and asking her to buy him the
same tight T-shirts and caps that she was getting for her boyfriend. Jackie
recalled, 'He used to try and model himself on Johnny because I would have
bought Johnny's clothes. He [McKeag] would have rung me and said, "If
you go into town will you buy me what you're getting him?" He liked the
way I dressed Johnny.'

McKeag, whose birthday was on April Fools' Day, had barely turned 22
when he shot Philomena Hanna. His utter lack of emotion as reported by
eyewitnesses and exhibited during interviews astonished the police. 'The
peelers used to say he was possessed, he was that crazy,' said 'Pete', another
C Coy gunman who was also amazed by McKeag's coolness. 'Everybody, no
matter who you were, got sweaty palms. But not Stevie. He just fucking
flew through it.' By the time he was arrested and charged with murder in
November 1993 he had killed more Catholics than anybody around him,
filling his comrades with admiration and awe. 'The first couple of times
you'd have went out and you'd have been nervous, but basically if it's in
you, it's in you,' boasted 'John'.

'It' was definitely in Stevie McKeag. According to C Coy sources, on 27
September 1992, nearly five months to the day after his first taste of blood,
McKeag shot dead an 18-year-old Catholic schoolboy at his home in New
Lodge in north Belfast. Gerard O'Hara, known as 'Soggy', had just popped
out to buy a packet of cigarettes and sweets and was about to settle down
to watch television with his mother, Bridie. She was looking forward to
spending a quiet Sunday evening with her son. Little did she realise that her
house was being watched by C Coy. Shortly before 5 p.m. McKeag and

another masked gunman burst into the house and opened fire, having observed the teenager return home from the hijacked car they were waiting in. O'Hara managed to shut the living-room door but one of the killers dropped onto his knees and shot him through a glass panel in the bottom of the door. Once he was on the floor, they finished him off in the same style as Philomena Hanna, firing into his head from point-blank range. He was hit 17 times.

Bridie had pleaded with one of the killers to stop. 'I asked him to stop – to shoot me instead. He looked me in the eye and then he went on shooting,' she said afterwards. Sandra, the dead boy's sister, added, 'My mother was standing at the top of the stairs and she shouted at them. Mummy begged them to shoot her instead, but they shot my brother.' The UFF's claim that Gerard O'Hara was an IRA member was attacked as 'downright lies' by Father Aidan Brankin. He told mourners at the funeral, 'Gerard was a quiet, loveable, innocent young fella who loved nothing more than playing with his young nephews, listening to music and watching television. The nearest he got to the Troubles and violence was watching through a window.'

According to high-grade police intelligence, the murder gang included Adair's friend and neighbour, Norman Green Jnr. The killing took place less than 100 yards from a street called Midland Close in the loyalist Tigers Bay area where Adair had set up a satellite team. They were such lowlifes that the UDA's north Belfast brigade had tried to expel them from its ranks. They included Stephen 'Dick' Dempsey, a small bisexual man with a ponytail and a tattoo of a naked lady devil on his left arm, and William 'Buff' Hunter. 'They were housebreakers and hoods and the UDA in north Belfast said it didn't want them: they said they had been knee-capping them and trying to sort them out,' commented one police officer. 'They would have shot their own mothers, but Adair still took them.'

The UDA insists to this day that there was a legitimate IRA target in the house that night. Their intelligence had come from a CID officer in Castlereagh police barracks, who told a C Coy gunman that one of O'Hara's brothers was an IRA member who had been involved in the killing of Damian Shackleton, a 24-year-old Scots Guard, in New Lodge in August. There was never any evidence to back up the RUC man's claim, but it was wrongly treated as fact by Adair. According to one C Coy hitman, one policeman in particular had a knack of casually letting things slip: 'Your man would just sit there with his shoes, Hush Puppies they were, up on the table, leaning back in his chair and just going, "Can you boys do nothing but kill innocent Catholics every fucking time?" You would maybe be able to hear what was going on in the other rooms and they'd be shouting next door at some guy they were questioning. "You fenian bastard, you fucking bastard," and your man would be saying to you, "He's in for killing that policeman so-and-so." And there were times when the window or the door would be open and you'd be able to see out. He'd be looking out and he's saying to you, "Did you see that guy there?" and you'd say, "Yes," and he's saying, "He's a cop killer. He kills policemen.'"

The fact that an RUC officer was supplying C Coy with titbits of intelligence is no great surprise, though given Gerard O'Hara's age and the circumstances of his murder it is particularly appalling. During interviews in Castlereagh the same officer later urged a C Coy gunman to target Sinn Fein and suggested several places they could attack, including a bar on the Falls Road and the party's headquarters in Andersonstown.

Even though he had shot the wrong person, nobody challenged Stevie McKeag. In fact, his attitude was generally admired. 'Sometimes all you would be told was that it was the cunt with the ginger hair that was the target and if you bounced in and saw somebody with ginger hair they got it,' said one gunman. 'You didn't like wasting a journey – if you couldn't get the target, get his brother or get the bloke walking down the road. It was terror. We were doing back to them [the republican community] what they were doing to us.'

McKeag revelled in the image he was acquiring. He was clearly the man of the moment. Less than a month after O'Hara's murder he cemented his reputation with an attack that went down as a glorious day for Johnny Adair and C Coy. In November, the UFF issued a statement responding to an IRA bomb blitz that had damaged hundreds of Protestant homes in Northern Ireland. Two months earlier, as the Provisionals stepped up their campaign in Britain with a firebomb attack on the Hyde Park Hilton Hotel, a 1,000 lb bomb had destroyed the Northern Ireland Forensic Science Laboratory in Belfast's loyalist Belvoir estate, wrecking 1,000 homes. In October, as IRA bombs continued to explode in central London, a 200 lb device ripped through the commercial heart of Bangor, Co. Down, while at least 100 homes were damaged when a car bomb exploded outside a police station in another Protestant town, Glengormley. In a telephoned statement to the BBC, the UFF warned that, as of midnight on 6 November, any further bombs in Protestant areas would be responded to with attacks against 'the republican community as a whole'. Its riposte, it said, would be similar to its action after the massacre at

TOP GUN

Teebane, a grim reference to the carnage at the Ormeau Road bookies.

Shortly before 11 p.m. on 13 November, a 500 lb IRA car bomb rocked the Unionist town of Coleraine, damaging 50 shops full of Christmas stock and leaving three pensioners injured. The following afternoon the UFF delivered its response. As customers inside James Murray's betting shop on the Oldpark Road watched the four o'clock race from Cheltenham, Stevie McKeag and another C Coy volunteer stepped out of their hijacked Ford Escort and strode into the bookies. It was, as loyalists called it, a 'spray job'. One pulled a machine gun from under his jacket and raked the place with gunfire, spraying steadily from left to right. The other then yelled, 'Youse deserve it, youse fenian bastards,' and tossed a grenade into the shop. All but four of the sixteen people inside, one of whom was a Protestant, were injured. Peter Orderly, 50, was hit by at least three bullets, while Francis Burns, 62, was shot four times and badly wounded by the grenade blast. Both died within seconds. A third man, 72-year-old John Lovett, who was hit in the chest, died the next day having been given 40 pints of blood in an attempt to save his life. He was a Second World War veteran who had been tortured by the Japanese as an RAF prisoner of war. As his sister said afterwards, 'Here was a man who served Britain, suffered terribly for it, and look what happens.'

It was a miracle more were not killed. A man who held the hand of one of the dying said, 'I counted about six bodies on the floor. They were all moaning and only one man spoke. He said to me, "Will we be all right?" I told him, "You're OK and don't worry." It was dreadful. One man's leg was practically hanging off, then a priest came and he anointed everybody.' Another customer, who was hit by three bullets, said, 'I saw a man standing in the door. He started firing. I could hear John Lovett saying, "Keep your calm, keep your calm." He got hit. He was in front of me and I knew I was next. Then I could feel myself getting hit a number of times.'

As the getaway car was being stolen earlier that afternoon, the hijackers told the owner, 'We have to pay back those fenian bastards for last night and the other times.' The betting shop, just yards from the 15-foot-high fence separating Catholics and Protestants in the Oldpark district, was a pathetically easy target. As the ambulances arrived, cheers rang out from across the peaceline. In its admission of responsibility the UFF predicted there would be more killings like it. 'We again warn . . . that the theatre of war will be full of casualties from the republican community in the coming weeks,' it said.

After the shooting the gunmen and their driver changed their clothes and washed themselves down at a house barely 100 yards from the killing, on the Protestant side of the peaceline. The house belonged to a close associate of Adair, who was rewarded with a bottle of vodka. After getting rid of their clothes, a large C Coy crowd, including one of the killers, went to celebrate at a club in south Belfast. Later that afternoon Adair phoned Jackie Robinson and asked her to join them in the Sandy Row Rangers Club. Although Adair was not one of the gunmen, he enjoyed taking credit for it. They were all sitting drinking when news of the murders came on the television. 'It came on the TV as a newsflash and they were cheering and shouting,' said Jackie. 'He [Adair] was hyper. I said, "I take it you've done the bookies?" He was slapping everybody on the back and shaking their hands.' Jackie was amazed that Johnny was so bold and open about what he claimed to have done. It astonished her that he was making it clear that he had been involved in the bookies murders.

McKeag, however, was nowhere to be seen. Although he would later turn to drugs in a major way, flamboyant parties were not his style in the early 1990s. At a party in the Avenue One Bar in east Belfast in 1993, leading UDA figure Jim Gray gave McKeag a bag of cocaine, but he flushed it down the toilet. He was not interested in anything that distracted him from killing. One former friend, in whom McKeag confided, revealed, 'He used to say, "At the end of the day I went out, I pulled the trigger and I came home and I didn't run round shouting and screaming about it." Whatever Stevie did he kept in his own head . . . He never expressed any regret. He saw himself as a soldier and that's the way it was. He believed what he did was right and he was hitting republican targets.' The same friend added, 'He was a very nice person, Stevie. He didn't come across as a bully – he never threw his weight about the way the others did. He was completely the opposite. Don't get me wrong, Stevie partied later on but he wasn't one that ran about like the rest of them saying what he'd done.'

Police officers, however, remember McKeag as anything but 'nice'. One detective who interviewed him in 1993 recalled, 'He was probably the most evil person that I've ever come across, and I've interviewed some super-dooper IRA and INLA men in my time. This guy would rank up amongst them. He would sit there, completely silent, just staring right through you. It was like, "Who do you think you are trying to talk to me?"'

Four months later, McKeag claimed his first republican victim. Peter Gallagher, a Sinn Fein supporter who helped to put up posters in his neighbourhood, was killed on 24 March 1993 as he arrived for work at a building yard in west Belfast. As he opened a storage unit, McKeag, who was hiding in bushes behind a fence, opened fire on the father of six with a 9mm Browning that had been used 24 hours earlier in a C Coy attack on the home of Gerard McGuigan, a Sinn Fein councillor. A detective told the inquest that the UFF had not claimed responsibility for the murder until the victim was identified in the media as a Sinn Fein supporter, raising the prospect that the terrorists may not have been aware of his republican credentials. But the fact that McKeag carried out the shooting alone, making his escape on a bicycle, won him the unabashed adulation of his colleagues. 'He pulled up on a pushbike and shot him through the railings. That was Stevie on his own – that was a good move, like,' said 'Davy'. 'He actually pedalled away on the bike, left the gun wherever he left it and got a lift home. That one always sticks in my mind because of the way it happened.'

By the time McKeag was imprisoned in November that year he had shot dead at least four more people, including an IRA member, a 17-year-old shop trainee and a hairdresser. Although he did not celebrate as wildly as the rest of them, he got his reward. As Adair took control in west Belfast, he made McKeag C Coy military commander. He also decided to expand the UDA's annual awards ceremony, turning it into a macabre evening of back-slapping at which C Coy's best killers were decorated as heroes. The first of these was held in 1993 after Adair took over as brigadier. 'The awards ceremony was hijacked by Johnny,' said one former friend. 'It started off as just a nice evening out for the LPA [Loyalist Prisoners' Aid], where they would recognise people for long-term service to the UDA and all that. Johnny hijacked it and turned it into an occasion to thank the men. There might be four or five who were handed out plaques for things like scouting work, minding weapons, and the ones who were doing robberies left, right and centre. And we wouldn't always know what they were getting the awards for.'

In the early 1990s the awards ceremony was held in The Berlin Arms on the Shankill, but in 1993 it moved to the Diamond Jubilee Bar further down the road. Everyone was expecting an ordinary night when all of a sudden four masked gunmen burst through the doors. Two were carrying AK-47s, one an Uzi and another a belt-fed M-60. As the gunmen stood in silence, Adair presented seven plaques for operations that had taken place that year, including one for Stevie McKeag. He was given the 'Top Gun' award for being the most outstanding killer of the year. According to one of McKeag's closest friends, 'Stevie always got Top Gun. He would have had plaques with his name on it saying he was Top Gun UFF for the year.'

Gradually the awards ceremony became a polished, slick event, with a buffet and drinks laid on, and a raffle that included bikes, televisions, camcorders and Sony PlayStations. The evening would begin with a pumping rendition by a local band of Tina Turner's 'Simply the Best', which Adair had adopted as his C Coy anthem, after which Adair was welcomed on to the stage to rapturous applause. But although the format changed, one thing stayed the same: the 'Top Gun' award, the most coveted prize, always went to McKeag. As the name stuck he had a special 'Top Gun' tattoo emblazoned on his left breast and another, of a masked gunman and the slogan 'UFF', on his right arm. Over the years his house on the lower Shankill estate became a shrine to his many awards. A large mirror took pride of place in the living room, bearing his name and the initials 'UFF' in frosted writing next to the image of a gunman. Scattered across the room were plaques, paintings and statuettes, many of which were presented to him by other UDA brigades, and photographs of McKeag and Johnny Adair.

By the time of his arrest in November 1993, McKeag had become one of the most prolific mass murderers of the Troubles. By the time of his death seven years later his colleagues believe he had killed over a dozen people. As 'Pete' explained, 'You can put Stevie down for about 14 hits. It became common knowledge how many hits people had done. You would have referred to the fact that J**** would have done two, S**** done three. People got associated with numbers rather than operations, and everybody knew Stevie did 14 . . . We would all have done a couple, do you know what I mean? But the main operator through all of this was McKeag. He set the standard.'

7. Money, Guns and South Armagh

'He said he was down in the Bandit Country a lot. "I've been down there," he says, "having a good old run about." And I went, "What for?" "I found a couple of rocket launchers lying in a field," he says, "with the cows."' – *Jackie 'Legs' Robinson*

'He [Adair] was told the Army had an observation post and he said, "Aye, that observation post, we'll get round that." He hadn't a big lot upstairs maybe, but he had balls.' – *Co. Armagh loyalist*

AT MIDNIGHT ON 10 AUGUST 1992, 21 YEARS OF SEMI-LEGALITY CAME TO AN end for the UDA when it was officially banned by Britain, ending the crass deceit that had allowed it to claim murders under its UFF cover name and get away with it. The decision was a direct result of the upsurge in UDA violence that followed the Stevens inquiry and a belated acknowledgment that the security forces could no longer control it. The fact that it was now joining the UVF, the IRA and Northern Ireland's other terrorist groups as a proscribed organisation was thanks in no small part to Johnny Adair. As Lord Mayhew of Twysden, the then Northern Ireland Secretary, told the authors, 'The test which was applied to proscription under the Act was whether an organisation in question was wholly or substantially committed to the use of violence for political purposes, and there were some where you could say they weren't, they did other things as well, but Mr Adair's organisation crossed the line.' As the deadline approached, Adair grew nervous. What if this was the beginning of a tough new crackdown on loyalists? After speaking to Jim Spence, his brigadier, and A Coy's Curtis Moorehead, the trio marched into Tennent Street police station and asked for Detective Sergeant Johnston Brown. To Brown's astonishment they admitted being members of the UDA up to that date but said they were now leaving. 'In one sense they were taking the mickey out of the fact that they were going to be proscribed and poking fun at the Secretary of State,' says Brown. 'But they were also concerned. They genuinely didn't know what was going to happen.' The statement was completely unsolicited, and duly noted as such. It was one of the stupidest things Adair had ever done and would later be thrown back in his face along with countless other boasts and admissions.

Although the ban led to cosmetic changes in the way the UDA did business, by now things were generally going well in west Belfast, particularly on the money side. Shortly after his release from prison in December 1990 Adair started to look for ways to improve C Coy's fundraising abilities, which had been all but neglected by Sammy Verner and his son, the unit's old welfare officers. He was not impressed by what he saw. C Coy was not extorting enough money from local businesses, while its only steady source of income was the Langley Street Social Club, the local UDA bar. Both A and B companies – the other divisions in west Belfast – were making far more. While A Coy ran a community centre-cum-bar and the Highfield Glasgow Rangers Club, B Coy had two bars, including the highly profitable UDA club in Heather Street.

While Spence set about reorganising the UDA's extortion rackets on the Shankill, Adair started to turn C Coy into a profitable enterprise. As well as strengthening his own power base there was another important motive for this: he wanted to send an unequivocal message to the UVF, which owned and operated far more than its loyalist rivals on the Shankill. 'The UVF had always had a stronghold, they had always had a supremacy in west Belfast,' said Ian Truesdale, a former C9 member and a close ally of Adair. 'So when the new brigade took over they stood up and put a firm hand down, letting the UVF know they were no longer going to be a soft touch. Johnny made it known that he wasn't Tucker Lyttle. Him and the new brigade weren't going to be stood on and walked over by the UVF.'

Truesdale himself was one of the first beneficiaries of the new approach. In April 1991, Adair gave him £10,000 of UDA cash to open a taxi depot on the Crumlin Road and to start making money for C Coy. No sooner was it up and running, however, than the UVF phoned Truesdale and ordered him to shut it down. As far as they were concerned, it was unwelcome competition for their own taxi firm on the Shankill Road. Knowing his boss would be furious, Truesdale told Adair what had happened. 'Johnny got on the phone to Bunter [the local UVF leader] and said it was a UDA taxi depot, it was staying open,' he recalled. The next day Ken Barrett, Adair and a number of his heavies, including Jackie Thompson, held a meeting with senior members of the UVF and told them in no uncertain terms that they could no longer dictate what took place on the Shankill. 'There was a lot of yelling. They [the UVF] thought they could run the place financially,' said one of those at the meeting. It was a rude awakening for the UVF and unmistakeable proof that the old days, when the UDA had been happy to sit back and let the UVF call the shots, were over.

Left alone to do Adair's bidding, Truesdale christened the firm Circle Taxis, although police soon nicknamed it 'Murder Cabs' because so many of its cars were being hijacked for C Coy operations. To many locals it was also known by another name: Dial-A-Drug. 'For Es you would have phoned Circle Taxis and they would have delivered them to you. If they knew who you were, there was no problem, they'd have brought them to your door,' said one former Shankill resident who was close to Adair for many years. As Adair built his fiefdom around him, drugs became increasingly important, not just as a source of personal enjoyment but also revenue. Special Branch later reported:

> Only one obvious weakness has become evident over the period of his [Adair's] command to date. He has increasingly turned to drug abuse in numerous forms, for whatever reason, and has become a habitual user of both 'E' tablets and various other narcotics. The extent of his drug abuse has been further accelerated by the fact that his team members are selling large quantities of drugs as a means of making substantial sums of money. The readily available supply of free drugs has caused him to develop an increasing habit.

Although the dates are unclear, Jackie Robinson, Adair's former girlfriend, believes it was in the early 1990s that a first-floor apartment on the lower Shankill was turned into a shebeen and another made into a 'dope flat'. To begin with, the dope flat mainly sold cannabis. 'You just knocked the window, somebody would have opened it and you would have handed the money and they would have passed out what you wanted,' said one old friend of Adair. 'You either got a 10 deal [£10 worth] or an eighth or whatever. There was no stop to it; it was open till two, three or four in the morning. The police would often sit watching it and filming people going in to get their stuff but they never did anything about it.' According to one senior police officer, by the late 1980s the UDA was already selling large quantities of cannabis across Belfast and by the early 1990s it had moved into harder drugs, including Es and cocaine. Those who tried to encroach on this lucrative market were dealt with brutally. On 17 January 1991, Thomas McCreery, a former UDA assassin from north Belfast who was now operating as a freelance drug dealer, was shot and seriously wounded as he got into a car outside Heather Street Social Club off the Shankill. As one former RUC officer involved in the case explained, 'He had gone to the club to meet senior UDA people to talk about the rights and wrongs of dealing drugs and to negotiate how much he was to pay them for being allowed to operate with impunity in and around the Shankill district. He went in, drank his pint and came back out and as he was getting into his car he was shot by a lone gunman.' His attempted killer was Ken Barrett.

By 1993, C Coy was making so much money that Adair was starting to get noticed. According to police records, in this year alone he bought five cars: an Audi 80, a Vauxhall Cavalier, a Ford Orion, a Rover and a Ford Sierra. They were all second hand and none was particularly expensive – the most he paid was £4,695 for the Cavalier – for the simple reason that Adair had to be able to cruise in and out of republican neighbourhoods without attracting attention to himself. But they were well beyond the means of a man officially unemployed and allegedly surviving on his income support of just £44 per week. The same year Adair would reward himself with two holidays, one to Tenerife with Gina Crossan, Jim Spence and B Coy's Geordie King, and the other to Butlin's in Scotland.

While C Coy and the 2nd Battalion prospered, Adair's killing squads were also busier than ever. They were given new impetus when Adair succeeded Spence as brigadier in west Belfast following his friend's arrest in March 1993 on extortion charges. For the rest of the year the tempo of attacks increased dramatically as Adair waged a two-pronged campaign in Belfast, combining targeted attacks on Sinn Fein with random murders of innocent Catholics. The new reign on the Shankill, however, started with a setback. On 10 March 1993, the IRA shot dead Ian Truesdale's brother, Norman, as he served a 12-year-old boy at a shop on the Oldpark Road. At the time of his death the 39-year-old, who had four children, was team commander of C9 and an active gunman. He was shot in the chest by a man with a handgun before a second gunman sprayed him with an AK-47. Thomas McWilliams, who fired the assault rifle, was given a life sentence after being convicted of the murder in 1995 but the other gunman was never caught, even though the entire murder was captured on the shop's security camera. The operation was put together and ordered from the Ardoyne, half a mile up the road. The Truesdale family, who have studied the video time and time again, believe to this day that the man with the handgun was a well-known republican from the area.

Two weeks later, C Coy hit back when Stevie McKeag shot dead Peter Gallagher, a Sinn Fein worker, in west Belfast. The following day, hours after the UFF's north Antrim brigade killed four Catholic workmen in Co. Derry, including the IRA's James Kelly, McKeag claimed another victim. Damien 'Didi' Walsh was closing up a fuel supplies shop in a shopping centre on the outskirts of nationalist west Belfast when he was shot dead. Witnesses said that one of two gunmen walked up behind him and held an automatic gun to his head, but the weapon jammed as he pulled the trigger. As he tried to run away the gunman managed to open fire, shooting him several times. Walsh, who died later in hospital, was just 17. A friend who was with him at the coal depot, where Walsh had been working on a youth-training scheme, said afterwards that one of the gunmen had also tried to kill him but his weapon had failed to fire. 'I heard it click four or five times and I saw him hitting the side of the gun with the side of his hand,' he told the inquest. He said that his friend had jumped up when he was shot but then fell dying on top of him. 'I said to Damien, "We'll have to get up and run at them." I got Damien's body off me and put it to the side. I lifted a footstool and the gunman went outside.'

The teenager's mother described her son as 'an innocent child . . . a typical wee lad. All he wanted was to enjoy himself. He had no interest in politics. My only hopes for Damien were that this job would be the making of him and that he'd find a nice girl. We have everybody in our family, Protestants, Catholics, Baha'is and atheists.' The following day, as police combed the scene of the shooting for clues, they found more than five tonnes of fertiliser of a type used by the IRA to make explosives. Although the killing had all the hallmarks of an indiscriminate sectarian attack, the UFF insists that the discovery of explosives justified its attack. In an interview with one of the authors, the back-up gunman, who waited outside the shop with a .357 Magnum, said that Walsh's name had been selected from a list of IRA suspects handed to him by a senior C Coy figure. The list included Walsh's address, date of birth, and said that he was a member of an IRA active service unit. The gunman had little doubt that the information came from the security forces. 'We spent a long time going through those names and I would have studied them day in and day out,' said 'Pete'. 'We were looking through them and I think it was the night before that Stevie and me said we were happy with that one. Johnny was up there scouting it out beforehand. He then took the driver up there to show him where we had to go, so he was up there twice in all.'

'Pete', who still lives on the Shankill but is no longer active in the UDA, said that the operation had been put together in a house off Agnes Street. He said McKeag was 'elated' as they drove away from the scene listening to rave music: 'We were all silent in the car going up. I don't care who you are, your mind is ticking over. The first words Stevie said on coming out were, "Right, that's it, let's go." The driver just said, "Is it a hit? Is it a hit?" And Stevie said, "Aye – go, go!" If you get somebody and they go down, you're elated, you were on a high. If you believe in what you were doing and that those bastards are killers then you're on a high. If you get to the stage when you're regretting it afterwards then you're doing the wrong job. If you actually did somebody you felt we were winning the war against the Provos. You felt a certain sense of pride.'

After the shooting 'Pete' lay in the back of the car on the floor (the sight of three men in the same vehicle always aroused the suspicions of the police), while McKeag sat in the front singing to the music. They went to three separate houses to change and wash before meeting in a bar on the Shankill. 'You would get changed and scrubbed down as quick as you could and then go down to a bar to make yourself seen,' said 'Pete'. 'Sometimes the bath was already run for you and there'd be a girl waiting to take your clothes. Sometimes you used lemon juice on cotton buds to wash out your ears and nose properly. A nailbrush was always very important as well. After a job, somebody had to go and tell Winkie or Johnny, and they'd often say, "There's a few hundred quid, now go and get full," but it wasn't that we were being paid for killing somebody – it was because they knew what we had done took balls.'

Over the next month Adair sent his teams out on operation after operation, including a mass murder attempt at Brian Graham's bookmakers on North Queen Street on Thursday, 29 April. Five Catholics were wounded, one of them seriously, in a gun attack by a team that, according to police intelligence, included Gary 'Smickers' Smith, a C14 volunteer in his early 30s who ran a pet shop on the Shankill. Smith had originally joined the UDA in the early 1980s but left in disgust after the INLA murdered Billy 'Bucky' McCullough, then west Belfast brigadier, in 1981. He wanted to avenge McCullough's death by mounting a gun attack on a Falls Road bus stop but his superiors blocked the idea. Twelve years later, his fearless desire to kill was exactly what Adair wanted, and over the next twelve months his role in C Coy would become increasingly important. Two days after the bookies mass murder attempt, at 5.45 p.m. on Saturday, 1 May 1993, C Coy's luck improved when it killed an IRA volunteer as he helped to build a porch at the Andersonstown home of Alex Maskey. Alan Lundy, a former republican prisoner from Ardoyne, was shot when McKeag and another gunman stepped out of a hijacked Ford Orion outside the house in Gartree Place and opened fire with rifles. After shooting Lundy, at least one of the killers ran into the house and up the stairs in an attempt to find Maskey, a Sinn Fein councillor and a hate figure among loyalists. The gunman searched the bedrooms but was unable to find the politician, who was hiding in the bathroom. Even though Maskey was untouched, for C Coy it went down as a 'good hit'. 'There were C Coy murders that were cowardly, but it takes fucking balls to go into Gartree Place,' said 'Pete', a C Coy gunman. 'You're looking at your family before you go and you know at the time you might not see them again.'

Maskey, whose house would again be attacked by C Coy the following January, was used to being targeted by loyalists and in an attempt on his life in 1987 took a shotgun bullet in the stomach. In a statement claiming responsibility for Lundy's murder, the UFF admitted its real target had been the Sinn Fein councillor. The terrorists also took the opportunity to make a broader comment on the political situation. They delivered their response to a joint statement by Gerry Adams and John Hume, leader of the nationalist SDLP, who a week earlier had agreed a number of principles that might pave the way for an end to IRA violence. Chief amongst them was a rejection of any internal solution to the conflict in Northern Ireland and the assertion that 'the Irish people as a whole have a right to national self-determination'. For loyalists it was proof of all they had feared since on-off political talks on Northern Ireland's future had started two years earlier. Like so often before, they suspected the Protestant community was about to be betrayed by Britain and that Downing Street was about to capitulate to a 'pan-nationalist' alliance between Sinn Fein, the SDLP and Dublin. The UFF's assessment of the Hume–Adams talks was exactly that. 'The UFF have studied closely the Hume–Adams nationalist self-determination statement and are now more confident of a pan-nationalist agenda,' it said.

From the spring Adair was going out of his way to terrorise nationalist politicians. In the early hours of 24 March, a C Coy unit threw a grenade into the Ardoyne home of Gerard McGuigan, a Sinn Fein councillor. The device smashed through an upstairs window and blasted a hole in the floor of the bedroom where McGuigan's wife lay sleeping. She and the councillor's three children were unhurt, while McGuigan himself was downstairs watching boxing on television. The address had been checked by Adair in person earlier that day. Wearing a hooded top, he had run through the area posing as a jogger, a trick he used on a number of occasions even though the IRA knew his face.

McGuigan recalled, 'What really sticks in my mind is the dust that came out of the house. All the dust came out of the plaster when it exploded. It was so thick that one of the neighbours was convinced it was smoke and climbed up the drainpipe to try and get us out.' It was C Coy's second attack on his home in a year. Hours later Peter Gallagher was shot dead, while the following day a grenade was thrown into the home of Joe Austin, another Sinn Fein councillor. It was a carbon copy of the attack on McGuigan, but again nobody was injured. On 17 May, 22-year-old Jamie Hill stepped out of a car outside a Sinn Fein advice centre in the New Lodge area of north Belfast and fired 20 shots through the window. The targets were Bobby Lavery and Denis O'Hagan, two well-known local republicans, and Gerard McGuigan. As O'Hagan said afterwards, 'I was sitting in the front office when a gunman fired shots through the bulletproof glass of the window and through the front door. When the first shot was fired, I got below the table and stayed there. When the shooting was over, there were bullets lodged in the internal walls. We were all very frightened.'

Things did not go the way C Coy intended. As Hill clambered back into a getaway car driven by his 27-year-old brother, Robert, a sharp-shooting British soldier opened fire from a nearby Army observation post and hit him in the back. The police found the wounded man in an alleyway just inside the loyalist Tigers Bay district, while his brother was arrested in a house in nearby Copperfield Street where he had gone to get washed down and changed. Both were later sentenced to 16 years.

MONEY, GUNS AND SOUTH ARMAGH

The attacks continued throughout the summer. At around midnight on 8 June, the wife and son of Gerry Adams escaped unhurt when a lone C Coy volunteer threw a grenade at the Sinn Fein leader's home, damaging the front door and porch. Adams himself, who was in the habit of sleeping elsewhere for security reasons, was not at home but condemned the attack as an 'indiscriminate attempt to murder members of my family'. The pace of activity was frenetic. As one C Coy 'operator' put it, 'It was relentless. We thought it was the only way we were going to avoid Protestants being slotted. The Provos have admitted it was the first time they were ever scared. They were sleeping with the settees behind the doors.' On 23 July, C Coy launched another attack on the Sinn Fein office in the New Lodge. A bomb was left outside the building but only partly exploded, and nobody was injured. Four days later, on 27 July, one of Adair's gunmen attempted to kill Annie Armstrong, a Sinn Fein councillor, at her home in Twinbrook on the outskirts of west Belfast. The gunman fired through a downstairs window, one of the bullets narrowly missing the politician's daughter and hitting the family's television set.

After so many near misses, it was just a matter of time before another life was lost. Shortly before 9.30 p.m. on 8 August, Sean Lavery, the son of Sinn Fein councillor Bobby Lavery, died in a hail of bullets as two gunmen raked the family home. The killers, who included Stevie McKeag, fired some 25 bullets into a downstairs room after their car pulled up outside the house on the Antrim Road in north Belfast. The wounded man managed to stagger upstairs to his father after being shot twice in the side, but died later in the Mater Hospital. Bobby Lavery, whose brother Martin had been shot dead by the UVF as he wrapped Christmas presents the previous December, described the shooting as a cowardly attempt to wipe out his family and a 'blatant attempt at mass murder'. Three months later C Coy would mount another gun attack on Lavery's home, but again they failed to shoot the councillor.

Although the carnage was piling up, Adair was far from done. On 30 August, a C Coy gunman murdered Marie Teresa Dowds de Mogollon, the Catholic wife of a Peruvian mechanic who had settled in Belfast many years earlier. She was shot in the head and neck when Stevie McKeag fired through a small glass window in the door of her semi-detached home in north Belfast. The real target had been her husband, Maximo, who had worked in a garage on the Oldpark Road at which a policeman, Raymond Carroll, was shot dead by the IRA in January 1972. Adair rowed with his fellow brigadiers about the murder and even threatened to shoot one of them, Joe English of south-east Antrim, if the UFF did not officially claim it. The following day it issued a statement admitting the dead woman had not been the target and expressing regret for 'last night's tragic events'.

While C Coy had been picky about its targets throughout the summer, now it was becoming sloppy. Eight days later, on Tuesday, 7 September, McKeag was one of two hitmen, a machine gun and a handgun under their jackets, who marched into the unisex Jon David hair salon on the Catholic Falls Road as children made their way home from school. Wearing sun glasses and baseball caps, they fired a single shot at a man in the first-floor hallway and pumped six more bullets into his body as he lay face down on the ground. Sean Hughes, who had run the salon from the same premises for 19 years, was 40 years old and had three children. He was mistaken for another hairdresser who worked elsewhere in Belfast called Frankie 'Studs' Lanigan, an INLA man. As McKeag left the salon he also opened fire on the male receptionist, who escaped injury by ducking under the counter. Before fleeing in a hijacked estate car, McKeag walked up to an hysterical woman outside the shop and sang 'Follow the Yellow Brick Road' from the *Wizard of Oz*. 'She was screaming and hysterical and he was just singing in her face in the middle of the Falls Road,' said 'Pete'. 'It was the middle of the afternoon and the place was completely packed. That was Stevie: he was just totally focused. He believed 199 per cent in what he was doing, that's why he was able to do things like that.'

While Adair's attacks on republicans won the admiration of the brigadiers on the UDA's ruling inner council, by late 1993 it was not just Joe English who was becoming concerned about C Coy. At 7.30 p.m. on Friday, 15 October 1993, Paddy McMahon, a 23-year-old Catholic, was shot dead in north Belfast when a gunman fired from a derelict house before climbing down the drainpipe to his escape. The killer, once again, was Stevie McKeag. Just over an hour and a half later, at 9.05 p.m., Adair quipped to a policeman at a checkpoint on the Shankill, 'Who shot the pizza man in the face? Who's killing all these taigs?' It was another random killing, and at least two of Adair's fellow brigadiers thought there had been too many. They were also wary of the power the Shankill Road loyalist was wielding. The UFF's military campaign in Belfast was becoming increasingly synonymous with one man alone, and it was starting to go to his head.

Once again Jim Spence, who was trying to restrain his friend from jail, feared his old military commander was running out of control. His worries were underlined four days later when an article appeared in *The Guardian* under the headline 'For Queen and Country'. Although it did not refer to Adair by name, reporter Maggie O'Kane painted a chilling picture of a mass murderer whose men were in the business of 'spraying taigs'. Asked whether he had ever had a Catholic in his car he joked, 'Only a dead one,' before adding, 'Once you get your first fenian blood it's easy after that.' Adair, who was introduced to O'Kane as the UFF's 'OC, west Belfast', was referred to throughout the article as 'Mad Dog'. It was the first time the 'Mad Dog' moniker had appeared in print. According to the reporter, the name came from the police, although friends of Adair insist that his only real nicknames at that time were 'Pitbull', 'the Wee Man' and 'Red Adair'. They say that O'Kane overheard a reference to another Shankill man, 'Mad Dog' Jackie McCarroll, but decided to put the name to better use. No matter how it originated, the effect was immediate. The press seized on it, and by the time he was jailed the following May the words Johnny Adair and Mad Dog had become inseparable.

Days later, in an interview with Belfast reporter Alan Murray in the *Irish Independent*, Adair taunted the IRA's commander in Ardoyne, describing him as a 'coward'. 'He's so frightened of the Ulster Freedom Fighters that he won't sleep in his house. I live in my house, but he runs and hides,' said Adair, who again was not named. Like *The Guardian* article, which made the wild claim that Adair had personally murdered 12 Catholics in two years, the *Irish Independent* continued to feed his ego. 'In one-to-one dialogue, the bundle of nervous energy talks fifteen to the dozen, racing along, flinging the names of IRA men in Belfast across the room. The addresses he personally knows because he has targeted their homes, cruising around the estates of west Belfast as well as the tightly knit nationalist streets in north Belfast . . . In recent weeks the top UFF man was spotted cruising through Ballymurphy and received the customary RUC examination. He doesn't admit that he is lining up potential targets, but they know, and he knows they know.'

Adair, whose obsession with the media would be central to his eventual downfall, was starting to believe his own propaganda. His appetite for power was growing by the day and it was manifesting itself in several different ways. According to former friends, as he established his power base in the early 1990s one thing above all started to preoccupy him: weapons. According to 'John', C Coy had comparatively few guns that could be relied upon in the early 1990s. Getting his hands on some good 'gear', as Adair called it, became his top priority, and he gradually set about expanding his arsenal. Although there was no single big weapons consignment, over the next few years Adair slowly improved the quantity and quality of C Coy's equipment. Occasionally he would swap weapons with other loyalist groups, trading a couple of handguns for an Uzi or vice versa. He also started to make approaches through mid-Ulster loyalists to a businessman in the predominantly Unionist town of Markethill in Co. Armagh. Although it is not clear exactly when these contacts began, by 1993 they were well advanced. The businessman controlled access to a hidden jewel, the very thought of which made Adair water at the mouth: concealed in farm buildings and hay sheds in the surrounding countryside was a vast cache of weapons, including handguns, assault rifles, grenades and RPG-7 rocket launchers. They were the property of Ulster Resistance (UR), a shadowy loyalist umbrella group established in 1986 following the Anglo-Irish Agreement. The arsenal represented roughly a third of a consignment supplied by a Lebanese gunrunner and smuggled into Northern Ireland in late 1987. Although the operation was run by Ulster Resistance, the arms were shared equally with the UDA and the UVF, each of whom received a third. But while the UVF's share was delivered safely to its dumps, the UDA had lost its entire allocation when three members of the organisation, including Davy Payne from north Belfast, turned up at the rendezvous point in January 1988 and insisted on taking all the UDA's guns in one go. With the weapons piled into the boots of two cars and the mud-flaps scraping along the ground, Payne and his colleagues were a dead giveaway. On their way back to Belfast they were stopped at an RUC checkpoint, where their cargo was quickly discovered and seized. They may as well have just handed the guns into a police station.

While the UVF put its weapons to good use, the Ulster Resistance guns were hidden away to defend Northern Ireland Protestants in a future 'Doomsday' scenario. Adair was desperate to get his hands on them. According to one Markethill loyalist familiar with the contacts, by 1993 Ulster Resistance had already supplied Adair with a number of weapons, including AK-47s. It is highly likely that C Coy's very first AK, acquired in 1991, came from this source. It was driven up from Portavogie in Co. Down, and to help him negotiate a police checkpoint the driver put a goat in the back of his car and cut it with a knife. When stopped, he said the animal had snagged itself on a fence and he was taking it to the vet. By the middle of 1993, however, Adair wanted something bigger and better than AKs, preferably that would make a loud bang. As rank-and-file loyalists became increasingly suspicious of Britain's intentions and a new nationalist alliance between Gerry Adams's Sinn Fein and John Hume's SDLP, the clamour for more weapons became irresistible. In November 1993, both the UFF and the UVF warned that, while they wanted peace, they were preparing for war. The following week a huge arms shipment, destined for the UVF, was intercepted on its way from Poland, including 320 AK-47 assault rifles, 500 hand grenades, 52 Russian-made pistols, 14,000 rounds of ammunition and two tonnes of high explosives. In December, the UFF, desperate to prove its firepower, released pictures of hooded men posing with a heavy duty belt-fed M-60 machine gun, AK-47s and SA-80 rifles. It was a sobering warning to John Major, the British Prime Minister, and Albert Reynolds, his Irish counterpart, of the problems they might face if they agreed a political settlement for Northern Ireland that was not to the liking of the wider Protestant community.

Behind the scenes, Adair was working constantly on his contacts in Markethill. On 26 September he let the cat out of the bag, telling Detective Sergeant Johnston Brown that he had got his hands on some powerful new equipment: RPG-7 rocket launchers. As they chatted outside the front door of his house in Hazelfield Street, Adair confessed to the detective that he had obtained the equipment from the Ulster Resistance. He gave the officer the impression that there were at least two rocket launchers, although there is no evidence to suggest that there was ever more than one. It had been hidden on a farm, as Brown soon learned. 'He put his hands out and he said, "Smell my hands," and I could smell nothing. I said to him, "What is it, gunpowder?" He said, "No, it's straw, smell the fresh straw." He said that he had bought them from the UR and that the UR told him the one condition was for them not to be pointed against a loyalist target or the security forces, that's all they asked him.' Also standing outside the house was Donald Hodgen, who as usual was perfectly quiet and starting to wish Adair would follow his example for a change. 'Adair said that Hodgen would go and hijack a Volvo estate and Hodgen would be coming out of a hole in the roof of the car with an RPG-7. He [Adair] said they were going to fire it at the Hole in the Wall Club in the Ardoyne,' remembers Detective Sergeant Brown. Adair also told Jackie Robinson, his long-term girlfriend, about the rockets. 'He said he was down in the Bandit Country a lot. "I've been down there," he says, "having a good old run about." And I went, "What for?" "I found a couple of rocket launchers lying in a field," he says, "with the cows."'

But while Adair's plan to fire rockets at republican targets would come to fruition the following year, he also wanted to extend his violent campaign by moving beyond the city. One area above all others fascinated him and filled him with almost uncontrollable excitement: south Armagh. Ever since the start of the Troubles, when the minority Protestant population along the border was deliberately targeted by the IRA, loyalist paramilitaries had been reluctant to mount attacks here. The area known as 'Bandit Country' was a place most ordinary Protestants entered with dread: overwhelmingly Catholic and virulently republican, it was home to the Provisionals' most ruthless unit, the south Armagh Brigade, and a virtual no-go area for the British Army, where the security forces could travel only by helicopter. The small number of Protestants who refused to move lived in constant fear and many put themselves further at risk by becoming part-time police officers or soldiers in the Ulster Defence Regiment. By the time Adair first visited Markethill, the idea of fighting the south Armagh IRA had long been abandoned by Britain, which instead sought only to contain it through a network of massive watchtowers along the border.

The fact that nobody else, not even Billy 'King Rat' Wright and his mid-Ulster UVF, would consider attacking the IRA in south Armagh was a large part of the thrill for Adair. Like so many of his schemes and plans it was motivated by the thought of writing himself into the history books. At a series of meetings near Markethill, Adair, always surrounded by two or three trusted cohorts, outlined his strategy to representatives of Ulster Resistance. At one of these, in a local farmhouse, he said his teams could be driven in and out of the border area to carry out attacks on specific republican targets. 'He said he was taking the war to the IRA in Belfast, he said he had Ardoyne nearly cleaned out. He said he was going all over west Belfast but he needed to stretch out further and wanted to start hitting south Armagh because that was the heartland,' revealed one of those at the meeting. He added: 'He reckoned he was taking it to the heartland of west Belfast and would do it in south Armagh. To be honest, there was a wee bit of logic in what he was saying because there were only three areas where the Provies were strong – west Belfast, south Armagh and Tyrone – and there wasn't much going on anywhere else . . . If he had have took it to the heartland of south Armagh, he'd have been classed a hero. Nobody would have been able to touch him . . . He was game for it. He was told the Army had an observation post and he said, "Aye, that observation post, we'll get round that." He hadn't a big lot upstairs maybe, but he had balls. He says, "Listen, all you have to do is get somebody to drive the cars and take the weapons away." He said, "My boys will do it, they're mad to get in here." He was bouncing about, rubbing his hands together.'

All Adair needed, he stressed, was local knowledge, drivers to take his teams to and from their targets and safe houses from which to mount attacks and clean up afterwards. The idea was simple enough. Although several of those present were instinctively wary of a man whose terrorist campaign had claimed many innocent lives, the plan was sufficiently appealing for them to give it further consideration. A provisional list of targets was discussed, including Thomas 'Slab' Murphy, the head of the IRA in south Armagh and a long-term member of its governing body, the seven-man 'Army Council'. But before the plan could go any further, local loyalists warned that an offensive in south Armagh would spark a strong riposte from the IRA and almost certainly lead to innocent Protestants being killed. 'I said, no way, it was madness,' said one of those present. 'Not that I was against shooting Provies to be honest with you, but because there would have been retaliations and innocent people losing their lives. He [Adair] didn't really accept that there would be Prods massacred, he said that for every one Protestant killed he would do two [Catholics].' Once again, reality was coming between Adair and his plans for greatness. Although he was disappointed, he had little choice but to accept the advice and return, his tail between his legs, to the Shankill. It would not be the last time he would seek to extend his power base outside of Belfast.

8. Big Mouth

'You mark my words, I get my hands on a good fucking bomb it's going right into there [a republican area], no fucking doubt about it . . . Nobody will stop me from detonating them anywhere.' – *Johnny Adair to a police officer wearing a wire, 24 October 1993, the day after a bomb on the Shankill Road claimed the lives of nine Protestants*

AT EXACTLY 2.30 P.M. ON MONDAY, 25 OCTOBER 1993, JOHNNY ADAIR stopped briefly to speak to a police officer as he was driving away from his house. He smiled as he wound down the electric window of his new car, a second-hand Rover 214 he had picked up on the cheap six weeks earlier. Then he looked the policeman in the eye and uttered a phrase that chilled the constable: 'I'm away to plan a mass murder.'

It was not idle banter. Seventeen hours and four minutes later, at 7.34 a.m. the next day, two hooded gunmen wearing masks and yellow binmen's jackets stepped out of a white Citroën they had hijacked from Ian Truesdale's taxi firm and into a refuse depot in nationalist west Belfast. Many of the refuse collectors and street cleaners were sipping tea in the canteen before their 7.45 a.m. start, while others were still arriving at the Kennedy Way site. James Cameron was closing the gate after letting another worker in when the C Coy gunmen pushed past. His heart skipped a beat. 'Take that, you bastards,' they yelled as they raised their weapons and let rip, one with a handgun and the other a machine gun. Around 25 people were in the yard as they rattled off 60 rounds in 3 short bursts.

There was no specific target. John McGeough, who arrived for work seconds after the gunmen fled, said afterwards, 'I was a wee bit late this morning and that saved my life. It was an unbelievable and sickening sight. When we got into the yard, one man was lying on his side covered in blood, obviously dead. A second fellow was lying by the side of a lorry. He had been shot in the back and the legs and there was another man behind a skip who had been shot in the stomach and legs.'

James Cameron, a 54-year-old road sweeper with three children, was killed as he tried to dive behind a skip. Mark Rodgers died as he took cover behind a lorry. 'Mark was standing in front of me,' said a colleague. 'I saw him sway, raise his hands to his chest and fall in front of me.' A man who lived nearby rushed to the depot when he heard the 'awful noise' of the shooting, not realising it was gunfire. 'At first I thought it was a mechanical hammer, but it went on and on,' he told a reporter. At the depot he found his friend Mark Rodgers lying dead, 'covered in diesel which was pouring from a tanker which had been pierced by bullets. I will never forget that sight as long as I live.' In the words of one eyewitness, 'They were lying there like slabs of beef.' A small boy, believed to be Rodgers's son, was later seen near the depot wailing, 'My daddy is dead, my daddy is dead.' As well as two dead, five were wounded, one losing his spleen, a kidney and part of an arm. According to another worker, one of the gunmen was trying to clear his weapon while standing with his foot on the back of a wounded man. The other was screaming frantically, 'Do the bastards – do them.'

The body count was not as high as Adair would have liked but as the assassins sped away they believed they had committed a massacre. According to senior UDA sources, the two gunmen were Gary 'Smickers' Smith and Robert 'Rab' Bradshaw. Driving that day was another C Company man, 21-year-old Tommy Beggs, who had rewarded himself for his efforts by stealing the car radio, an act of petty crime that later enabled police to convict him of the murders. Beggs, who worked at a gentlemen's clothing shop in the centre of Belfast, was known as 'the suit-and-tie man' because he was always immaculately turned out. He went to special sartorial efforts whenever he was out murdering for C Coy. That day, as usual, he was dressed in his most respectable suit and a pair of smart black shoes he had polished beforehand. Like his companions, he was anxious to please Adair, not just because of the praise they would receive but because it was his boss's 30th birthday the next day and they wanted to give him a special present.

At about 4 a.m. on 27 October, Adair, Donald Hodgen, Paddy Patterson and several other C Coy henchmen turned up at Jackie Robinson's home in south Belfast wanting to party. Adair was indeed enjoying his birthday. 'They'd been out partying all night. They were laughing, drunk,' said Jackie. Although Adair was his 'usual cocky self', he said nothing about the murders in Kennedy Way, preferring to leave that to one of his sidekicks. Referring to another individual, Jackie said, 'He was laughing about the expressions on their faces when they bounced in . . . There was a whole big laughing joke about, "Did you see the expressions on their faces?" That was the big fun for them, the fear. They got off on people's fear.'

For three days before the attack a furious Adair had been desperate to get his teams into nationalist areas of Belfast to avenge the murder of nine Protestants in a bomb attack on the Shankill Road. On 23 October, as shoppers thronged the street on a busy Saturday afternoon, IRA volunteers Thomas Begley and Sean Kelly walked into Frizzell's fish shop dressed as delivery men and carrying a white box containing a bomb. It was meant to be on a fuse long enough to allow customers to escape but short enough to trap loyalists understood by the IRA to be meeting in the UDA's local headquarters above the shop. At least, that was what the IRA claimed afterwards. As Begley placed the device on the counter it exploded, blowing him apart and reducing the shop to rubble. Among the dead were four women and two children. Seven-year-old Michelle Baird died with her mother, Evelyn, aged 27. Leanne Murray, a 13-year-old schoolgirl, had left her mother, Gina, in the shop next door to buy a tub of whelks. Gina Murray said later, 'Leanne had just left me to go into the fish shop. Suddenly there was this huge bang. We ran screaming for Leanne. We couldn't find her. No one had seen her. There were people lying in the street covered in blood. My little girl was under all that rubble. We started clawing at it with our bare hands. I was screaming her name but it was no use. My little daughter was dead.' According to a police officer who was one of the first to arrive, 'As the rubble was being removed – and it will stay with me until I die – I saw a young girl's foot. I knew it was a young girl's foot because her shoe size was about three or four. It poked through the rubble, and I wanted to stop digging then, because I knew I was going to see quite a horrendous sight, and in fact I did.'

Some 58 people were hurt, many sustaining horrific injuries. One man described seeing a badly injured old woman in the middle of the road. 'She had no face. She was 60, 70 years of age. Her face was gone. Someone put paper towels on to staunch the blood. I was throwing bricks away, people were trying to get through the rubble. It was a slaughterhouse.' None of the dead had any links to paramilitaries, and the UDA office at 275a Shankill Road – the IRA's target – had been virtually empty at the time of the blast. Herbie Millar, a young C Coy member, had just hit the buzzer to enter the building when he was blown across the street. He suffered perforated eardrums and a dislocated collarbone as well as needing a number of stitches. 'Everything went completely quiet. I just looked across the road and there was a man lying with a hole in his throat,' he recalled. In a statement, the IRA said it had identified known members of the UFF entering the UDA office, a veiled reference to Johnny Adair and Winkie Dodds. Both had been spotted going in earlier that day, although by the time the bomb exploded Adair was 15 miles away visiting Sam 'Skelly' McCrory in the Maze Prison.

The attack came just four days after *The Guardian* printed Adair's boasts about being a mass murderer and a day after he taunted the IRA's Eddie Copeland in the *Irish Independent*. To his mind there was no doubt the Provisionals, who had issued a 'death warrant' for him in *An Phoblacht*, the republican newspaper, took the risk they did because they were determined to kill him. They had already come close three times that year. On at least one other occasion Special Branch, which was attempting to ingratiate itself with Adair, also warned him that the IRA were planning to murder him as he collected his children from school. Twice an IRA unit from Ardoyne took over No. 54 at Upper Glenfarne Street, which overlooked the front of Adair's house in Hazelfield Street. They did not realise that it belonged to another C Coy volunteer and one of Adair's closest cohorts, Norman Green, otherwise they would certainly have shot him. Though Adair's car was outside his house on the first occasion, he was in fact at the Belfast Motor Show with Paul Orr, his welfare officer. Seven months later, on 15 September, the IRA staged an identical operation but fled when one of Green's friends pulled out a handgun.

The most serious attempt came on 6 March, when an IRA gunman fired a number of shots at Adair and Donald Hodgen as they sat in Adair's car off the Shankill. Adair's white Vauxhall Cavalier was riddled with bullets, but miraculously the two escaped without serious injury, Adair being hit in the leg and Hodgen in the shoulder. Several weeks later, when Adair's car came back from the garage, the first thing he did was drive up to the Ardoyne home of Eddie Copeland. For several minutes he sat in the car outside Copeland's front door, beeping the horn and shouting insults at his arch enemy. Four days before the Shankill bomb, on the same day as *The Guardian* article, two INLA suspects were arrested after police gave chase to a car acting suspiciously in a road parallel to Hazelfield Street, where Adair lived. A fully loaded rifle and a sawn-off shotgun were recovered from the car, and although neither suspect made admissions to police, there was little doubt they were after Adair. By now he was so notorious that different republican terrorist groups were competing to murder him, and Adair himself knew that his days were probably numbered.

By all accounts Adair flew into a fit of rage when he returned to the Shankill after visiting Skelly at the Maze. 'James', an active C Coy operator at this time, remembered, 'He fucking went mad. I went round to see him and he'd only just pulled the car up but he was squealing blue murder.' Another friend recalled, 'He was gutted, fuming, sickened. He wanted immediate revenge but because of the security presence nobody got moving. Everybody was pegged into a corner, there was roadblocks everywhere, the peelers knew something was going to happen.' The next day Adair was ranting incoherently when he spoke to a police officer wearing a wire. 'At the end of the day do you see if the UFF – I'm just saying this – or the UDA ever were in there, sure they [the IRA] were always killing fucking ten innocent people before they were getting to them [UDA members] and see when they were getting to them they weren't even killing any of them uns. You see, of the three people that was in UDA headquarters, there were only three slightly injured so there you are.' He went on: 'I know what happened. They spotted me going in earlier. Whoever it was on the Shankill spotted me and Winkie going into it earlier on. You read the statement there [the IRA's claim of responsibility], there's three statements. You get the whole text of the statements. There was somebody on the road yesterday, either a man, male or female, in the café or standing about the road who witnessed me and Winkie Dodds going in but all we done was went in, picked up a pass [to visit Skelly in jail] . . . Whoever it was now they're right, they're right what they said, their statement, their first statement was they identified known members of the Ulster Freedom Fighters going into there and they brought their plan forward, whatever they meant by that, so whoever was there, there's Adair and Dodds away in now and – and we're in. We just collected a pass to go up and see McCrory and we left. We weren't in any more than five minutes but whoever watched us knew that we'd went in and thought maybe the UFF's having a meeting.'

Once again Adair had cheated death, but this time he knew the consequences would be huge. 'They'll [the IRA] have to answer for what they do and shortly after,' he told the policeman, adding ominously, 'You mark my words, I get my hands on a good fucking bomb, it's going right into there [a republican area] no fucking doubt about it . . . Nobody will stop me from detonating them anywhere.'

The UFF's response to the Shankill bomb was chilling. In a statement issued within hours of the blast it said all its units would be 'fully mobilised' by six o'clock that evening. 'John Hume, Gerry Adams and the nationalist electorate will pay a heavy, heavy price for today's atrocity,' it warned. 'To the perpetrators of this atrocity we say: "There will be no hiding place. Time is on our side."'

John Major, the Prime Minister, summed up the anger felt by many when he dismissed an IRA statement expressing regret as 'cold comfort' for the victims and denounced the attack as 'premeditated murder'. At a stroke the fledgling peace process, which was making slow progress through John Hume's attempts to push Sinn Fein and Gerry Adams away from violence, appeared to be sunk. In a departure from his usual refusal to speak out against IRA violence, Adams described the bombing as a 'disaster'. 'It was wrong,' he said. 'It cannot be excused.' Unionist leaders demanded that Hume put an end to his dialogue with Adams and called for internment without trial to be reintroduced. Facing criticism on all sides, Hume insisted that the talks go on. 'What I am doing is talking, and talking in a situation where I believe and still believe that there is real hope of achieving a lasting peace.' His party's MP for west Belfast, Joe Hendron, had to be given police protection when he visited the Shankill the next day and was jeered by an angry crowd.

Meanwhile, loyalists were thirsting for revenge. At least a dozen older C Coy militants who had drifted away from taking part in operations joined a long queue of those wanting to hit back. Hours after the bombing, in a move that was not sanctioned by Adair, two of his men, Freddie Douglas and Peter Gilliland, attacked the Boundary Bar in the Catholic Bawnmore district, shooting a man in the arm but failing to cause him serious injury. The following day two Catholics were shot dead, one by the UFF in south Belfast and the other, on the outskirts of north Belfast, by the UVF. Two days later a loyalist gunman tried to massacre patrons of a bar in the town of Lisburn, Co. Antrim, but his rifle jammed. After the attempted mass murder at the cleansing depot in Kennedy Way, fear in nationalist areas of

BIG MOUTH

Belfast was now so intense that many families refused to leave their homes. One man in Ardoyne, who was too afraid to give his name, told *The Times*, 'Everyone is expecting something to happen here, especially with the [Shankill] bomber coming from the area. There is extra security on the bookies and locals are asking strangers to identify themselves.' He said the loyalist killer known as 'Mad Dog' had already been sighted. 'He was on one of his dummy runs. People tried to catch him but he was too quick and the police can't do anything because he is clever enough not to carry guns.'

Adair was desperate to retaliate on a larger scale but when the UFF's *coup de grâce* came he was in police detention, having been arrested on 28 October in a determined effort to keep him off the streets. It was the UDA's brigade in Derry and north Antrim that evened the score. A senior UDA figure suspected of planning the retaliation told one of the authors, 'We had the resources and we had the personnel, but most importantly we had the discipline and capability to reply at any time. Very little had happened in this region for a long time, mainly due to the fact that the IRA in this area had more or less quit offensive action, but the Shankill bomb in Belfast was to change all that.' He dismissed the IRA's claim that it believed a UDA meeting was being held above the shop and said the bombing was a naked act of sectarianism. 'The IRA is an extremely professional organisation and there is just no way they believed that UDA brigadiers were meeting upstairs when they placed a bomb on the counter of Frizzell's fish shop. That venue had not been used for [UDA] inner council meetings for a long time. On a Saturday it was a place where women left prams and buggies before boarding a bus to visit their husbands who were languishing in jail. It was clearly a sectarian act. There could have been no other outcome.'

Around 60 people were packed into the Rising Sun bar on Saturday, 30 October 1993 when two masked gunmen wearing balaclavas and boiler suits walked in and shouted 'Trick or treat?' Thinking it was a Halloween prank, 19-year-old Karen Thompson told them sternly, 'That's not funny,' but the words had barely come out of her mouth when the killers opened fire. Stephen Irwin, a 24-year-old member of the UFF's most prized murder team outside Belfast, pointed his AK-47 and began shooting, keeping his finger firmly on the trigger as he sprayed a group of women out on a hen night before opening up on the dance floor. His colleague, Jeffrey Deeney, let rip with a Browning automatic pistol but managed only one shot before it jammed, saving the death toll from climbing into double figures. Deeney could only watch and marvel while his fellow assassin raked the room and the third member of the team, Torrens Knight, kept guard at the pub door with a double-barrel shotgun. There had never been anything like it in Greysteel, a quiet, predominantly Catholic village seven miles outside Derry. One of Northern Ireland's most experienced detectives, Detective Chief Superintendent Eric Anderson, said that bodies were everywhere when police arrived at the scene. 'That sight will live with me until the day I die. It was unbelievable. I've witnessed some awful tragedies, but Greysteel was . . . well, I never want to see anything like it again.'

It was a massacre every bit as appalling as the Shankill bomb. Six Catholics and a Protestant were killed, among them Karen Thompson and her boyfriend, Steven Mullan, who had hoped to marry shortly. John Moyne was hit as he threw his wife to the ground to protect her, while John Burns, a 54-year-old Protestant, was on his way to the toilet. A 17-year-old girl said later, 'When they came in through the door and shouted, "Trick or treat," he [Burns] started to laugh and shout, but then he was hit in the stomach. He was in a really bad way. John was lying there and he told me everything would be all right and told me to look after his daughter and make sure she was OK. I bent down and kissed him on the head and told him he was going to be all right, but I knew he was dying because he was so cold. It was awful. I have not been able to sleep. Every time I closed my eyes all I could see was the dead bodies.' The oldest of the dead was 81-year-old James Moore, the father of the bar owner, while six months after the attack another pensioner, 76-year-old Samuel Montgomery, who was treated for a fractured thigh bone after being shot, collapsed with a blood clot and died.

In its admission of responsibility, the UFF declared, 'This is the continuation of our threats against the nationalist electorate that they would pay a heavy price for last Saturday's slaughter of nine Protestants.' Although the killers were later jailed for life, the commander who ordered the attack was never charged. One of those questioned by police recalled, 'As I was being released, an officer screamed at me, "Maybe, and just maybe, some good will come out of this." He threw down a copy of the *News Letter* [a Belfast newspaper]. There was an article where Gerry Adams had called on loyalist paramilitaries to invoke an immediate ceasefire to see what could happen. That was the first mention of "ceasefire" and the IRA called one the following August.'

In all, 28 people had been killed in October, 16 by loyalists, and a seemingly endless procession of funerals bore testimony to a society teetering on the brink. To his annoyance, Adair himself was forced to sit out the main event of Greysteel in jail. For seven days he was held in Castlereagh holding centre while police quizzed him about the murders and a number of other attacks. Asked why he had been arrested along with a handful of senior west Belfast UDA figures he replied, 'To keep me and a couple of others off the streets so that the Catholics can do their shopping.' He jibed, 'It's great, a clear head, nothing going on every half hour – time to plan for the next couple of weeks.' According to police notes, he even thanked them for arresting him. 'Unprompted, he said he was 30 years old last week,' police recorded. 'He said that he has run long and hard and didn't even realise that he was under pressure till he came in here and got his head clear. He said if he hadn't come in here he might have got caught.' He went on to make a series of staggering admissions that came close to implicating himself in murder:

> Discussing the recent murders of both loyalists and nationalists, he spoke freely and stated he was bitter against republicans because they have blown the fuck out of Belfast and killed innocent Prods. He stated as far as he knew the troubles would stop if the IRA stood down. He stated he did not agree with loyalists murdering but stated some good ones had been killed, referring to leading republicans.

Adair refused even to contemplate peace:

> When the futility of recent murders was put to him, he stated it was sad. He also stated that the Prods had to even the score for the bomb on the Shankill and that he thought that there would be no more murders unless the Provies start it again . . . When it was put to him that the loyalist community was losing the sympathy of the world because of the senseless murders of innocent Roman Catholics, he scoffed and stated that we had the sympathy of the world before for La Mon and Enniskillen and Teebane massacres by the IRA. He said they could shove their sympathy and added that he did not agree with turning the other cheek. He stated that he believed that the IRA should be kept on the run. He said he is not a criminal now, nor a racketeer and added that the UFF are now all young blood taking the war to the IRA.

MAD DOG

According to detectives who interviewed him, Adair's cockiness stemmed from a belief that the police would never touch him. One officer who interviewed him after he was arrested in the wake of Pat Finucane's murder in February 1989, remembered, 'He was a cocky bastard, an arrogant little so-and-so. Johnny would talk away, joke away with you but he would always stop short of admitting anything.' At around this time Detective Sergeant Johnston Brown also questioned Adair for the first time and was amazed by how much information the loyalist revealed – not about the UDA, but the UVF. It was obvious Adair's mouth was his Achilles heel. 'There was one particular company of the UVF, B Coy 1st Battalion, who were known as the Liverpool team because they were based in the Liverpool Club on the Shankill,' said Brown. 'Adair professed his admiration for B Coy and sought to model UDA C Coy on them.' In particular the young terrorist was impressed by the UVF's rocket attack on a Sinn Fein office in May 1989. 'Adair and the UDA used to refer to them as the Mujahideen because of the RPG-7s they fired. They were the first loyalists to use those weapons,' said Brown.

In 1990, some three years before the RUC launched its investigation into Adair, Brown told his superiors that the loyalist's tendency to brag could be used to snare him. His view was based on intimate first-hand knowledge. Early that year the detective sergeant made a conscious decision to befriend Adair and before long he was dropping into the loyalist's Hazelfield Street home on his way to or from Tennent Street RUC station off the Shankill, where he was based. He would sit in Adair's front room dangling his young son Jonathan from his knee and being plied with tea and biscuits by Gina Crossan. While many of his friends were wary of the police officer, Adair was too flattered to realise that a member of the security forces was trying to set him up. He thought the detective was great company. On one occasion, when Adair and his mates were all talking at once, Brown told them to be quiet and pointed to the lampshade on the ceiling light. 'Don't all be talking at once,' he said, 'because the bug in that light won't pick it up.' Adair howled with laughter. Back at his police station later that day, however, a Special Branch officer pulled Brown aside. 'Johnston, I wish you hadn't said that about the bug in the light in Adair's house. We do have a bug there, but it's not in the light.'

Given Adair's notoriously volatile temper, it was a risky strategy. One day Brown, who also cultivated a number of Adair's friends, was sitting chatting to Gerry Drumgoole, Adair's neighbour, when Adair turned up with Winkie Dodds and Paddy Patterson. Adair stormed in and started telling Brown that he was going to kill a police sergeant who was annoying him, even jibing that he was minded to borrow a coffee jar bomb from the IRA to do the job. 'It was frightening. He could blow hot and cold just like that,' recalled Brown. On another occasion he was talking to Adair and several others, who had just returned from Norman Truesdale's funeral. Dressed in smart suits and ties, they could have been mistaken for CID officers themselves. As they stood in the street, however, Stevie McKeag noticed a flashing red light inside the policeman's car. 'He's taping us, he's taping us,' he yelled. Donald Hodgen and Winkie Dodds, no longer the respectable men in suits, pinned Brown against a wall while Adair ordered him to explain himself. The detective knew his life was in danger. He calmly explained that the light was part of an under-car booby trap alarm system – it flashed once to check the front driver's side, twice the front passenger side, three times the rear driver's side and so on. Adair took a look for himself, saw that Brown was telling the truth and let him go. For the RUC man it was a sobering reminder of the people he was dealing with. 'One minute you were their mate, the next they were about to kill you,' he reflected.

But the strategy paid off as the officer kept coming back, causing alarm among his more conservative colleagues, many of whom believed that he had recruited Adair as one of his informants. Amid the moments of bone-chilling fear there was also a lighter side to Brown's encounters with Adair. On 5 December 1992, after a row between C Coy and the UDA in north Belfast over a group of petty criminals Adair had recruited as an extension to his power base, the detective decided to take a spin down the Shankill. According to Brown's notes, at 10.43 p.m. he drove into Hazelfield Street:

> I was aware that there had been, and we suspected that there would
> be further, confrontation between the loyalist UDA elements from
> the Shankill estate and UDA elements from Tigers Bay. I drove into
> Hazelfield Street, Belfast. I was alone in the police car. I stopped
> outside number 10, the home of John Adair. I was aware that Adair
> might be involved in street disturbances. As I drew up outside
> number 10 I became aware that there was a large gathering of people
> inside Adair's home. The front door opened and Adair jumped into
> the front passenger seat of the police car. He told me to wait – he
> said a few of his friends were coming behind him. I noted that he

was drunk. He believed that he was seated in a taxi. I made Adair aware of who I was and we were then joined immediately by three to four others who jumped into the back of the police car, obviously thinking it was a taxi.

That night Jonty Brown believes he prevented a murder bid from taking place. He recorded:

> Adair spoke of being Officer Commanding – he referred to this as OC. When the remainder of Adair's friends realised that it was a police car they became agitated. Adair ordered them to go away. There were approximately six to one dozen people and all went indoors immediately and without question. Adair made reference to the fact that he was going to get his men to take out a taig but he cancelled it. I noted that Adair was dressed in jeans and had on a green combat jacket, black gloves etc. I also noted that there was a very large contingent of UDA/UFF in the area. I later attended Tennent Street CID Office . . . I warned the Inspector that all persons present at Hazelfield Street appeared to be sober except Adair. I believed this to be sinister and that it may be a prelude to a UDA/UFF feud or to a sectarian murder bid in the Oldpark area. Later, at 23.20 hours on the same date, riots developed at the Mount Bar [in Tigers Bay] and Adair and 60 to 70 others were involved in the fracas.

Thanks to his persistent visits to Adair's neighbourhood, the RUC man was able to gain an extraordinary insight into the way the terrorist operated. 'I think he really trusted Jonty Brown, he thought he was on his side,' said Jackie Robinson. Thinking he was a rogue cop, Adair constantly pestered the detective for intelligence on IRA figures and was undeterred when Brown consistently failed to oblige. On one occasion, in November 1992, Brown asked to be allowed to wear a wire after Adair and his brigadier, Jim Spence, offered him money for photographs of republican suspects. The request was turned down. 'I was telling my superiors that there was sufficient evidence to prosecute Johnny Adair, that I was meticulously noting my conversations with him and his admissions.' While the political will to go after Adair did not exist, the detective also believes there was a cultural explanation for the lack of activity. 'Some of my [Special Branch] colleagues were quite content to do nothing,' he said. 'They would say, "But he's got the Sinners [Sinn Fein] on the run."'

But by the second half of 1993 the political situation had changed entirely. While Downing Street conducted secret peace talks with the IRA, John Hume's ongoing dialogue with Gerry Adams held out the prospect of luring Sinn Fein into the political mainstream. As the carnage on the streets intensified and peace seemed further away than ever, the urgency to find a solution became all the greater. Lord Mayhew of Twysden, the then Secretary of State, recalled, 'I responded to the situation with a determination to uphold the law, to support the security forces and to try to demonstrate on my own part a degree of steadiness rather than volatile reaction, while at the same time proceeding with the development of a political alternative to direct rule that would be fair and hold out a better way for the Province to conduct its affairs.' The next few months, culminating in the IRA's historic ceasefire the following August, would prove critical but there was a dangerously delicate balance between progress away from violence and a descent into civil war. Holding the key to which way the Province would sway were the likes of Johnny Adair, hotheads and extremists on both sides with an inbred lust for bloodshed and a mindset that viewed any let-up in the killings as weakness. The time had come for a robust response from the security forces. In Lord Mayhew's words, 'There was a determination to deal with paramilitaries even-handedly and to not appear to condone violence on one side but to condemn it on the other, which we never did.'

By the time of the Shankill bomb, a dedicated police inquiry team had been set up under the overall command of Detective Chief Superintendent Derek Martindale, head of the CID in Belfast, but the day-to-day control of Acting Detective Chief Inspector Brian McArthur. The team, initially based in the RUC station in North Queen Street and then Antrim Road in north Belfast, had been put together earlier that year to probe a number of unsolved murders. In the early autumn, however, the call came through to drop everything and focus solely on Adair. 'The word came right from the top: stop what you're doing and put all you can into getting Johnny Adair behind bars,' recalled one detective on the case. 'It came straight from the NIO to the top of the RUC.'

The team's sole task was to put Johnny Adair in jail. They examined every aspect of his life and started to collate evidence going back three years, much of it drawn from Jonty Brown's notebooks and those of other officers who had had dealings with Adair. In the introduction to the RUC's preliminary report into Adair, McArthur noted:

> Adair, since joining the UDA in the mid 1980s, has forced his way up through the ranks to his present high position. He is the most revered and the most feared leader within the UDA/UFF hierarchy. He sits on and is the most influential figure on the UDA Inner Council, the ruling body of the organisation. Adair's loyalist fanaticism and outright hatred of the republican/nationalist (and indeed, simply Roman Catholic) sections of the community cannot be overstated. To this end, during recent years and particularly from 1990, through his personal endeavours and through procurement of others, Adair can be said to have waged an almost personal war against the nationalist community in Belfast and has been directly responsible for countless murders and attempted murders during that time.

He also dispelled the notion that Adair was a simpleton:

> Adair has an extrovert and forceful personality. Although he had no significant schooling, he is an extremely bright and intelligent character. Adair is a streetwise and cunning individual who has, for a number of years, eluded police efforts to bring him to justice. All of the above combine to create in the eyes of his followers a heroic, charismatic leader. Adair thrives on the reputation he has built up and wastes no opportunity to enhance it. He adores the adulation of his followers and the fear he inspires in those he perceives to be his enemies. In short, Adair is not only the most influential and ruthless leader within the UDA, but (and this aspect has been most important to this inquiry) he wants everyone to be aware of that fact.

The RUC set out to prove two things: not only Adair's membership of the UDA/UFF but also his role as its most powerful leader. As well as his frequent sightings in the company of convicted loyalists and visits to prisoners, it clocked his comings and goings at the UDA's Shankill Road headquarters both before and after the group was banned. Repeated attempts to kill him by the IRA and INLA were a good indication of his perceived status as a leading loyalist terrorist, while further signs of this were gleaned from searches of his house.

On 11 January 1994, the inquiry team carried out a search of 10 Hazelfield Street and found security arrangements deemed by McArthur to be 'excessive for the average citizen'. Inside the heavy PVC front door were three Chubb dead bolts and a metal plate fixed to the door itself. Behind was a steel shutter to be pulled down at night, an arrangement that was also in place for the back door. There was security lighting at the front and rear, while at the front there was also a CCTV camera/monitoring system (the equipment that had been stolen from a workshop by Adair's mole at the Police Authority). The downstairs windows were all fitted with bulletproof glass. Following his arrest the same day Adair told police that he had spent £2,000 on the bulletproof windows and that 'if he ever left 10 Hazelfield Street he would try an AK-47 on the glass'. During the search, officers also discovered a number of incriminating items. In the kitchen, a bundle of 74 UFF calendars was found featuring photos of armed and masked men. In the top right-hand corner of one Adair had written, 'From the boys of Shankill – Johnny 2 Batt C/Coy'. Also seized was a photocopy of a business card on which was the simple message:

Ulster Freedom Fighter
West Belfast
2nd Battalion
YE HA
Fuck the RA [IRA]

As well as the attempts on his life by republicans, the evidence against Adair also included the loyalist's bitter feud with Eddie Copeland in Ardoyne. On the evening of 25 August 1993, the two arch enemies came face to face as their cars pulled up alongside each other at traffic lights on Clifton Road in north Belfast. According to a conversation between Copeland and a police officer later that night, Adair pointed at the republican and shouted, 'You're a dead man,' before screaming to the other occupants of the car, 'We're going to get you, we're going to get all you fenian bastards.' At 10 p.m. that night several shots were fired into the Ardoyne home of Eddie Copeland's sister. The following day the UFF admitted Copeland had been their intended target. The next month a C Coy team went back to Ardoyne and shot up the house they believed the republican shared with his mother. In fact, they had hit the wrong address: Eddie Copeland's mother lived next door. The only casualty of either attack was a dog, which was shot dead as it ran behind a sofa. In typical Adair style, he later claimed that one of his men then forced their way into the house and tucked the blood-soaked animal into an upstairs bed in a gesture reminiscent of the mafia film, *The Godfather*.

The police case against Adair detailed every recorded sighting of him in republican areas from April 1991 until March 1994, when the preliminary investigation was completed. McArthur wrote:

> On many of these occasions Adair was stopped and spoken to by police. Taken at its most basic, the frequent sightings of Adair in republican areas raise questions for a 'loyalist' being in such areas on a regular basis. When one adds to that the numerous comments that he has made to police on such occasions, such as reciting to police the name and address of a known republican personality who lives close to where Adair had been stopped, and take all the other matters outlined in this report into consideration, then there can be little doubt that Adair's frequent forays into republican areas have a more sinister connotation and leaves little room for doubt that he is in fact targeting future victims of UFF murder gangs.

During the search of his house in January 1994 police seized, amongst other material, a six-inch cardboard cut-out of a Celtic football player, the very same that Adair would hang from his back windscreen before driving into Belfast's Catholic ghettos. Many of the sightings coincided closely with murders or attempted murders. For instance, in April 1992 Adair was spotted in the Falls Road/Lanark Way area of west Belfast close to where Philomena Hanna was gunned down just days later. Four days before Gerard O'Hara's death in September of that year he was seen at 7.30 p.m. driving into the Catholic New Lodge district where O'Hara lived. On 24 October 1993, two days before C Coy's 'spray job' at the council refuse depot, Adair was spotted in Kennedy Way. Less than 24 hours after the Shankill bomb, the loyalist was obviously eyeing his target.

The police notes show that Winkie Dodds was often in the car as well and that Adair occasionally wore body armour. When stopped by police, he did not even try to hide what he was doing. At 8.15 p.m. on 3 July 1992 he was pulled over at a checkpoint on the Crumlin Road and asked about an

Ordnance Survey map in his car. According to police records, he said it was to find his way round republican areas. At 10.40 p.m. on 1 September 1993, he told police in Glenbryn, a Protestant area neighbouring the Ardoyne, that he'd 'heard through the grapevine it's going to be a bad month for sectarian murders'. Two days after the Shankill bomb, at 8.45 a.m. on 25 October, he was stopped with Winkie Dodds in Rosapenna Street in the Catholic Oldpark district. The police notes show that he 'stated he was looking for the bombers, the instigators like C******* and M********* [authors' amendment to names]. He suspected he might catch them out in a girl's house in Rosapenna or Lower Cliftonville.' Pulled over in his Rover 214 at 6.40 p.m. on 18 November he told a reserve constable, 'I may visit a Sinn Fein man's house.' At 9 p.m. on 3 December, a joint police and Army patrol searched his car at the junction of the Andersonstown Road and Kennedy Way in nationalist west Belfast. A soldier recorded Adair's details and upon completing the form asked him to sign it. Adair said, 'I'm protecting the public of Great Britain,' and signed the form 'Johnny, 2nd Batt, UFF'.

On 19 February 1994, Adair, driving a Mazda 323 with Winkie Dodds in the car, was stopped by police near nationalist Lenadoon. The constable who spoke to him said he 'stated that he was going "up to take a look at the Donegal Celtic. I'm told there's a lot of bad boys drink about there."' Asked whom, Adair replied, 'You should know, sure youse are in collusion with us.' Commenting about police suddenly appearing and stopping him, he referred to a C Coy gun attack on Sinn Fein's headquarters the previous day. 'Aye, it looks like I'm going to have to change my plan, but you weren't about when we popped up the other day.' It was typical of many of Adair's remarks to the security forces – he was winding them up, but he was also basically telling the truth. On 10 March 1994, he was again stopped and his car searched. According to police records:

> He said he would be killing as many PIRA as possible shortly, he asked for info about Brian Gillen's new address, he said he wished to kill Gillen personally. He was frustrated that the recent attacks against Sinn Fein in Ardmore and A'Town [Andersonstown] had not been more successful. He said it was a waste of time soldiers searching his car, as he was not stupid enough to carry stuff on him and added that he has people to do that for him.

As Adair became more powerful he found bragging harder than ever to resist. As he entered Crumlin Road Courthouse on 10 September 1993, he boasted to a police sergeant, 'You know, I'm on a 365-day-a-year, 52-weeks, 24-hours-a-day operation. We're making the running, the taigs will have to do something.' On 18 October, he spoke to a policeman outside the Times Bar in the loyalist Tigers Bay area of north Belfast. Told to have a nice day, he said, 'I will when I spill some fenian's blood.' It was a joke, but it was also true. Two days later he was stopped by police near the Shankill and threatened to kill Eddie Copeland. 'Copeland is afraid to live in the Ardoyne and is calling the shots from the New Lodge. I'll put a bullet in his head.'

In October 1993, Detective Chief Superintendent Derek Martindale asked Johnston Brown if he would wear a wire to tape his conversations with Adair, but despite his earlier request to do so, the detective now said no. Were it to be discovered on him it would not only destroy the relationship he had cultivated with Adair and his colleagues, but also leave his family vulnerable to attack from the UFF, who knew where he lived. Instead, the task fell to a young community policeman who was ambitious to transfer to Special Branch. He was already covertly recording Adair at the time of the Shankill bomb and was able to capture his frenzied reaction to it. The following month the policeman struck up another conversation with him and asked him about the prospect of peace. 'Are we gonna get peace? Not while I'm about,' came the response. 'I have to tell you, I'll never have peace.' Adair then confessed:

> I've tried my hand at everything but no good, so I had to go to terrorism and build my way up through the ranks. A couple of dirty ones and then a couple of good ones to the top of the ladder, untouched too. I've got them all. The ball's at my foot. If I say 'Go' it goes. I say stop it stops. I say, 'Make the bombs, we'll scare the peelers for 48 hours,' the ball's at my foot. I've some fucking power, I'll tell you. How did I get to the top? Scratching my balls do you think? Do you think I bluffed my way to the top?

Adair, who was standing with Norman Green Jnr, then asked to see the officer's Ruger handgun. He was messing with the policeman. 'Let's have a look at that Ruger. I'm getting a few of them. Let's see,' he said as he admired the gun. 'Norman, here's these weapons we're getting. Ruger,

there's it there. Fuck sake, show him. We're getting a load of these . . .
that's them there, paid for and all.' Whether seriously or in jest, Adair
continued, 'Look at the gear I'm getting in at the minute,' at which point
Green chipped in, 'You've got more gear than Tennent Street barracks
has.' Asked by the policeman whether anything had happened while Adair
was being held in Castlereagh the previous month, the terrorist replied,
'No . . . sure, fuck, if I go away for 48 hours there's not a shot fired. I went
to Spain and there wasn't a shot fired [a reference to his holiday in August
1993]. All the fucking wee men were taking drugs and going mad.' On the
question of peace, Adair said he longed for it:

> So would I [want peace]. We all would like. Nobody wants to fucking
> run seven days a week targeting Provos, killing innocent people,
> killing Sinn Feiners, nobody wants to do that . . . all their lives. No,
> we want to go home and watch *Coronation Street* like the rest of them.
> We're all human. We're balls and heart like the rest of youse. We
> wanna go away to the beach at the summer . . . Do you think I
> honestly want this war to go on? I want peace as much as the next
> man wants it, know what I mean, but I'll not sit back and let our
> fucking people get fucking walked on, do you know what I mean?

In another taped conversation, Adair asked the police officer:

> What's happening, is all quiet?
> *Policeman*: At the minute, aye.
> *Adair*: Some UFF cell running about now. They're right and tight,
> aren't they?
> *Policeman*: What?
> *Adair*: It's a good UFF cell running about now. They're very tight.
> *Policeman*: What do you mean by tight, Johnny?
> *Adair*: Well, they're slaughtering a lot in west Belfast.

Challenged by the policeman to explain his views, Adair went on:

> Well put it like this. There's been over 3,000 killed and youse can't
> stop it, so I think that's not quite good enough. So, if people want
> to take the law into their own hands, fair play to them.
> *Policeman*: No, no, you can't do that.

MAD DOG

Adair: Well, everybody has their own opinion and my opinion is, they who live by the sword will die by the sword – it's the answer to the Troubles.

Although his taped remarks may ultimately have been deemed inadmissible as evidence, one thing is clear: Adair was so consistently blatant in his boasting that it is hard to believe that he was not already behind bars. Only in the topsy-turvy world of Northern Ireland, where justice tends to coincide with Britain's wider political agenda, could such a man have freely walked the streets for so many years.

Although he knew roughly how far he could go, on many occasions Adair appeared to cross the line, even while in police custody and officially under caution. Immediately after his arrest on 11 January 1994, he attempted to phone Winkie Dodds but couldn't get through. 'You can't get these gunmen when you're looking for them,' he told the detective sergeant. 'Is Winkie not a bit over the hill to be a gunman?' asked the police officer, to which Adair replied, 'Nobody's over the hill when I shout at them and put a gun in their hand.' As his picture was being taken at Castlereagh holding centre, he was asked whether the name on the photo card was correct. 'That's right, I'm Mad Dog,' he said. According to police notes of the conversation, 'A comment was passed that Mad Dog was Dominic McGlinchey [the INLA gunman]. Adair retorted, "The difference between me and McGlinchey is that he killed policemen but I kill taigs."' Told to wipe his hands for fingerprinting, Adair said, 'These are some hands. They can do anything – pull the trigger, point the finger, anything.'

During one of many interviews Adair was asked about a £25,000 robbery by his men a few days earlier. His remarks and the subsequent turn of events incriminated him as somebody who clearly had influence over the UFF on the Shankill. The police appealed to his vanity and he fell for it:

Discussing a robbery at Shankill Road Post Office, Adair was informed that when the family of the postmistress were being held by UFF men in their home, the culprits had stolen items of personal property, i.e. a charm bracelet, a gold bracelet and two watches. Adair was obviously displeased at the news and said that if that was the case he would see that the family got their stuff back. (The property was, in fact, delivered anonymously to Shankill Road Post Office on Friday, 14 January 1994, within 48 hours of his release.)

BIG MOUTH

During two days in Castlereagh Adair made several further admissions, all of which were carefully noted as the police continued to build their case against him:

> He said, unprompted, that his visits to Castlereagh Police Office allowed him to clear his head, think of things and get matters into order. He said the last time he was lifted for the seven days there wasn't a shot fired by the UFF but when he got out he got the boys together and told them that if he disappeared from the scene again, they are to carry on. He said he was 60 per cent sure that there would be an incident from C Company UFF while he was in custody, maybe even tonight.

According to the notes, 'It was put to him that he had murdered people. His reply, "I've never murdered anybody." He smiled and said, "Or I've never been caught."' In another interview:

> Having denied being a UDA godfather, he stated that he enjoyed deciding what would be news tonight or tomorrow. He said he had projected the UFF to a high level. He said he was worried about a C1(3) inquiry regarding his financial status, that it was dragging his wife Gina into it and she is innocent.

And well he might be worried. A list of the contents of his house in Hazelfield Street included a £1,650 black leather suite, a built-in tropical fish tank, a newly fitted kitchen and televisions in every room, even that of his two-year-old baby son. It did not suggest the lifestyle of a couple struggling to get by on income support. An examination of Adair's finances became an increasingly important part of the inquiry. Between July 1991 and January 1994 more than £40,000 passed through the hands of Johnny Adair and Gina Crossan, an amount of money that could not be explained through their known income. The majority, over £22,000, was deposited in Gina's bank account. There was also evidence that Adair was cashing cheques through third-party accounts for his own benefit and that this money was almost certainly coming from racketeering. As Adair himself put it to a police officer on 19 November 1993:

I don't need money. I get eight pounds a fortnight on the 'bureau' and I get a few quid day to day. As long as I've petrol in the car, food in the cupboard, I don't give two fucks. Certainly, I get a few quid if I do the odd robbery. We do the odd robbery: it's a bonus, isn't it? If the odd businessman comes up and says, 'There's a cheque for 20 grand', certainly there you are, know what I mean, we don't need money.

Brian McArthur was right. The police were not dealing with an 'average citizen'.

9. UFF Rocket Team on Tour

'It was the fucking best that loyalists had ever had. For once in their lives they got their act together under good leadership. There's no doubt about that. The war went straight to their [republicans'] fucking doorsteps, right in and they didn't like it.' – *Johnny Adair on C Coy*

EVERY TIME JOHNNY ADAIR WAS HELD IN CASTLEREAGH BARRACKS HE complained to his closest friends that police tormented him about his sisters, Lizzie and Etta, both of whom suffered from severe learning disabilities. Although older than him, the constant stream of abuse they had received since childhood made Adair highly protective of them and alert to the slightest insult. It was a pity, then, that his brotherly compassion did not extend to others with similar mental problems. On a freezing December night in 1993, Adair changed into a smart black jacket and black shoes before entering a derelict flat in Boundary Walk, just a few doors down from the C Coy shebeen. There, with a young UDA member standing alongside him, he stood in front of a large man on his knees and pronounced a sentence of death. Summoning his sternest voice, he declared, 'The Ulster Freedom Fighters finds you guilty of treason and as such sentences you to the ultimate penalty – death.' He tapped the silencer on his Magnum 10 Pistol, put it against the man's head and squeezed the trigger. As his victim slumped sideways to the floor, Adair thought he caught a glimpse of the life draining from his eyes and for a second or two he stood watching as the blood gushed out of his head. Despite all his boasts about being a killer and a gunman, Adair's big secret – which only his closest friends knew – was that he had never killed anybody. Up to that point he had relied on the likes of 'Fat Jackie' Thompson, Stevie 'Top Gun' McKeag and Sam 'Skelly' McCrory to do this for him. Despite his many attempts to take life, this was the first time he had shot someone from point-blank range in the head and for a brief moment he did not know what to do. At least he had done it now, he thought to himself, then dragged his gaze away from the body in front of him. He walked quickly out of the flat, where Gary McMaster, another C Coy man, was waiting. 'Move!' he barked as he handed him the gun.

At 9.30 a.m. on 13 December 1993, a neighbour, hearing groans from the flat, pushed open the front door to reveal an appalling sight. More than 12 hours after he had been shot, 26-year-old Noel Alexander Cardwell lay in a pool of blood, still alive but only just. It had been so cold during the night that his blood had been prevented from flowing at a normal rate, delaying his death and prolonging his pain by a few extra hours. After being rushed to hospital, his body started to heat up and he died at 10.20 a.m., barely 50 minutes after being found. McMaster was later given a life sentence for his role in the murder, though Adair has never been charged with the killing. In a telephoned admission of responsibility, the UFF said Cardwell had been executed by the terrorist group's 'Special Assassination Section'. It said he was a Special Branch informer and blamed him for a series of recent weapons finds, including at least one on the Shankill Road. The claim was a lie. Noel Cardwell had been assassinated because Adair could not resist the opportunity to look ruthless in front of his men. Every now and then, he believed, it was good to make them afraid of him. Even if he had wanted to, Cardwell would not have been able to disclose much to police because he was not a UDA member. There was also one other fact that made him an unlikely candidate for a police informer: he had the mental age of a 12-year-old. 'He used to play about with the kids outside,' said a relative after the shooting. 'He would do anything they asked, he was so soft . . . All he lived for were his three sisters. He lived with one of his sisters – you couldn't let him live on his own. Whoever did it, I hope they can't sleep in their beds at night. I know I couldn't.'

Noel Cardwell, a 6 ft 4 in. friendly giant, was guilty of exactly the same 'crime' as Johnny Adair's two sisters: he wanted to hang around the local hero and be part of his gang. Jackie Robinson, Adair's former girlfriend, remembers 'Big Noel' as a harmless young fellow who collected glasses in the Diamond Jubilee Bar on the lower Shankill. 'He was very simple-minded,' said Jackie. 'All he wanted was to be in with the big boys. He just wanted to be liked and he thought it was great to be around Johnny and his clique.' Jackie has a vivid memory of the night Cardwell was shot. She was having a cup of tea in a friend's house on the estate when she saw Adair pull up in his car with Donald Hodgen, the C Coy commander, and Winkie Dodds, C Coy's second-in-command. 'He saw my car so he came in and said, "What are you doing?" He wanted me out of the way; he wanted me to go home. He never wanted me to think bad of him. I said, "Where are you going?" He said, "I'm just going up the road here." I knew that flat was used for interrogations and as I saw him walking towards it I knew. I just felt sick and went home.'

By the time Adair arrived in the flat, a hood had been placed over Cardwell's head and he had been badly beaten about the face and body during a lengthy interrogation. The Belfast *News Letter* reported afterwards that his knees had been smashed. Cardwell had been abducted by two C Coy henchmen earlier that day shortly after checking out of the Royal Victoria Hospital on the Falls Road, where he had spent the night after some of Adair's friends spiked his drink in a bar. In a typically callous prank, they wanted to see what effect an Ecstasy tablet would have on the young man, who was on daily medication for a nervous complaint. Whilst in hospital, however, Cardwell received a visit from the police, who, due to the suspicious circumstances under which he had been admitted, were keen to find out who he had been drinking with. Not thinking he was doing anything wrong, Cardwell named two UDA men who were then arrested, questioned and released without charge. His simple-mindedness cost him his life. After being picked up from the hospital by his sister he headed to the Buff's Club on the Oldpark Road for a quick game of snooker with his friends. He never made it home.

The ruthless manner in which Adair dealt with Noel Cardwell was a reflection of his pathological hatred of informers, which dated back to the Tucker Lyttle era when the UDA in west Belfast was riddled with them. Given Adair's big mouth it was ironic that he should be so hard on people who talked to the authorities. Despite the claims of many of his enemies, Adair himself was never a paid police agent. Unwittingly, however, he became a casual informer for at least one officer who filed source contact reports based on his information using the codename 'Sid' after Sid Vicious, the punk rocker. On one occasion a gun was recovered based on Adair's intelligence, though Adair had no idea he had helped to pinpoint its whereabouts. He did not see any contradiction between boasting to police about his importance and his loathing of informers. Indeed, he always liked to spell out in graphic terms what would happen if his men were caught feeding information to the security forces. Few were left in any doubt that this meant a bullet behind the ear or, as Adair put it, 'a head job'. As one senior Special Branch officer explained, 'He had a terrible habit of unsettling people. He would just grab somebody in a pub and say, "You're a tout." They'd all be sitting there thinking, "Is he going to pick on me this week?"'

Following the arrest of the 'Dream Team' in July 1992, Adair became convinced that details of their operation had been betrayed to the security forces. In an attempt to prevent a repeat of this, he set up what became known as C Coy's 'Internal Security Unit'. Like many of Adair's military innovations it was modelled on the Provisional IRA, in this case its notorious 'nutting squad'. According to 'Pete', 'It was some time in late 1992 or early 1993 that it was set up. There would have been certain people pulled in and had guns put in their mouths and questioned . . . To my knowledge there were four on the internal security unit, Johnny at the head of it. But it was very secretive, we didn't know much of what it was about.' 'Pete' recalls at least three C Coy gunmen being questioned by the unit in 1993–4, the period in which he was active. 'They would talk to you if you'd had an approach from the peelers or if maybe you'd been caught doing a petty crime like shoplifting.' One of those on the unit recalled seeing fully grown men whimper with terror after having tea towels wrapped around their heads – to deaden the noise of a gun blast and to limit the spray of blood: 'There were guys pulled in after an operation had gone wrong and no matter who they were they were all questioned. They'd be there with a gun in their mouth and a tea towel over their head. They'd be there in tears and you'd be joking with whoever was with you, "Do you want to shoot him or shall I?" and they'd be shouting out, "I'm not a tout, I'm not a tout."'

Adair had a knack of knowing when his units were most vulnerable to penetration by the police. After the influx of older volunteers following the Shankill bomb, he took special care, according to 'Pete'. 'Johnny knew exactly what the peelers would be doing. He said, "We'll have to be careful here because the peelers will be trying to get their £10 touts." He knew every move the peelers were going to make. He was ahead of them every time.'

As a result the police became increasingly frustrated and more and more blatant in their attempts to 'turn' Adair and his colleagues. Despite his boasts to the police, most of this information was of little use to them; what they needed was hard intelligence. On one occasion Special Branch officers arrived at Adair's house with a briefcase full of money but were turned away by the loyalist, who laughed in their faces and said the offer was nowhere near enough. Special Branch was also harassing Adair's associates, and on several occasions they approached Gary 'Smickers' Smith in the pet shop he ran on the Shankill Road and offered him money and even a house. Another C Coy veteran recalls a policeman holding up a bulging envelope in which he said there was £30,000 in cash for him if he became an informer. The man had no intention of betraying his colleagues but every intention of taking the money and bolting. He grabbed the envelope and ran but only managed a few yards before the officer rugby-tackled him to the ground.

Adair's crackdown on 'touts' was part of a wider restructuring of the UFF in west Belfast. Although a cell structure had existed before, knowledge of operations was often shared with ordinary UDA members who had nothing to do with the military side and did little more than pay their dues. 'Johnny changed it into more of a military structure,' said 'Pete'. 'There were ASUs before but the knowledge would have extended to the teams themselves and the ordinary C Coy team members. Under Johnny it was kept within the military. Before, you could have walked into a bar on the Shankill and found out who was doing what, there was that much loose talk.' In another attempt to reduce the risk of betrayal, ASU members were all made to stay together in one place after they had been called together for an operation and they were often briefed just minutes before it was due to begin. 'Pete' explained: 'Johnny would say, "Right, there's going to be an operation on such and such. The car's going to be here in 15 minutes, there's how you get in, there's how you get out, here's your driver." Very often that would be the first you knew about it. The next thing the guns were brought to the house, the driver came, you got in the car and the thing was done. The whole thing was kept tight.'

Cardwell's murder was a grisly example of Adair's new approach, but it was not the first time Adair had taken the lead in shooting a suspected informer. In May 1992, he had come close to killing Billy Stobie, the UDA's west Belfast quartermaster, after correctly suspecting that he was a police agent. A close friend had tipped him off about Stobie after police raided the office of Circle Taxis, where Stobie worked as a clerk, and inquired about a pick-up from a house in the Glencairn estate. The taxi had been hijacked by the UVF but the planned attack did not go ahead and the taxi was returned.

As a precaution, Stobie, who recorded every order, was instructed by his boss to tear out the relevant page of the logbook and rewrite it from scratch, minus the call. As far as anybody else was concerned, a taxi was never sent to that address. But the fact that the police asked questions about that particular job made Stobie's colleague smell a rat, and Adair was duly informed. It was a small detail, but enough to seal Stobie's fate.

In the early hours of 21 May 1992, Stobie was summoned to a house in Snugville Street where Adair, Donald Hodgen, Tommy Potts and several others were partying. The party was at Jackie Thompson's house, who was celebrating his release on bail earlier that day. He had been in jail since the previous autumn when police had found radio scanners in his house. With a few drinks inside them, Adair and his friends had started talking about 'touts' and Stobie's name was mentioned. Acting totally on impulse, Adair phoned Ian Truesdale, who drove up to collect him while a gun was sent for. As he pulled up outside the house, Stobie was dragged out of the car by Hodgen and Thompson. 'If it's about my loan, I'll pay the loan,' he blurted, referring to a sum of UDA money he had been lent several months earlier. As he was dragged towards an alleyway, a bullet whizzed past the side of Thompson's head between him and Stobie. While Thompson turned to see what was going on, Stobie seized his chance, wriggling free and bolting down the alley as fast as he could. Adair, who was standing with a Magnum in his hands, fired five more shots, hitting Stobie in the legs and back. Thompson and Hodgen could not believe it. All six bullets in the gun had been used; it should have been a simple question of walking up to him and shooting him in the head from point-blank range.

Adair later told Jonty Brown that he had been aiming for Stobie's spine because he was a 'spineless bastard'. It was not true: Adair had been desperate to impress his friends by showing them he could kill somebody, but he had failed. Adair never forgot that night. Over the next nine years Stobie's role as a Special Branch agent gradually came to light as he told police investigating the 1989 murder of Pat Finucane about his role in the UDA. He had committed the ultimate crime, and as far as Adair was concerned the only fitting punishment was death. No matter how long he had to wait, he would have his retribution.

While most Shankill loyalists had turned a blind eye to the Stobie incident, many were quietly appalled by the shooting of Noel Cardwell. It sent a chilling message to Adair's men but it also sickened many ordinary Protestants, though none dared to speak out. 'See, to be honest with you at that time the whole estate was 100 per cent behind Johnny and when it came out that the wee lad had a mental age of 12 you'd have got the odd one against it but nobody said anything out loud,' said one C Coy veteran. 'Johnny was God. Anything he done he was worshipped.' Some time later, when Adair was inside the Maze Prison, Jackie Robinson told him how disgusted she felt about Noel Cardwell's murder. 'He phoned me from the Maze one day and we were actually having an argument about it and I said I was disgusted. He said, "Jackie, why would you say that? Gina would never bring up anything like that with me." He didn't try to give an explanation, he didn't try to give a reason. I knew he had two mentally retarded sisters and I think they all knew themselves that that kid was fine.' According to local sources, Stevie McKeag was also briefly in the room before the murder but did not expect Noel Cardwell to be killed. He, too, told close friends that he had reservations about it. Also appalled when he heard was Jim Spence, Adair's old brigadier, who was now in jail. It was one thing shooting innocent Catholics, but another entirely killing ordinary Protestants. Spence and A Coy's Matt Kincaid, who had been in prison since 1991, asked Adair to come up to the jail and explain himself. 'Nobody else wanted it [Cardwell's murder], just Johnny Adair,' said one detective. 'Spence and Kincaid invited Adair to come up and explain what was going on but he wouldn't go.' As a last resort the pair even considered having a gun planted in Adair's house so that they could talk sense to him inside jail. They never went through with the idea.

Adair did not dwell on Cardwell's murder. 'Johnny has a state of mind where he can cut off reality, he can make believe that he was not a part of something,' explained Jackie Robinson. 'He can convince himself that he hasn't done these things and just switch himself off in his head.' Instead he threw himself into preparations for Christmas, his favourite time of year. As usual there was a party for the prisoners' wives and children in the Ainsworth Avenue community centre at the top of the Shankill, with free drink and food for the women and presents for the kids. At home, he helped Gina put lights up in all the downstairs windows and decorate the Christmas tree. Gina above all was fastidious about Christmas and took care with her decorations, although they were nothing like as elaborate as those of Stevie McKeag, whose house, with flashing plastic reindeer on the roof and Christmas figurines in the front garden, resembled Santa's grotto. On Christmas Day 1993, Gina's mother, Georgina, came for dinner as usual and the family sat down for their meal after opening their presents. It was a particularly special day for Jonathan, who had turned nine that August. Dejected because he had no more presents, the boy was sent outside by his father to get some more coal for the fire. In the shed he found a brand new bike. 'Johnny kept telling me about the expression on that boy's face,' said Jackie. 'When it came to Christmas, or anything that involved giving presents, Johnny was the biggest kid of all.'

But after a couple of weeks off it was back to work for Adair and his colleagues. The year 1994 opened against a backdrop of increasing worry for loyalists, who feared yet again that Britain was about to sell their country down the river. In December, John Major, the Prime Minister, and Albert Reynolds, his Irish counterpart, had signed the so-called 'Downing Street Declaration', a direct response to the talks between Gerry Adams and John Hume. It promised to allow 'the people of the island of Ireland alone, by agreement between the two parts respectively, to exercise their right of self-determination on the basis of consent, freely and concurrently given, North and South, to bring about a united Ireland, if that is their wish.' Although the document effectively guaranteed the union with Britain as long as there was a Protestant majority in Ulster, its deliberate ambiguity caused widespread suspicion among loyalists. In their eyes, the Government was bending over backwards to accommodate militant republicanism, and the belief that the world was against them was confirmed again in February 1994 when Adams was fêted by a naive American media after being granted a two-day visa to enter the United States.

Back home, Adair was determined to intensify his campaign against Sinn Fein. On 2 January, his gunmen fired several shots at the home of Alex Maskey, the party's leader on Belfast City Council, the fourth attack on his home in eight years. Maskey's wife, Liz, and a son escaped uninjured while the councillor himself was out at the time. The next day Adair wrongfooted the police by sending the team back up, but the car broke down on the way and they were forced to walk back to the Shankill. Three days later Adair sent a team into Catholic west Belfast to kill Una Gillespie, another Sinn Fein councillor. Shortly after 6 p.m. on 6 January, three men forced their way into a house in Benwee Park in the nationalist Lenadoon district. They believed that Gillespie lived opposite. Claiming they were from the Provisional IRA, one of the men gestured at the occupants with a handgun and ordered them to stay downstairs. The two others took automatic weapons from a bag and went upstairs. The house takeover was another tried and tested method lifted straight from the IRA. On this occasion, however, the team decided to abort their operation 45 minutes later after learning that an Army foot patrol had entered the neighbourhood. But they did not leave without spilling blood. As they were on their way out, a 21-year-old Catholic man, the son of the couple who owned the house, was shot in the arm and back. While he underwent surgery later that night his elderly father was treated for shock. One C Coy 'operator' recalls, 'The ASU came into the house saying they were Provos. On their way out the fella says, "I'm one of youse 'uns," and that's when they shot him.' 'Davy', another C Coy gunman, recalled, 'There was a unit actually sitting in a house. They [the ASU] just rapped the door and told the people, "Provisional IRA," and that was it, they let us in. They saw the guns and whatever and the hooded men and then we told them it was the Ulster Freedom Fighters.'

Five days later, Johnny Adair unleashed his brand-new toy, which was better than anything he had been given at Christmas. More than 50 people were enjoying a quiet drink in the Rock Bar on the Falls Road when they became C Coy's latest targets. Shortly after 6 p.m. on 10 January 1994, a dark-blue Ford Escort pulled up and did a U-turn outside the pub. Two masked men got out of the car and fired a shoulder-held RPG-7 from the middle of the road. The rocket, which was aimed at the upstairs lounge, bounced off a protective window grille and detonated in the street, causing two deafening explosions. Had it penetrated the building there would have been multiple fatalities. The attack was audacious but indiscriminate, and as the car sped away the team opened fire on the bar with automatic rifles. Nobody was hit, though several were treated for shock while others received cuts and bruises after being showered with flying glass. In a statement the UFF admitted responsibility and claimed that senior republicans had been meeting in the bar, a claim that was dismissed as ridiculous by republican sources. The attack was a propaganda coup for C Coy but it worried the security forces, who feared it was only a matter of time before Adair caused the massacre he was trying to achieve. In an attempt to calm things down, the loyalist was arrested at home the following day and held in Castlereagh for 48 hours. 'Are youse not worried about us having a rocket?' he asked the detective sergeant who detained him. 'Does anybody know how to use it?' replied the police officer, to which Adair smiled and said proudly, 'Didn't it make a bang?'

On 7 February, Gary Whitty McMaster, a 29-year-old Protestant originally from east Belfast, was tested with another job by Adair, who was trying to suss out the quality of his new recruit. He planted a grenade in a shrubbery outside Sinn Fein's headquarters in Andersonstown in west Belfast and fixed a trip wire to the building's front gate. It was spotted by Alex Maskey as he arrived for work and made safe by the Army's bomb-disposal experts. Adair gave McMaster £100 in cash but the new recruit was keen to do more. He wanted the money but he also wanted to rival a close friend who had already made a name for himself in the UFF. As a sign of his commitment he had a special tattoo emblazoned on his forearm. Beneath a clenched fist it read, 'UFF – Till Death Do Us Part'.

McMaster did not have to wait long for another taste of action. At 7.30 p.m. the following day he took part in a gun attack on the home of a republican suspect in Hatfield Street in south Belfast. At least 20 shots were fired from an automatic rifle but none hit the target. As one C Coy gunman explained, McMaster was a classic example of an inexperienced operator who fell briefly into Adair's favour, showed great enthusiasm but 'failed to get the job done'. He said, 'People do things in a certain way. If there's 14 in a magazine and it's somebody inexperienced you'll be lucky if they fire seven. With the experienced ones it's up close and personal, in the face, close up.' Again McMaster received £100 from Adair and again he wanted more. With nine children to feed, cash was a big part of his motivation. Four days later, on 12 February, he secured himself a place in loyalist mythology by taking part in Johnny Adair's finest hour. Earlier that Saturday morning Adair drove into west Belfast and past the Sinn Fein headquarters, checking for additional security on the building and signs of undercover police or soldiers. He then returned to the Shankill and set his plan in motion. His chosen team that day consisted of McMaster, Robert 'Rab' Bradshaw (who later hanged himself in jail) and at least one other C Coy man. Adair briefed them all in a safe house before dispatching them on a mission that he hoped would ensure his place in the pantheon of great loyalist heroes. Barely ten minutes after heading off in a hijacked silver Toyota, the team stopped outside the Sinn Fein office and fired a rocket at an upstairs room used for meetings of the party's Belfast executive. The missile smashed through a window and lodged in a wall at the back of the building, causing extensive damage and a loud explosion. Mercifully, there was nobody in the office at the time because it was closed as a security precaution. 'The building would normally have been crowded on a Saturday morning. If it hadn't been shut there would have been a massacre,' said a Sinn Fein spokesman. Nobody was injured, but the attack made international news and received an extended mention by, amongst others, the *Pittsburgh Post-Gazette* in Pennsylvania and the Xinhua News Agency in China. Though disappointed nobody was killed, McMaster's brigadier was delighted with the publicity and again gave him £100.

Adair was starting to enjoy himself. He had made the decision to attack Sinn Fein's headquarters after a CID officer in Castlereagh – the same policeman who had linked Gerard O'Hara's family to the IRA – floated the idea to a C Coy volunteer. In the same interview he had also suggested targeting the Rock Bar, alleging that IRA meetings were held there. At least one further piece of information came from the rogue RUC man. He let it slip that Gerry Adams and Alex Maskey were among a group of Sinn Fein politicians attending meetings at a building in Poleglass while renovations were being carried out on the party's main offices. According to a close friend of Adair, C Coy monitored the building and observed Gerry Adams turning up in a black taxi. Because the car was almost certainly armour-plated, there was only one way for Adair to attack it and be sure of success: by using a rocket. Fortunately for Adams, the operation never got off the ground. 'They never actually got the RPG up into the area. The meeting was never tied down closely enough so it never got going,' said one of those involved in the plans.

For every successful operation there were many aborted and many more that failed. On Valentine's Day, Adair's volunteers left a bomb on the doorstep of a house in west Belfast in a heart-shaped chocolate box with a bouquet of flowers next to it. A male occupant in the house became suspicious and threw the box into the garden, where it exploded without causing injury. It is not clear for whom it was intended. On 18 February, the day after an RUC constable was killed in Belfast when an IRA rocket ripped through his armoured car, Adair launched one last attack on the Sinn Fein offices. Shortly after 11 a.m. McMaster jumped out of a car and opened fire on a number of workmen who were repairing the damage caused by the RPG-7 attack. Three were hurt, one seriously after being hit in the leg and stomach. They were standing on scaffolding when the gunman struck. 'There were quite a few shots. We ran out and found the three men lying on the ground,' said one eyewitness. 'There was quite a lot of blood but they were all able to speak.' It was the third attack on the Sinn Fein headquarters in two weeks. 'Johnny was running rings round the cops. They were scratching their heads,' said 'Pete'. 'The cops didn't expect him to go back to the same place two days later and attack it with a rocket, and then they didn't expect him to go back after another couple of days and attack it again.' Quite literally, Adair was taking the 'war' to the doorstep of the republican movement and the police appeared powerless to stop him.

The following day, Adair was arrested after the RUC carried out a search of his house and seized stolen CCTV cameras. Unprompted, Adair started to talk about the gun attack the previous day. 'I know every minute and every second of that operation,' he bragged. He then told police about his next plan:

> He went on to speak about a kamikaze operation on a bar just above Rosapenna Street where the job would be done with a grenade and AK-47s. He stated, 'We might take a loss but there will be three or four fatalities.' He then remarked that he had stood all the boys down and that there would be no operations tonight or until he got out. He stated, 'Everybody needs one day off.'

When Adair got out, this time after just a day in custody, the lull in activity continued as he basked in his success. He paid McMaster another £100 and threw a party in his honour. Like Gary 'Smickers' Smith, McMaster loved the glamour of being seen with Adair. By now, with Stevie McKeag in prison, Smickers was C Coy's most reliable gunman and was duly rewarded for his loyalty. According to former allies of Adair, the terror chief bought Smickers a car and showered him with gifts. He even took him on a visit to the Maze Prison to show him off to Skelly, Jackie Thompson and Tommy Potts and to let them know that, while they were behind bars, other young militants were carrying on the war.

Although some of his oldest friends were in jail and he had lost Stevie McKeag, things were going well for Adair. He had transformed C Coy into a ruthless terrorist unit based around a small clique of individuals who had successfully resisted police efforts to penetrate them. Adair's power base consisted of around a dozen people, including C Coy's most active gunmen. His trusted friends Donald Hodgen and Winkie Dodds were respectively C Coy commander and second-in-command. McKeag had been military commander until he was arrested and charged with the murder of Sean Hughes in the autumn of 1993. While in prison he was replaced by Gary 'Smickers' Smith, though he resumed his role following his acquittal in December 1994.

UFF ROCKET TEAM ON TOUR

Outside the inner core, up to 30 others formed a dependable pool of volunteers to be used on the fringes of military operations such as hijackings, house takeovers, and 'mop-up' duties. Many others played occasional roles, but the main activities of C Coy were carried out by a very small number of individuals. By the start of 1994, many of C Coy's leading 'operators' genuinely believed that they were winning the war against the IRA in Belfast. Their relentless campaign against Sinn Fein members and their families had become too much for many republicans. At the same time, the odd indiscriminate attack on Catholics increased the sense of despair within the broader nationalist community and put new pressure on the republican movement to find a way of ending the violence.

The only slight drawback for Adair was his relationship with the UDA's 'inner council', the group's governing body composed of all six brigadiers. While for the most part they were happy to let Adair do what he wanted, some of them were occasionally alarmed by his behaviour, above all Joe English, leader of the UDA's south-east Antrim brigade. Adair's relationship with English was becoming increasingly fraught, and in late 1993 he questioned Adair about rumours that he was planning to walk into an inner council meeting, pull a gun on his colleagues and shoot them all. As Adair's rival commanders would discover nearly ten years later, the idea sounded preposterous but it was not beyond him. During his interviews in Castlereagh in January, Adair showed his open contempt for English and the other four inner council members. According to police notes:

> Speaking about UDA/UFF personalities he said that Brigadier Joe English is a political man, a thinker, a talker, not military. He added that when the police seized the weapons from the flats at Rathcoole recently, that was all the weapons the UDA/UFF had there.

Adair had more to say:

> Still speaking about Joe English and his position in the UDA/UFF he laughed and said that English would ring him up after shootings and ask him was that them in the top right – English was referring to the UFF emblem being at the top right corner of the UDA badge. He said that English and the rest of the Inner Council are old ginnies but he needs them too.

In another interview during the same period of detention he derided his fellow brigadiers as 'cardboard cut-outs'. Even at this stage it was obvious that Adair had no time for politics. As the IRA cooled down its activities at the start of 1994, he was desperate to keep piling on the pressure. While his fellow commanders knew they would probably have to escalate their campaign further, they were also more alert to the changing mood in London and Dublin and the pressures from their political wing, the Ulster Democratic Party. According to Davy Adams, one of the UDP's leaders, the UDA was slowly realising that it had to embrace a political future. He recalled, 'My sense of it was that, although on the surface things were almost as bad, if not as bad as they had been years earlier, beneath that there was a real sense that things were moving towards some sort of ceasefire situation all round that would pave the way for politics to take the place of violence.' In January, Britain ended a ban on ministers meeting Sinn Fein, the UDP and the UVF's political arm, the Progressive Unionist Party (PUP) and announced that IRA weapons decommissioning was not a precondition to talks with Sinn Fein. Previously secret peace talks were now being conducted openly, and the momentum towards a settlement was fast becoming unstoppable.

Of the six brigadiers on the inner council, Johnny Adair alone could not be reasoned with. English, who chaired the meetings, attempted to cool him down but every time he tried Adair looked away and shrugged his shoulders. Like the others, English was afraid of Adair and was careful not to push him too far. Tom Reid, the UDA's brigadier in north Belfast, and Gary Matthews from the east of the city both scented the coming changes and realised that they had to prepare for an end to violence. The two biggest question marks hung over Billy McFarland, brigadier in Derry and north Antrim, and Alec Kerr from south Belfast. Both gave the impression of being signed up to English's way of thinking, but they also believed that the increase in UDA violence was directly linked to the IRA's peace moves. By far the most militant was Adair. Whenever politics came up in conversation, his eyes drifted elsewhere in the room and he never said a word. He would begin to fidget like a bored child, with a look of mischief on his face that reminded his colleagues of Just William, the famous schoolboy. Although at this stage he tried to remain on good terms with them, he had little respect for any of the brigadiers. Neither English nor Reid knew the first thing about military operations, while Gary Matthews' stomping ground in east Belfast was so inactive that Adair dubbed it 'the

Silent Valley'. Although Billy McFarland's brigade had put in some good operations in the early 1990s, Adair regarded him as a redneck from the country. As for Alec Kerr, he simply couldn't be trusted, largely because of the July 1992 ambush on Finaghy Road North, in the heart of his turf.

Looking back, it is not hard to see why Adair was not interested in peace. Here was a man who, with little by way of education or qualifications, would have had no potential in life had he been born in any other city in the world. On Belfast's Shankill Road, however, he was acclaimed as a god. As winter turned into spring he showed no sign of letting this go. There were six murders by loyalists in March and April 1994, three of them by the UFF in Belfast, plunging the city into a new security crisis. Two, those of Joseph McCloskey on 26 April and Liam Thompson the very next day, were blamed on Adair's brigade. The third was Theresa Clinton, the wife of Sinn Fein activist Jim Clinton, who was shot on 14 April at the couple's home in the Ormeau district of south Belfast, an area where Adair exerted considerable influence through his friendship with Joe Bratty, the UDA's local commander.

At around this time Adair was also stepping up his attempts to kill Brian Gillen, his old enemy. Derek Adgey, the Royal Marine who was passing intelligence to Adair, gave him information on a safe house where Gillen was staying in Andersonstown. A team from C Coy watched an Army patrol go through the street before taking over a house that faced the address. They waited an hour and a half but just as Gillen and a female republican arrived at the house, another Army patrol entered the street. By the time the Army had left, Gillen and his colleagues had also moved on. Not to be deterred, on the evening of 5 May Adair sent another team to murder Gillen, consisting of Gary 'Smickers' Smith, Robert 'Rab' Bradshaw and Richard Calderwood. Glen Esdale, a south Belfast UDA man, organised a safe house where the team could set out from and return to afterwards, but in an uncanny repeat of July 1992 all four were arrested before they reached their destination. As in 1992, the unit had been monitored by undercover police, apparently following a tip-off from an informer. Adair was livid that the unit had been compromised. Once again the police appeared to be protecting Gillen and once again Adair had been robbed of his best operator, this time Gary Smith. In February 1995, Smickers, Bradshaw and Calderwood were sentenced to 16 years for conspiracy to murder and having guns. At a delicate moment in the peace process, one of the most dedicated murderers in Northern Ireland had been conveniently removed from circulation. As the security forces celebrated Smith's arrest they knew that their work would not be finished until Adair himself was behind bars. It would not be enough to take him off the street for a few days and then, like so often in the past, have to let him go. This time the evidence would have to stick.

10. Prison

'His own sanity was going and he talked about killing himself and everything. Johnny wanted to hang himself, he couldn't stick it.'
– Jackie 'Legs' Robinson

JUST BEFORE 7 A.M. ON MONDAY, 16 MAY 1994, A FLEET OF SIX GREY RUC Land-Rovers pulled up outside 10 Hazelfield Street off the Shankill Road. Across west Belfast a similar scene was being enacted at more than a dozen addresses. Up to 20 of Adair's colleagues were scooped, including C Coy's Winkie Dodds, Paddy Patterson and Donald Hodgen. As the police arrived in Hazelfield Street (pronounced 'Hazeyfield' on the Shankill), they believed they were lopping off the head of loyalist terrorism in the city. The unmistakable whine of the Land-Rover engines had already wakened Adair from his sleep and he was almost completely dressed by the time he answered the door. After a senior officer read him his rights, Adair was arrested on suspicion of directing terrorism and membership of the UFF. It was an historic moment in the battle against terrorism in Northern Ireland.

Determined to put the squeeze on Adair in as many ways as possible, they also arrested Gina Crossan, his common-law wife. After being allowed to make arrangements for the couple's three children, she was driven to Gough Barracks in Armagh, while her husband was taken to Castlereagh in east Belfast. At Gough, Gina was interviewed by Detective Sergeant Alan Cormack, the number two on the investigation team. He had interviewed her on a number of occasions and had always found her easy to get on with. Today, however, she was cold and uncommunicative. In an attempt to break the stalemate, Cormack decided to try a different tack. Knowing Adair and his partner had extravagant tastes and plenty of money, he started talking about food. To his delight, Gina responded.

He recalled: 'Gina was saying nothing. I had interviewed her a number of times before and she had always been extremely helpful and quite chatty. It was as if she sensed something was different this time. I don't know what made me do it, but I decided to talk about food. I said I liked Chinese food and Gina said she also liked Chinese. I then mentioned that I had one or two favourite Chinese restaurants and I think Gina said her favourite was on the Shankill. I remember saying I thought most people from this part of the world experimented with Oriental cooking in a similar way. You know, they start off trying something simple and then become more adventurous as their experience and confidence grows. You kind of work your way up the ladder. I then asked Gina what her favourite Chinese dish was. In my own mind I was expecting to hear something like sizzling Peking duck with Szechuan sauce, spring onion and water chestnuts, but all Gina said was, "Curried chips." Clearly she was still on the first rung . . . After that she refused to answer any more questions and a couple of days later she was released. I was then transferred up to Castlereagh to join the team dealing with Johnny.'

The drama unfolding in east Belfast was a world away from the one that had just ended at Gough Barracks. This was the big picture. The Adair inquiry team included the cream of the CID and had been hand-picked by Ronnie Flanagan, the Assistant Chief Constable for Belfast, and Detective Chief Superintendent Derek Martindale. Flanagan had been born and brought up just a few streets from Adair and had witnessed the 25-year devastation which had turned a once-decent district into a killing field. His team, known as the Terrorist Intelligence Link Team (TILT), was headed by Acting Detective Chief Inspector Brian McArthur.

By the time of Adair's arrest, most of the hard work had already been done. In a highly unusual move, McArthur and Cormack had visited the offices of the Director of Public Prosecutions (DPP) several weeks earlier and presented the police case against Adair. They were accompanied by the most senior officers in Northern Ireland: Chief Constable Sir Hugh Annesley, ACC Belfast Ronnie Flanagan, and the head of CID and Acting ACC Crime, George Caskey. Senior DPP legal advisers listened intently as Cormack, using flipcharts and statistics, outlined the evidence that would be available to the Crown if a prosecution were mounted. The detective did not mince his words, telling the DPP bluntly, 'We want to bring a charge of directing terrorism against this man.' McArthur and Cormack were quietly confident that the presentation had gone well. After three weeks they were informed that, on the basis of what the DPP had been told, the Crown would be prepared to run with the case.

When Adair was arrested, he was convinced it was just another routine exercise to keep him off the streets. On the evening of Thursday, 19 May, after four days in Castlereagh, he was told he would be required to undergo a medical examination, where he would be able to put any allegations of ill treatment to a doctor. Believing he was about to be released, Adair was in good spirits as the doctor gave him the once over. But his happy confidence vanished at a stroke when he noticed one of the custody suite officers writing in the log under his name, 'On the instructions of DI Brian McArthur, transferred to Antrim Road for charging.'

Belfast's rush-hour traffic had scarcely died down when police mobile support units from Strandtown RUC Station arrived to take Adair across the city to north Belfast. Adair had lived all his life in the policing area known as 'D' Division and it would be there, in Antrim Road police station, that he would be formally charged with being a director of terror. Once the prisoner was safely inside the protected building, word was sent to McArthur and Cormack. Not a word passed between them as they descended the stairs to the custody suite, but the importance of the moment wasn't lost on either officer. They were about to pass another important milestone on the road to putting Adair behind bars. The detectives entered the room where Adair was being held and formally identified themselves. As the senior investigating officer, McArthur informed Adair of his rights before charging him with directing acts of terrorism by the UFF and membership of the same organisation. The prisoner was given the opportunity to respond to the charges, but he declined. He was then informed that he would be required at a remand hearing at Belfast Magistrates' Court the next morning and was returned to his cell.

On the Shankill, word of Adair's predicament spread quickly and groups of his supporters gathered to discuss the situation. Most were convinced it was just another ruse by the police to get him off the street and Winkie Dodds even compared it to the attempt four years earlier to turn Kathy Spruce, Adair's one-time girlfriend, against him. They vowed to turn up in force at court the following day to show him their support. Back in his cell,

Adair contemplated his future and fell into a fit of depression. He started to worry about all the things he had said to police officers and, in particular, what he had told Detective Sergeant Jonty Brown. The truth was that he could not remember what he had said. It was not until he received a message from his girlfriend, Jackie 'Legs' Robinson, that he started to cheer up slightly. She recalled: 'I actually phoned Antrim Road police station after they brought him back there and I said, "Look, can I come and see my boyfriend?" And the policeman who answered says, "Sorry, his girlfriend's just been nicked." And he asked who I was and I says, "Jackie Legs." And he started laughing because everybody knew me. He said, "Gina's just left, Jackie, we can't." I says, "Will you do me a favour?" And he says, "Yeah, what is it, love?" He was really nice, this policeman. And I said, "Just go and tell him I love him, I'm sorry, and I'll hear from him soon." And he did go and pass the message on because when I spoke to him [Adair] a couple of weeks later he says to me, "When that door opened and they told me what you said, Jackie, it really picked me up."'

Anticipating a loyalist show of solidarity the next morning, the RUC mounted an unprecedented security operation around Belfast Magistrates' Court. As the press waited for the appearance in the dock of Johnny 'Mad Dog' Adair, the atmosphere became increasingly tense. Two dozen burly police officers filed into court to be eyeballed and verbally abused by Adair's supporters. When he finally entered the room, they cheered and waved. Their idol, wearing a maroon jacket over a white vest and denim shirt, waved back. To those who had never set eyes on him before, the diminutive bleached blond, a gold hoop earring in one ear, seemed an unlikely director of terrorism. He smiled again a few minutes later when he was charged with belonging to the outlawed UFF and the commissioning of acts of terrorism between October 1993 and May 1994. He was only the second person in Northern Ireland to be charged with directing terrorism under a piece of legislation brought to the statute books two years earlier. It was the newest weapon in the armoury of the security forces, aimed at bringing the leaders of terrorist organisations to justice. In March 1994, the charge had been tagged on to a case against Laurence Maguire, a close colleague of Billy 'King Rat' Wright in the mid-Ulster UVF, but this would be the first time it was tested out properly.

It was only when McArthur took the stand that the real nature of the case against Adair was glimpsed for the first time. Under cross-examination from Billy McNulty, Adair's solicitor, the detective revealed that the evidence consisted largely of tape-recorded conversations with police officers and admissions by the accused during previous periods in police detention. Sensing the police case was moving into uncharted waters, McNulty asked McArthur, 'Can you indicate if the alleged tape recorded conversations and certain comments made on the street were made under caution or not?' 'They were not,' replied the officer. His answer provoked angry outbursts from Adair's supporters. Cries of 'It's a joke!' and 'Bastards!' rang out from the public gallery. McNulty told the court his client would be strenuously denying the charges. He said it was obvious the prosecution case had been cobbled together on speculation, innuendo and hearsay. Ending the ten-minute hearing, Magistrate Tom Travers ruled that the accused be remanded in custody until 3 June. Clearly delighted with the eloquence of his solicitor, Adair raised his right arm and waved to his friends who clapped and cheered as he was led back to the cells.

Adair's first night on the remand wing of HMP Belfast sparked a wave of violent reaction across the loyalist heartlands of north and west Belfast. Two people were arrested during a night of major disturbances. Police patrols came under gun and petrol bomb attacks and several vehicles, including a bus, were hijacked. As he lay in his cell at the 'Crum', as the prison was known because of its location on the Crumlin Road, Adair was delighted at the outrage his incarceration had caused. The thick walls of the decaying Victorian jail failed to prevent the violent city sounds drifting through the cell windows. Adair could hear practically every bullet fired and every petrol bomb thrown. The disturbances died down in the early hours, but residents in loyalist areas woke the next day to scenes of devastation on their doorsteps. Burnt-out cars and vans littered the streets and a lingering smell of smoke filled the air. Johnny Adair had spent less than 24 hours behind bars as a remand prisoner, but already the compensation bills were mounting.

After the initial flurry surrounding his arrival at Crumlin Road, Adair settled down and held a number of meetings with his solicitor, Billy McNulty. McNulty engaged the services of Tony Cinnamond, a leading local barrister, and together they prepared a strategy for Adair's next remand hearing on 3 June. The day before the case was to be heard, an accident 13 miles off the Antrim coast made international news and dealt a devastating blow to Northern Ireland's anti-terrorist agencies. A Chinook helicopter carrying 25 senior figures from the intelligence community plunged in thick fog into a hillside on the southern tip of the Mull of

Kintyre. All those on board, including Detective Chief Superintendent Brian Fitzsimons, head of the RUC Special Branch, died instantly. While the security forces went into a state of shock, the terrorists were delighted. As Adair's supporters arrived at court the next morning, a large crowd of C Coy men taunted RUC detectives by singing 'Mull Of Kintyre', the one-time hit by Paul McCartney and Wings. The situation almost boiled over as two officers lost their tempers and squared up to Adair's men. However, the defendant's luck was no better this time. Having examined the papers, Magistrate Travers was convinced there was more than ample evidence for him to answer and he was again remanded to Crumlin Road Prison.

On the outside, republicans were busy taking the 'war' to the Shankill Road. On 16 June, three UVF men, Colin 'Crazy' Craig, David Hamilton and Trevor King, were chatting in the street when they fell under a fusillade of gunfire from a weapon fired by one of Adair's old enemies, the INLA's Gino Gallagher. Craig, 31, died at the scene and Hamilton, 43, the following day. King, 41, lost his battle for survival three weeks later. The attack took place as the Shankill Road was crowded with lunchtime shoppers, sparking memories of the bomb in Frizzell's fish shop eight months earlier. As it decided how to respond, the UVF leadership took a leaf out of the UFF book. Once again, the Shankill was the focus of a major security clampdown and military action by the UVF in the area was deemed too risky. But there was no security at all when, two days later, two UVF gunmen walked into the Heights Bar in the Co. Down village of Loughinisland and opened fire on customers as they watched the Republic of Ireland playing Italy in the World Cup. Six Catholics, including an 87-year-old, were killed and five others seriously wounded in the Saturday night attack.

On 11 July, the IRA shot dead Ray Smallwoods, the UDA's political strategist and chairman of its political wing, the Ulster Democratic Party, in the garden of his home in Lisburn, Co. Antrim. Although Adair had little time for politics, he had always admired Smallwoods for his role in one of the UFF's most audacious murder attempts. Back in 1981, he had been part of a hand-picked assassination squad which came tantalisingly close to murdering former nationalist MP Bernadette McAliskey and her husband. McAliskey was shot seven times as she was dressing her children and would probably have died had an undercover Army unit not given her first aid. The loyalists were intercepted by the soldiers as they fled the couple's farmhouse home. Smallwoods, who was the driver, received a 15-year jail term for his part in the attack. Since leaving prison after serving half his sentence he had dedicated himself to political work and was regarded as one of the UDA's most important strategists. Like John McMichael seven years earlier, he was singled out by the IRA because he was an articulate spokesman for working-class loyalism and a threat to the republican movement's domination of the political debate in Northern Ireland. After the shooting, Smallwoods' widow, who had witnessed the attack, helped the police to construct a photofit of one of the gunmen. At an identity parade she identified a senior Belfast IRA figure as the man who murdered her husband. Despite her evidence, no prosecution was ever mounted.

Inside Crumlin Road Prison, Adair paced restlessly in his cell as he heard the news from outside. He could hardly believe it as the days went by without a UFF response to Smallwoods' murder. He was also starting to worry about his personal life. For some reason he and Gina had started rowing during her visits to the prison, possibly because Gina knew Jackie Robinson was coming over to see him every time she left the visitors' hall. 'I used to go and visit somebody else at the jail, that's the way we got to see each other at the Crum,' said Jackie. 'I couldn't go up and visit him because she had all the visits, but I would have been in the visit and then when she went we would have had a talk. It was one big room in those days, you'd probably have got 50 tables in it. Johnny couldn't do his whack, he couldn't do his whack at all. Regardless of what anybody says I was the one that had to listen to him whimpering and crying. He was up and down, very up and down. See to be honest, it's like putting a wild bird in a cage, isn't it?'

Soon, however, Adair found something to distract him. For years trouble had been brewing inside the jail. Some 800 remand prisoners were crammed into its small and dingy cells and its inmates had none of the freedom they enjoyed at the Maze, where loyalists and republicans were segregated from each other. In 1990, inmates smashed up their cells in protest at having to share facilities. In November 1991, the IRA took advantage of the integrated conditions to plant a bomb behind a radiator in the dining room of C Wing, killing two Shankill loyalists, Robert Skey, a 27-year-old UFF man, and Colin Caldwell, a 23-year-old UVF prisoner. In December 1992, the UVF fired an RPG-7 rocket at a wing housing republican prisoners, blasting a two-foot hole in the wall but failing to injure anybody. On 1 September 1993, hooded UVF gunmen broke into a house in the Oldpark, less than a third of a mile from the prison, and shot James Peacock in the back. The 44-year-old, who was only the second prison officer to be killed by loyalists, died in the arms of his 13-year-old daughter. After the attack the UVF warned that prison staff would continue to be targeted until its prisoners were segregated and 'permitted to serve their sentences with dignity and in safety'.

Although the ingredients for full-scale disorder were already in place, Adair's presence in the jail sent it over the edge. Shortly after 7.30 p.m. on Thursday, 7 July, he was among more than 100 loyalists who smashed their way onto the prison's roof during a recreation period. As the police and Army moved to seal off the area, the prisoners bombarded them with slates and roof tiles. Shouting words of encouragement, relatives and friends of the protesters began to assemble outside the prison walls. A loyalist band struck up in a side street, while a huge cheer erupted as the inmates rigged up a loudspeaker and played 'Rule Britannia'. After mediation by two Shankill councillors, Joe Coggle and the Reverend Eric Smyth, the loyalists were persuaded to come down and at 10.30 p.m. they returned to their cells. In an honourable compromise, the Prison Service agreed to look into the prisoners' complaints and agreed that no action would be taken against protesters. Adair, however, felt no need to back off. Sensing that the authorities were on the back foot, loyalists on two of the prison wings started another protest nine days later. Under Adair's instructions, they removed bricks from the jail's internal walls, giving them access to each other's cells and spreading panic among the prison staff. According to one police officer: 'Before Adair went in there were sporadic protests but in the main the Crum was holding its prisoners and doing its function. He found out that the prison walls were crumbling. The limestone and the mortar were crumbling so he was able to use crude utensils and once you had one brick or two bricks out the rest just followed and they went from cell to cell in a very short time. Adair was one of the main instigators in bringing the thing to a conclusion by getting them all moved to the Maze. Until that little bastard got there the problem had been containable.'

Within days nearly 70 cells had been so badly trashed that they could no longer be used and 80 prisoners, including Adair, were transferred to the Maze. Jackie Robinson believes that the move was entirely Adair's doing: 'You've got to hand it to him – they'd been trying to get up to that Maze for years. He was only in there for about two months and they were all away, you know what I mean? I mean that was funny, I have to admit. I got the phone call, "Put the telly on, put the telly on," and I put the telly on and they were up on the roof. The programme showed them all up on the roof rioting and there was Johnny. He had his wee vest on and his wee shorts. He was standing there screaming and shouting and yo-hoing and laughing. Johnny is a redhead, but in certain light his hair looks darker. He was standing on the roof with others standing behind him. That was him, the exhibitionist. That's why I said you've got to hand it to him because he did everything they set out to do. Within a few weeks of that they were moved up to the Maze and they thought it was a holiday camp because they had all these pool tables and TVs.'

As Adair was settling into life inside the Maze, the IRA continued to pick off senior loyalists. On Sunday, 31 July, the Provisionals shot dead Raymond 'Snowy' Elder and Joe 'Chinky' Bratty in broad daylight on the Ormeau Road. The men, both senior figures in the UFF in south Belfast, had just left the Kimberley Bar and were returning to their car when the gunmen struck. As they approached the vehicle, two IRA men brandishing AK-47 assault rifles sprang from a white van and opened fire. Elder had been charged with the UFF gun attack on Sean Graham's Bookmaker's shop in February 1992, but the charges were later dropped. Residents in the Catholic lower Ormeau Road area believe Bratty, who was the UFF commander in the district, was part of a murder gang that shot dead Theresa Clinton in April 1994. Like Adair, he was a local hero and was later commemorated in a little-known UFF song:

> What can I say about Joe Bratty?
> Well how can I talk of this man's life?
> His love for his country and his men
> But first came his family and his wife
>
> Well he always knew some day they'd get him
> But we won't forget the way he died
> It's hard to accept our friend is gone
> But we will remember him with pride
>
> To all of his men he was a hero
> A man you were proud was on your side
> So lift up your glass and toast Joe Bratty
> He's with us today although he's died

In July 2003, Adair, who had been friendly with Bratty, expressed to one of the authors his disgust at the UFF's failure to retaliate for the murders.

'When 1994 came and I was in prison, Brian Gillen went, "Let's test these UFF bastards." They murdered Joe Bratty – there was no response. They murdered Ray Smallwoods – there was no response.' In an egotistical reference to himself, he added, 'They knew the fucking brains and balls was in jail. If I had been out it would have been different.'

By September 1994, Adair's personal life was unravelling. Unbeknownst to him, Gina had been having an affair with Paul Orr, C Coy's welfare officer, and then Ian 'Fuzzie' Cousins, a UDA man from south Belfast. Adair suspected Gina was playing around, though with whom he did not know. It was only when Cousins was spotted pulling handbrake turns in Adair's brand-new Ford Orion that he was identified as Gina's lover. While Cousins was visiting Gina in Hazelfield Street one day, several of Adair's friends tried to force their way into the house to give him a hiding. After failing to break in, they set fire to his car, burning to death his Lurcher hunting dog. Adair gave his colleagues in south Belfast an ultimatum, telling them that unless they gave Cousins a beating, C Coy would shoot him. A senior UDA commander in south Belfast confided to the authors, 'I went up to the jail to see Johnny and I asked him if he wanted him shot. He shook his head and said no – but he wanted him taught a lesson.' For anybody else this would have meant a painful beating and probably one or two broken legs, but Cousins' father was widely respected in UDA circles. As a result, he managed to get his son off the hook on condition that he wear a plaster cast on his arm and pretend he had been beaten.

The discovery of her secret love life was a savage blow for Gina. She had confided to friends that Cousins was the love of her life and had even intended to move in with him. Within weeks of finding out about Cousins, Adair also discovered that she had been seeing Paul Orr. Devastated that one of his closest C Coy colleagues could betray him in such a manner, he ordered Donald Hodgen and Paddy Patterson to give him a beating he would never forget. One night in early 1995, Orr was dragged from his house in Ballysillan in north Belfast and taken to nearby waste ground where he was set upon with iron bars and sticks studded with nails. It was a grisly ritual, but one that would be repeated many times as C Coy degenerated into a ramshackle private army used mainly for settling old scores and maiming Adair's sexual rivals.

Adair's personal life became even more complicated when Cousins told Gina about his long-term affair with Jackie Robinson. Gina and Johnny had always been unfaithful to each other, but until now she had managed to delude herself that nothing was going on with Jackie. Jackie recalls: 'The old doll with the nice figure – that's what Gina used to call me. It was Fuzzie that told her, who confirmed that Johnny and I were going together. But I said to him, "The best thing you can do is just stay with her and I'll step out of the equation," and he was going, "No, you can't do that, you can't do that." So he was sort of stuck, like a child not knowing which way to go. He didn't want to be without me, he didn't want to be without her. So I told him to go to her and he cracked up because he couldn't be without me. Then it came to a head. Winkie and Spencer [Jim Spence] went down to her and got her in the house, gave her a couple of slaps and said, "Right, get on the phone, tell him the truth." And after that happened I started visiting him in the jail. It was a Friday afternoon, I was sitting in the bedroom and my phone went and it was him, all excited. "Do you want to visit me tomorrow?" And I nearly fell through the floor. He says, "Do you want to come up and see me?" I says, "You're joking me." He says, "That bastard's going with somebody." I says, "Yeah, I know."'

In early November, Adair asked Jackie to marry him during a telephone conversation from jail. He offered her £1,000 for a ring but she refused to take more than £300. Winkie Dodds, who had been appointed brigadier in Adair's absence, gave her the money but she spent less than half of it, finding a 9-carat gold ring for just £125. Two nights later Dodds threw a party for her at the Diamond Jubilee Bar on the Shankill. His wife, Maureen, remembers, 'Johnny phoned Winkie on a Saturday morning and told him he had just got engaged to Jackie. He asked Winkie to host a wee celebration for Jackie in the Jubilee Bar that night. I made food for it and as I remember it was a great night. Winkie Dodds gave us free drink all night – it was great.' When Gina found out about the engagement she was heartbroken. In all the years they had been together Adair had never asked her to marry him. 'That broke Gina's heart. It really hit her hard when he got engaged to Jackie,' said Maureen.

For the next eight weeks Adair was blissfully happy, though in early 1995 he called off the engagement and got back together with Gina after she sent him a copy of Celine Dion's 'Think Twice'. Recalls Jackie, 'She sent him that song and that day he decided to go back to her. "My head's telling me no but my heart's telling me yes," he said.' Over the next year Jackie was caught in the middle of a bizarre love triangle as Northern Ireland's most notorious loyalist terrorist struggled to decide which woman he wanted. He was in constant touch with both his girlfriends using a mobile phone that had been smuggled into the jail. According to Maureen Dodds, 'He was always ringing Jackie up at all hours. I got a mobile phone out in my name and it was smuggled into the jail for the prisoners. Sometimes the monthly bill would be £1,000–£1,200. Very few of them got to use it 'cause Johnny was always on it.'

Listening to Adair's emotional problems drove Jackie round the bend: 'He used to drive me crazy, he used to be on the phone all night. I used to be sitting and begging him sometimes, "Fuck off and leave me alone." And then I'd pull the plug out of the wall and the next morning, 9 o'clock, I'd put the plug in and he'd be at the other end of the phone. It was unbelievable. I would be screaming, "Fuck off, you fat bastard," and he'd be, "Jackie, don't talk like that, that's not like you." He'd be strong one minute and he'd say, "Soldiers don't cry," and I'd say, "Well you're a fucking whimpering bastard, you fucking never stop."'

As Adair was transferred to the Maze in July 1994, speculation was mounting about an imminent IRA ceasefire, though the terrorist group obviously had some loose ends to tie up first. On 8 August it killed Trelford Withers, a part-time member of the locally recruited Royal Irish Regiment. The 46-year-old father of five was shot dead at his butcher's shop in Crossgar, Co. Down. Ten days later the Provos were back in action, this time in Dublin. Martin Cahill, the notorious Irish criminal known as 'the General', was gunned down as he navigated his car through the city's mid-afternoon traffic. In a statement admitting responsibility the IRA claimed that Cahill, a 45-year-old with five children, had collaborated with the UVF in an attack on a Dublin pub and accused him of having links with Billy 'King Rat' Wright.

Three days before the Cahill killing, details of the Crown case against Johnny Adair emerged at a remand hearing at Belfast Magistrates' Court. Adair's solicitor, Billy McNulty, complained about the prosecution's failure to disclose the nature of its evidence against his client. As a result of McNulty's agitation, Magistrate Travers asked the Crown to furnish him with a report on the police investigation. Outlining the case, a representative from the DPP told the court that seven detectives were working full-time on a file that would run to over 1,000 statements and a similar number of exhibits. Areas being looked at, the court was told, included Adair's financial position, material seized in his house, sightings with convicted terrorists, and records of his conversations with police. The investigation was so complex, the Crown lawyer explained, that the RUC would need up to 10 more weeks while a further 300 statements were taken.

It was the first time a full explanation of the case against Adair had been heard. McNulty voiced concerns about the denial of his client's liberty, suggesting large parts of the Crown case were unlikely to be admissible. He asked for a time limit to be imposed on the police investigation to prevent further unnecessary delay. Although the magistrate said it would be unfair to impose a deadline, he agreed that progress in the case should be closely monitored and Adair was again remanded in custody.

While Adair considered his fate, on 31 August the IRA announced a 'complete cessation' of its armed campaign. By any standards it was a bizarre event. Unionists reacted suspiciously, convinced that the British had done a secret deal with the terrorists. Among republicans, however, there was unbridled euphoria. A cavalcade of black taxis swept up and down the Falls Road with IRA supporters leaning out of the windows cheering and waving Irish tricolours. Despite having failed in its objective of driving the British out of Ireland, the Provos were behaving like a victorious army. It was a world away from 1986, when Martin McGuinness, head of the IRA's Northern Command, had told the Sinn Fein annual meeting in Dublin, 'Our position is clear and it will never, never, never, change. The war against British rule must continue until freedom is achieved.' As time progressed it became clear that the IRA had called a ceasefire without securing any major concessions from the British on the future of Northern Ireland.

Although the UVF had carried out a spate of murders over the summer, following Adair's arrest the UFF in west Belfast had killed just one person, a 20-year-old landscape gardener by the name of Sean Monaghan. On 14 August, Monaghan was walking home when he was abducted by a B Coy murder gang cruising the Falls Road for a victim. They tricked him into getting into their car by telling him they were from the IRA, then took him to a flat in Disraeli Street off the Shankill where he was beaten and tortured. During a break in the proceedings, one of his captors took pity on Monaghan and allowed him to escape out of a window. He ran to the house of a 69-year-old woman who listened intently as he explained his predicament and then telephoned her daughter. Minutes later she arrived at her mother's house accompanied by her boyfriend, William Graham. Instead of leading Monaghan to safety as they had promised, the couple took the young man back to her flat, where he was handed back to his captors, bound and gagged with black tape and driven to nearby waste ground where he was shot in the head. Monaghan had endured a brutal final few hours. As the police pathologist was examining the corpse he discovered large amounts of unexplained white gunge in the victim's lungs. On closer inspection it turned out to be kitchen roll that had been stuffed into his mouth to stifle his screams. It had been rammed in so hard that some of it had gone down his windpipe. In March 1996, four men, including William Graham, who was sentenced to life imprisonment, were convicted in connection with the murder. David Burrows, a 31-year-old B Coy volunteer, taunted Monaghan's family as he too was jailed for life. Cupping his hand as if gripping a gun, he pointed at his head and screamed at Monaghan's mother, 'I shot your fucking son. Four in the back of the head. Yo!'

On 1 September 1994, the first full day of the IRA ceasefire, a UFF team from north Belfast shot dead 32-year-old John O'Hanlon as he helped a friend to change the wheel of a car. Like the Monaghan killing, the murder was purely sectarian. It was meant as a statement by loyalists that they were not going to be bounced into ending their campaign. Three days later a UVF car bomb exploded outside Sinn Fein's offices on the Falls Road, though thankfully nobody was injured. Despite intense political pressure to reciprocate the IRA's unilateral action, loyalist paramilitaries of all hues appeared determined to drag out the violence, despite no longer having an enemy to fight. They were not prepared to jump until they were convinced the IRA was genuine.

Unionist politicians were also edgy. They looked on with dismay as republicans in border areas encouraged local people to reopen roads that had been closed by the security forces. Television pictures of Gerry Adams standing on the steps of the Dail, smiling and shaking hands with Albert Reynolds, reinforced fears that what Unionists called the 'Pan Nationalist Front' had struck a secret deal with John Major. The same day, DUP leader Ian Paisley and other senior members of his party were shown the door at 10 Downing Street after Paisley refused to accept Major's assertion that there was no deal with the IRA.

On 8 September, the Combined Loyalist Military Command (CLMC), which spoke for the UDA/UFF, UVF and Red Hand Commando, issued a list of assurances it would require before it could recommend a ceasefire. Chief among them was the need to be satisfied that the IRA's cessation was permanent and that Britain had not sold them out. Although there was still huge uncertainty about the position of the UVF and UDA, as the weeks went by it became increasingly clear that the union with Britain was safe, at least for now. With a complete absence of republican violence, the level of loyalist attacks also fell sharply. On 12 September, the UVF admitted responsibility for a bomb on the Belfast-to-Dublin train, which was intended to go off as it arrived in Connolly Station in the Irish capital but failed to ignite properly. It was a final gesture of defiance, aimed at convincing militant loyalists across Northern Ireland that they were going into a ceasefire from a position of strength. Things were moving fast behind the scenes. By the middle of September, two officials from the Northern Ireland Office had opened a channel of dialogue with both the UDA and the UVF through their political representatives.

After a period of consultation with loyalist prisoners inside the Maze, on 10 October political representatives of both the UDA and UVF went into the prison for separate meetings with their inmates. They received a positive response about a possible ceasefire, paving the way for an historic announcement by the CLMC three days later. The venue, Fernhill House, a small mansion overlooking west Belfast, was itself significant. It was here that the original Ulster Volunteer Force had drilled and trained during the Home Rule crisis of 1912. Issuing the ceasefire statement, Augustus 'Gusty' Spence, the veteran UVF leader who had served 18 years for murder, said the CLMC had received 'confirmation and guarantees in relation to Northern Ireland's constitutional position within the United Kingdom'. 'The Union is safe,' he declared. In a move that went far beyond anything in the IRA's ceasefire announcement, Spence offered 'abject and true remorse' to the hundreds of victims of loyalist paramilitary violence.

Adair himself was fully behind the move, though he had only recently come on board. When the IRA had declared its cessation, he was against a reciprocal gesture from loyalists, though he changed his mind when he saw which way the wind was blowing. Adair never had any thought-out political arguments of his own and was always highly impressionable on this count. According to Jackie 'Legs' Robinson: 'He was going on about these peace talks and saying, "I'm not going to support them." I'm almost sure it was in September and he was really giving it rock on about them talks. He says to me, "Over my dead body," and I says to him, "Johnny, why don't you do me a favour?" And he says, "What?" I said, "Why don't you go away and why don't you sit and think. Think. Do you want your son carried away in a box, 'cause that's what's going to happen?" I said, "Give it a chance and listen to what they've got to say. Just listen and think." And he did. He phoned me back a few weeks later and he says, "You're right, I think I'll go for it," and that's what he did.'

At the back of his mind Adair had another reason for supporting the loyalist ceasefire. He was becoming increasingly worried about his trial and naively hoped that, if he threw his weight behind the peace talks, the Government would put pressure on the prosecution to drop its case against him. He was cruelly deluded. In reality, the Government was more preoccupied with the problems posed by Billy Wright in mid-Ulster and the prospect of a split in the UVF than it ever was with Adair. As his trial loomed closer, it slowly dawned on him that he was staring a long prison sentence in the face. The thought of spending the best years of his life behind bars terrified him. What if he was unable to see his children growing up? On at least one occasion in 1995, Adair's worries about the trial and his turbulent personal life drove him to consider suicide. Jackie Robinson recalls: 'He phoned me one night at about one o'clock in the morning, not long before his trial. Gina was giving him a hard time with the kids. She'd stopped the kids going up to see him because of me. I was the one visiting him, and she said she didn't want them going up to the jail with that "old whore". And then he was phoning her and he was getting all upset and he phoned me one night at about one o'clock in the morning. "Why is she doing this to me?" And I was trying to talk him down – "She's playing games, she's playing emotional games, the only weapon she has to get at you are your three children and you're playing into her hands." He was like a puppy, he was like a real wee soppy puppy. And he just says to me, "I just feel like putting the sheets up, Jackie, I've had enough," and I was trying to talk him round. I says, "You can't do that because of the kids." I spent two, three hours on that phone and he was running around getting other phone cards. He kept running around, getting another phone card and coming back.'

The day Adair had been dreading duly came on 6 September 1995. As he showered and dressed, Detective Inspector Brian McArthur and Detective Sergeant Alan Cormack were already at Belfast Crown Court. They, too, knew it was a big day and turned up early to prepare themselves. They helped to carry in hundreds of files and documents, which were delivered to the Crumlin Road Courthouse in three police cars. They were expecting this to be the first day in a trial likely to last up to three months, to cost more than £1 million and to become a litmus test for the police's ability to snare Northern Ireland's shadowy terrorist godfathers.

A hush fell over the famous Court No. 1 as the case of the Crown vs John

PRISON

Adair was called before Mr Justice Anthony Campbell. The public gallery was packed with about 40 of the loyalist's supporters, friends and relatives. They waved and smiled at Adair, who waved once and then stood calmly with his hands behind his back. He was dressed in a pink-and-white silk shirt given to him for the occasion by Jackie 'Legs' Robinson, a black woollen waistcoat and jeans. Watching him from behind a bulletproof glass screen were the remnants of the UFF in west Belfast. They included Jim Spence, Winkie Dodds, Donald Hodgen and Paddy Patterson. Jackie Robinson sat next to Adair's mother, Mabel, and two of his sisters, Lizzie and Jeanie. The group also included several Shankill women who fancied Adair (including the mother of two of his volunteers) and a prostitute from Tigers Bay who frequently entertained his men. Gina, who had split with him, stayed at home. Although Adair's closest friends knew what was coming next, the police did not. There was a deafening silence as his barrister, Tony Cinnamond, stood up to address the court.

According to former Detective Sergeant Alan Cormack: 'The thing kicked off and the charges were put. Adair's barrister got to his feet and entered a guilty plea on all charges. The court rose and I looked at Brian McArthur and he looked at me. We both looked at Derek Martindale and I think I said, "What do we do now?" We were stunned, totally stunned. It was the biggest anti-climax I had ever experienced.'

Jackie Robinson believes that her former boyfriend had been pressured into changing his plea. Four weeks earlier she had gone to visit him at the jail: 'He says to me, "You're too good for me, I'm getting 30 years," and he was crying like a child. And I was trying to convince him that they were just playing mind games. But he couldn't be sure of what he'd told them, he couldn't be sure of everything he'd said. And I was trying to get him to understand – "They're playing games with you, don't fall into the trap."'

She went on: 'I got the phone call two days before the case that he had taken a deal. It was Spencer [Jim Spence] that phoned me and says, "Look, Jackie, I want to meet you." And I went, met him and he says, "He's taken a deal for 16 years." He says, "We've tried to talk him out of it," but they couldn't. I was trying to talk him out of it as well because I knew what was going on.'

Thanks to Adair's big mouth, Northern Ireland had been saved what was expected to be one of its longest trials under anti-terrorist legislation. The entire hearing lasted under 90 minutes. Journalists were treated to a few juicy glimpses of the police evidence as the court went through the motions. In a quote that would follow Adair for the rest of his life, Pat Lynch, for the Crown, described him as a sinister and manipulative terrorist who was 'dedicated to his cause, which was nakedly sectarian in its hatred of those it regarded as militant republicans – among whom he had lumped almost the entire Catholic population'.

The QC said that Adair held sway over his subordinates 'with a combination of force of personality and the ability to inspire fear'. He quoted from a transcript of him telling a police officer, 'The threat of one [a bullet] behind the ear keeps them in line.' In a short speech, Adair's barrister dismissed the tape-recorded evidence as 'weird conversations with the police' and said his client was a victim of circumstance, growing up in a divided and violent society. Adair, he said, had paid a heavy price for his involvement in terrorism, suffering no fewer than seven attempts on his life.

Jailing Adair for 16 years, Mr Justice Campbell applauded the police for the risks they had taken to bring him to justice. Apparently unmoved by the sentence, the 31-year-old director of terrorism turned towards the press and gave a clenched-fist salute. 'I applaud the dedication of all the young men of the 2nd Battalion,' he said calmly, adding that his men would 'deal' with Detective Sergeant Jonty Brown. As he was being led away, Jackie Robinson shouted at her boyfriend across the crowded courtroom. 'Johnny, I love you. I'll wait for you, I'll see you soon,' she yelled. She was screaming at the top of her voice, but Johnny Adair did not hear her. Despite his bravura performance, beneath the relaxed exterior he was a broken man, and as he left the court he could hear nothing at all.

11. Hallion Battalion

'He wasn't like you or me. There was nothing normal about his sexual relationships. It was literally another world listening to him and Gina on the telephone and hearing some of the kinky filth they said to each other.' – *a senior Northern Ireland prison official*

AFTER SPLITTING WITH JOHNNY ADAIR, GINA CROSSAN DESCENDED INTO A haze of drink and drugs as her life started to fall apart. She got herself into debt and owed money to UDA men from the Shore Road, who took her income support book off her as a means of ensuring she honoured her debts. After a string of affairs, Gina started seeing a man from the Mount Vernon area of north Belfast and began taunting Adair by boasting about the size of her new lover's manhood and their depraved sex games. As usual, she knew how to torment her old boyfriend. As Jackie 'Legs' Robinson recalled, 'Johnny phoned me up one night and said, "Jackie, what does candle wax do?" I said, "What?" He said, "Candle wax." I said, "Who's asking?" He said, "Gina." Your man in Mount Vernon was dripping candle wax on her and she was doing it to him. He was running a knife down her back and slicing her. She was telling Johnny all these things on the phone.'

As Gina drifted from one party to another, she also started to hang around with a young neighbour from Hazelfield Street who worked as a prostitute and topped up her income by peddling small amounts of cannabis. 'Jeanie' (not her real name) looked after Gina's daughter Chloe whenever Gina stayed with her boyfriend. As well as Chloe, 'Jeanie' also had another guest in her house: her brother, who was on the run from prison.

When Adair discovered who was taking care of his daughter, he was furious. As a close friend recalled, 'His words were, "She had my child in that house and her brother's on the run and she's a prostitute selling cannabis."' Adair, who was always concerned for the welfare of his three children, was so angry that he could barely bring himself to speak to Gina. He complained to his friends and sisters that his kids were in danger of becoming victims of neglect. Gina, who always had a trick up her sleeve, protested that she had been led astray and that the real culprit – the person who had forced her to go out partying for days on end – was 'Jeanie'. Within days C Coy was mobilised. In early 1995, 'Jeanie' and her brother were beaten by Adair's colleagues and her house in Hazelfield Street ransacked. The pair were ordered never to return to the Shankill.

The attack was typical of the activities that were starting to define the post-ceasefire C Coy. With Adair in jail and the 'war' effectively over, the UFF's supposedly elite unit degenerated to such an extent that police nicknamed it the 'Hallion Battalion' ('Hallion' is Northern Irish slang for a lowlife or savage). As well as beating and shooting Adair's love rivals, it was also called upon to make sure his approved drug dealers stayed in line. In the summer of 1995, a dealer living in the Highfield estate at the top of the Shankill was instructed to leave Northern Ireland after C Coy found that he had been trading dope and E-tabs off his own back. According to an old friend of Adair, 'What happened was he [the dealer] was dealing drugs for Johnny but he got greedy and he was dealing with a Catholic guy and he was picking his own drugs up. So he was selling his own drugs plus the drugs for Johnny, and pocketing the extra money. When they [Adair's friends] found out, they put him out of the country. They fined him £20,000 and then they tried to fine him more and he said he wasn't paying so they were going to shoot him and that's why he left.'

Several months later another Shankill drug dealer was beaten, fined £50,000 and forced to leave the area after C Coy accused him of setting up his own supply line. According to Jackie 'Legs' Robinson: 'They [C Coy] trusted him to go and do whatever he was doing but he was also buying his own supply. They found out what he was doing and they took him up into [UDA] headquarters and he done a runner – he jumped out of the window. But that night his girlfriend, she brought this brown holdall up to me and she said, "Would you do us a favour, would you look after that?" And I've never seen so much money in my life, honest to God. It took three of us to push it up into the loft, but later I took it back down to have a look. The whole bag was full of money. Now somebody found out and that's when they asked him for 50 grand to get back on the road. So he paid them 50 grand and they let him back on the road. But then they demanded more money off him. They cleaned him out and he eventually had to move off the road and he was given an awful beating that night.'

In another incident, the home of the Green family, who had been friends and neighbours of Adair throughout the early 1990s, was attacked after a row between Johnny and Norman Green Jnr inside the Maze. Green Jnr, a member of C13, was jailed for 16 years in October 1995 after he and another volunteer, Tommy Porter, were rammed by a police car whilst cruising for a random Catholic to kill in north Belfast. Like many of Adair's recruits, Green Jnr was little more than a thief and a glorified thug. In July 1992, he was arrested in connection with a robbery at a local bookmakers and discovered with money and replica guns in his house. He told police that he had bought the replica as an ornament and had won the money at cards. On another occasion, Green Jnr was convicted of indecent behaviour after masturbating during a police interview in Castlereagh barracks. 'Listen Norman, I'm fucking telling you now – if you bring that out again I'll bite if off,' he was told by one detective. Even among C Coy circles he was seen as a loud-mouthed nuisance and in the autumn of 1992 he was kneecapped twice.

Green Jnr was still on remand and in charge of reading the trial depositions for all C Coy prisoners when he fell out with Adair. He asked to see the depositions for his commander's case but Adair, worried that his friends would see just how much he had been bragging to police, refused. He concocted a story about Green and his father being informers and had the prisoner beaten up and thrown off the block. In November 1995, Norman Green Snr, anxious to relieve the pressure on his family, sought to play down speculation of a rift after a Belfast newspaper received a letter purporting to come from one of his sons and describing the bust-up inside the Maze. 'My family is not involved in any dispute with Mr Adair,' insisted Green Snr. 'We have had no disagreement with him whatsoever. My son Norman was not ordered out of the Maze. He went to Maghaberry Prison because he wanted to do certain studies there. Somebody did fire a shotgun into the house and a car was set on fire. But my family have not been forced to leave. We have no idea what is behind these attacks and we have never for one moment thought it had anything to do with Mr Adair.' At about the same time, Adair also had another old friend, Gerry Drumgoole, slung off the Shankill. Drumgoole, whose family were related to the Greens, challenged Adair about the way he had treated them. Adair reacted by denouncing him too as an informer. The accusation was an easy one to make: Drumgoole's wife was Jacqueline Nelson, the sister of the British Army agent who had penetrated the UDA in the late 1980s.

Ironically, as Adair accused those around him of being informers, he was becoming increasingly concerned that it was only a matter of time before the extent of his own boasts and admissions to police was made public. On 22 January 1996, as part of a 7-part series titled *Inside the RUC*, Ulster Television broadcast a 30-minute programme called *The Crown Versus John Adair*. It blamed Adair for the murder of 72 people during the early 1990s, an exaggeration based on Special Branch's incorrect belief that Adair held the rank of 'Officer Commanding, Northern Ireland' for the whole of the UFF (in fact, no such rank existed at this time). More significantly, the documentary featured recordings of conversations between the loyalist and a wired police officer. As the Monday night transmission time approached, Adair became panicky and booked himself into the hospital wing at the Maze. He feared he was about to face his ultimate nightmare: being made to look like a tout in front of his friends. The day before the programme he telephoned Jackie Robinson, who was alarmed to hear her boyfriend again considering suicide. 'Just before that programme went out he got himself booked down the hospital wing,' she said. 'He was upset about that and I said, "What's wrong?" And he said, "Jackie, I can't remember what I've said."' Jackie, who frequently referred to herself as Adair's 'agony aunt', tried to assure him that his friends would stick by him. 'After the programme, he was on the phone to me again and he said, "You were right, you were right," because they gave him a hero's welcome when he went back to the wing.'

After his trial, Adair was moved from the Maze's H Block 1, where the UDA's remand prisoners were housed, to H7. Set on 130 acres of land 15 miles south-west of Belfast, the top-security Maze was like a prisoner-of-war camp, where up to 800 terrorist prisoners organised themselves along military lines. By 1995, H7 was home to more than 80 convicted prisoners, with two of the four wings controlled by UDA volunteers from west Belfast. Sam 'Skelly' McCrory was the 'Officer Commanding' in charge of the entire block, though in reality he was just a mouthpiece for Adair. Skelly was also head of 'C' Wing, while 'D' Wing was headed by 'Fat Jackie' Thompson. Bobby Philpott, from Lisburn, was in charge of 'A' Wing, which held men from the UDA's south Belfast and south-east Antrim brigades. 'B' Wing, for east Belfast prisoners, was run by Michael Stone, the loyalist assassin who in 1988 had killed three people in a solo gun and grenade attack on Belfast's Milltown Cemetery.

By 1995, the police had done a good job of mopping up C Coy. Along with Adair, Skelly and Thompson, the prisoners inside the Maze included Tommy Potts, Gary 'Smickers' Smith, Norman Green Jnr, Tommy Beggs, Jamie and Robert Hill, Robert 'Rab' Bradshaw (who later hanged himself) and Richard Calderwood. They also included Colin and Gary Hall, who were serving ten years for taking over a house in February 1993 while the occupants' car was stolen and used in a gun attack on black-taxi drivers. The Hall brothers were nicknamed the 'Telly Addicts' because they had been so glued to an episode of *Coronation Street* that they had failed to leave the house before the police arrived.

Jackie Robinson maintains that her influence over Adair at this time changed him into a softer person, leading his friends to dub him 'Tame Cat' after he began listening to sentimental love songs she brought to the jail. Many of the prisoners had their own CD players, supplied by family and friends on the outside, and Adair was no different. 'I took him CDs all the time,' said Jackie. 'We would be talking about songs, and there was a Celine Dion one he liked at that time. He used to say to me, "God, that's you, that is." It was "Because You Love Me – I'm everything I am because you loved me". I had him listening to all those love songs. One of his favourites was Madonna's "You'll See". I had him tamed and that's why they called him Tame Cat.'

For his first 18 months inside the Maze, Adair was emotionally vulnerable and on the verge of a breakdown. But while he showed a tender side to Jackie, he maintained a tough exterior in front of his colleagues. As always, he took pleasure in winding them up and playing the joker. He and his friends played some brutal jokes, particularly on new inmates. Jackie recalled: 'If somebody was brought in they'd have been sat down in front of four or so of them and all the rules were laid down and all. He [Adair] played practical jokes on them when they came in. He done it with one young lad and I went mad at him 'cause the kid was going to kill himself. What happened was Johnny had phoned me up, he was pissing himself. He says to me, "Wait till you hear this." He said the four of them were sitting and this wee lad was marched in and he went to sit down and he [Adair] started screaming at him not to sit down so the wee lad obviously crapped himself. And he says, "What are you in for?" and the wee lad told him even though they already knew. So he started telling them and he [Adair] says, "Right, sit down," and he handed him a load of tablets and says, "Now we know you're a fucking tout. I'm advising you to go and take an overdose or the lads are going to hang you later on." He thought that was hilarious but I knew the kid would do it 'cause he didn't know the way they were. They let him stew for a while before they told him.'

Playing jokes helped to improve the quality of life in prison and brought Adair closer to his old friends, whose camaraderie he had thrived upon throughout the early 1990s. As a morale booster, Adair persuaded a number of women he knew to send photographs to the jail showing them in compromising positions with sex toys. A prostitute in Tigers Bay in north Belfast, who had the message 'Johnny's been here' tattooed above her genitalia, was particularly obliging and provided Adair with sleazy home videos of her and her friends. The amount of material smuggled into the prison was staggering. On one occasion a blow-up doll was brought in for Adair and his friends, while in October 1995 the prison authorities discovered a sedated Patterdale Terrier pup down the trousers of one of his visitors. Porn, E-tabs, vodka (inside balloons) and mobile phones were all successfully smuggled in. According to Jackie: 'I said to him when they got the mobiles in, "You know, your mobile, do the screws not hear it?" and he said, "Yeah, but they'll not come in here, we'll break their fingers." They knew those mobiles were there but they couldn't come in. And what used to take me to the fair was, if they wanted to come in and search the cell they had to notify the commanders on the wings which gave them time to get rid of everything.'

Also secretly brought into the jail were steroids for Adair and his colleagues. During a search of one of his visitors, a phial marked 'For Animal Use Only' was found by prison authorities. Despite considerable risk to his health, Adair was injecting horse steroids straight into his arms and legs. Having for years hankered after a more muscular physique, he now seized his chance. He spent hours every day in the gym and started a high-protein diet that included four boiled eggs and two bananas every night. He and Skelly, who was also into the weights, shaved off their body hair and even rubbed baby oil on each other's bodies. On one occasion Jackie Robinson received a phone call from Jim Spence warning that her boyfriend was in danger of making a fool of himself: 'I got the call from Spencer to say, "Get on the phone and tell him he's making a laughing stock of himself."

They [Adair and Skelly] were taking photographs and they were sending them out all round the place. And in the photos they're both standing there in these fucking cowboy boots and these red leather shorts. Johnny couldn't understand why everybody was getting so worked up about it. I said, "You're making yourself look like a complete idiot here," and he did eventually start realising that what I said was true . . . Him and Skelly were always together in jail. Skelly was obsessed with him and sometimes he used to frighten Johnny. He [Adair] would have said, "Sometimes I wake up in the middle of the night and he's sitting on the end of the bed, just sitting there."'

The fact that Skelly was gay (his boyfriend, Harry Cowan, frequently visited from Scotland) led to endless speculation about Adair's sexuality and there was a strong homoerotic undercurrent between the pair. Ever the wind-up merchant, Adair even encouraged the gossip and on at least one occasion in the early 1990s pretended to be having an affair with C Coy's Stephen 'Dick' Dempsey. According to Michael Stone, Adair was nicknamed 'Willy Watcher' by the other prisoners because he was always looking to see how well endowed they were in the communal showers. While this is almost certainly true, in his autobiography, *None Shall Divide Us*, Stone also makes the claim that Adair had a homosexual lover in prison. There is no evidence to support this.

Although many of Stone's claims are exaggerated, he is astute in his analysis of Adair's character. On the same H Block for several years, he had plenty of time to observe the Shankill man and to watch what made him tick. Adair, who initially idolised Stone for his attack at Milltown, visited him in jail in the early 1990s and had been desperate to impress him. Gradually, however, he came to resent his colleague's fame and saw it as a threat to his own reputation. There was no way the two biggest egos in loyalism could live happily side by side. They were destined to fall out, and at one stage it was even reported that UDA mediators had been forced to visit the jail in order to calm tensions between the two. According to a prison official, 'They hated each other. Things got so bad that the prison was convinced Adair was going to march over to Stone's wing and kick him out or kill him. We were put on a state of high alert and a special riot team placed on stand-by.'

Stone describes Adair as a 'complex and deeply insecure personality' whose many personas include 'Mr Showbiz' (the wannabe celebrity), 'Mad Dog' (the ruthless terrorist), 'Daft Dog' (politically clueless) and 'Wee

Johnny' (vulnerable and childlike). Adair's friends and former friends confirm this volatile mixture. To them, the person they liked best was a dedicated loyalist terrorist but also a generous friend. 'If he'd had money on him and you didn't, he'd have shared it with you or bought you something,' recalled one old colleague. 'But that was before his head went and his ego took over.'

Although Stone is wrong in his assertion that Adair lacked street sense, he correctly deduced that he had 'never cut the mustard as an operator'. He also claims to have spotted the lust for power that would ultimately lead to his downfall. 'Mikey, what the UDA needs is one good man to run the organisation,' Adair is alleged to have told him.

It is often observed that republican prisoners used their time in jail to study, while loyalists either pumped iron or found God. Although Adair thought about doing a psychology course and discussed the idea with Jackie Robinson, it was little more than a passing phase. The idea of Adair even reading a book would have staggered prison officials. Although he was always polite and addressed the Governor as 'Sir', he and his friends made little effort (with the exception of Tommy Potts, who was a voracious reader) to improve their minds. They were known to prison staff as a group of sexual degenerates who regularly phoned sex lines even though every call from the prison telephones was monitored. Adair was no different from his friends, some of whom regularly masturbated in the phone booth. On several occasions he was monitored having phone sex with Gina.

According to one prison official, Adair was a 'sexual deviant'. The source explained, 'He wasn't like you or me. There was nothing normal about his sexual relationships. It was literally another world listening to him and Gina on the telephone and hearing some of the kinky filth they said to each other. Gina would routinely read out lists of people she had slept with and taunt him by revealing intimate details about what she had done with them. I remember one time in particular, Gina must have reeled off a list of about ten people she had been sleeping with. But the thing that annoyed Johnny wasn't the fact that she had been with all these people, it was that one of them was better endowed than him.' Between 1995 and 1997 Adair was constantly breaking up with Gina, getting back with Jackie and then going back to Gina again. In 1995, after patching things up with Gina, he broke up with her after discovering that she was pregnant. He knew immediately that the baby wasn't his. According to Winkie Dodds, who had taken over as brigadier in west Belfast, Adair told him to give her £500 for an abortion. 'She said she was going to England to see her sister, but it was for a wee operation, an abortion,' recalled Winkie.

In June 1996, Adair's father, Jimmy, died after suffering a heart attack. By the time he was released on parole for the funeral, Adair was back with Gina, though he was still agonising over the two women in his life. When Jackie arrived at his parents' house to pay her respects, she entered the living room to see Johnny and Gina sitting together on the sofa. Gina, who had never openly challenged Jackie, sat and stared at her rival as she went over to the coffin and kissed the dead man on the forehead. Incredibly, Adair was oblivious to the tension between the two women. He had his mind on one thing and one thing only. 'His dad was lying by the window in a coffin,' said Jackie. 'I went and gave him a kiss on the head. Johnny then jumped up and said, "Come and see the flowers," and we went outside and he started getting really familiar. He said, "Fuck, you see when you were bending over that coffin I just wanted to ram it up you."'

In March 1996, the Hallion Battalion was back in action when Andrew Green, Norman Jnr's brother, was attacked on the Shankill. It was the latest instalment in Adair's feud with the Green family. In September, Dick Dempsey, another former friend of Adair, was given a punishment beating by C Coy after a row over drugs. Three days before Christmas the unit proved it could still carry out planned military attacks when it planted a booby-trap bomb under the car of Eddie Copeland, the Ardoyne republican. The 25-year-old, who in 1994 had been named in Parliament as an IRA godfather, suffered leg and arm injuries when the bomb detonated as he started his Honda Civic outside his mother's house. The attack came two days after the IRA attempted to kill the Democratic Unionist Party's Nigel Dodds as he was visiting his sick son in the Royal Victoria Hospital on the Falls Road. The loyalists had held their ceasefires since the IRA bombed London's Canary Wharf in February, but this time there was bound to be retaliation. The bomb was intended to kill Copeland, but the explosive charge was not strong enough. According to 'Pete', who was closely involved in the operation, 'The bomb had been in a safe house in the lower Shankill for five or six days. They were just waiting for the right moment because Copeland had got away that many times.'

Adair was delighted by the bomb attack, though he wished Copeland had been killed. He missed the adrenalin rush of the early 1990s and the respect he had enjoyed from his friends and comrades. But by early 1997 he had something else to preoccupy him. For some time he had been smouldering over the fact that his children were growing up without his surname and had repeatedly begged Gina to change their name to Adair. Sensing a possible bargaining chip, she had always refused. The only way she would consider this, she told him, was if he was prepared to put a wedding ring on her finger.

After an on-off relationship lasting 17 years, Johnny Adair married Gina Crossan in the Maze Prison on 21 February 1997. She had hoped to get married on Valentine's Day, but had to settle for a week later because the prison authorities were unable to fit in with her romantic plan. Gina, who wore a full-length white gown and veil, was collected from her home in Manor Court in the Oldpark in a white limousine. By the time she arrived at the jail the cream of C Coy and the west Belfast UDA was already waiting in a small church inside the prison grounds. The ceremony was no different from thousands of others across the United Kingdom that week except that in this church there were bars on the windows. Afterwards, around 20 guests attended the reception in a Portakabin, where they were served a three-tier wedding cake baked by prison orderlies and sausage rolls and sandwiches. Those from outside the jail included Winkie Dodds, Donald Hodgen, Jim Spence and the veteran UDA man Derek 'Snow' Hamilton. Several of Adair's fellow prisoners also attended, including Skelly, who was best man, and whose boyfriend Harry had travelled from Scotland for the occasion. Maureen Dodds, Winkie's wife and a close friend of the happy couple, was also a guest. She recalled: 'Gina bought her dress in Jean Millar's Bridal Boutique on Royal Avenue. It was a traditional white wedding dress and I think it cost around £500, but she hated it and she never once afterwards looked at the pictures of her wedding. We all travelled down to the Maze and a minister married them in a small church inside the prison. Skelly was the best man and Johnny wore a grey morning suit with top hat and tails. Natalie and Chloe [Adair's daughters] were flower girls and young Jonathan also wore a top hat and tails, but he couldn't get home quick enough to change. There were no speeches or anything like that, but they brought a ghetto blaster down from the wings for music and Johnny and Gina had a wee dance to Tina Turner singing "Simply The Best". It was a great day out.'

Although the reception was held within the confines of the United Kingdom's most secure prison, it did not prevent the groom from ensuring his guests had proper alcoholic drinks to toast his bride. According to Winkie Dodds, 'Johnny arranged for a load of vodka to be smuggled into the jail. There were plenty of soft drinks like orange and coke, so we used them as mixers when Johnny got the vodka down from the wings.' Dodds says the reception lasted around three hours, but despite the traditional attire of the bride and groom, all other formalities, including speeches, were dispensed with. 'Everyone was too drunk,' said Winkie with a droll smile. The only sour note in the entire proceedings was when Adair let Gina see a card he had received from Jackie Robinson. In it, his former fiancée had written, 'To Johnny and Gina – Infidelity is one of the worst things in a marriage. Love, Jackie Legs'. Gina ripped the card to shreds and threw the pieces on the floor as her bemused wedding guests looked on.

Another incident brought an element of hilarity to the proceedings. Halfway through the reception one of the guests suddenly noticed that Skelly and his boyfriend were nowhere to be seen. While everyone else had been busy drinking, the couple had slipped off to steal a few moments of intimacy. 'Skelly and Harry disappeared a couple of times and when they came back they were both tucking their shirts in,' said Maureen. 'Everyone was laughing, though some got a bit embarrassed. No one said a word about it.'

12. Back to the Brink

'He [a friend] told me that if I stick my dick in the fire it will hurt and that's the same thing as admitting anything to you boys. Would you eat yellow snow, Jonty?' – *Keith Winward, a robber who became involved with Johnny Adair, to Detective Sergeant Johnston Brown*

GARY McMICHAEL'S FACE SAID IT ALL. FOR WEEKS HE AND DAVY ADAMS HAD been struggling to keep their UDA comrades on board as they moved towards an historic compromise between the diametrically opposed positions of unionism and nationalism. As senior figures in the Ulster Democratic Party, McMichael and Adams had striven hard to create a political voice for working-class loyalists, but now it looked as though their efforts may have been in vain. On Wednesday, 7 January 1998, they travelled to London for an emergency meeting with Mo Mowlam, the charismatic and controversial Northern Ireland Secretary known for her informal approach. McMichael had pushed Mo for an urgent appointment because he could see a crisis looming that could very well end up with the UDA pulling out of the already fragile peace process.

McMichael enjoyed a good relationship with the Secretary of State and the pair, who were both known for their sense of humour, got on well when they met at informal social functions. It was probably because of this that the UDP leader felt comfortable asking to meet Mowlam away from the prying eyes and ears of senior civil servants. The reason for the meeting was an event that had taken place 11 days earlier inside the Maze. Billy 'King Rat' Wright, a former UVF killer who broke away to form the hardline Loyalist Volunteer Force, was gunned down by the equally fanatical INLA. He was sitting in a prison van with Norman Green Jnr, Adair's former friend who had defected to the LVF, when three INLA prisoners shot him with two guns they had smuggled into the jail. Although Wright was detested by the majority of Unionists, to many ordinary Protestants his clinical assassination behind the 20-foot-high walls of the United Kingdom's most secure prison smacked of something more sinister. More than 5,000 people turned out on a dreary December day for Wright's funeral and leading Unionists called for Mowlam's resignation.

Twelve hours after Wright's murder, an LVF hit team drove into the car park of the Glengannon Hotel in Dungannon, Co. Tyrone, in the heart of Billy Wright's mid-Ulster killing fields. Two gunmen opened fire on a crowd of people at the hotel entrance. Seamus Dillon, a 45-year-old former republican prisoner who had served a life sentence after pleading guilty to two IRA murders, was cut down in a hail of bullets and died shortly after arriving in hospital. He had been working as a doorman when he was killed, letting teenagers in for a late-night disco. Although he had cut his links with his former terrorist colleagues, the hotel was attacked because the LVF knew that several republican ex-prisoners worked as bouncers at the disco and that they were bound to kill at least one of them. Three other staff were also seriously injured, including a 14-year-old waiter.

Four days later, on 31 December, Eddie Treanor was enjoying a New Year's Eve drink with his girlfriend in the Clifton Tavern, on Belfast's Cliftonville Road. The doormen were just about to stop letting people in and to pull down the steel shutters when the gunmen struck. At 9.07 p.m. a white Vauxhall Senator pulled up in front of the bar and two men in balaclavas stepped out, one clutching an Israeli-made Uzi sub-machine gun and the other a pistol. As they walked up to the bar, one nodded to the doormen outside and said, 'All right, lads,' before opening fire. Seven people were hit, including Treanor, a 31-year-old Catholic who worked as a civil servant in Belfast's Housing Executive. He was shot in the head and pronounced dead in hospital a few minutes before the New Year began. In a statement, the LVF claimed the killing was in retaliation for the murder of its leader, adding the chilling warning, 'This is not the end.'

The peace process was unravelling. On Sunday, 4 January, the UDA/UFF prisoners inside the Maze – by far the largest loyalist paramilitary faction, with 130 inmates – held a vote to establish whether they still supported it.

Sixty per cent voted 'no', and McMichael and his colleagues knew they had a crisis on their hands. As she listened to their anxious voices in her office in Millbank Tower by the River Thames, Mo Mowlam immediately sensed the seriousness of the situation. To her dismay, she noticed that McMichael's normally relaxed and confident demeanour had gone. He looked the Secretary of State straight in the eye and told her that the people he and his colleagues represented no longer had faith in the process. Their confidence had been shaken to the core by Billy Wright's murder but even before that there had been too many concessions to republicans, including the repatriation of IRA prisoners from British to Irish jails and a trip to Downing Street by Sinn Fein's Gerry Adams and Martin McGuinness.

McMichael explained that he and his colleagues were totally opposed to the LVF campaign, but that many working-class Protestants respected Billy Wright because he had stood up to the IRA. The fact that he had been shot dead by republicans whilst in Her Majesty's protective custody had set all sorts of alarm bells ringing. Mowlam listened intently as the UDP delegation freely admitted it was facing enormous difficulties. McMichael said that he needed help, her help, and he needed it there and then if there was to be any possibility of retrieving the situation. He then asked her to go into the Maze and to speak directly with the UDA prisoners. There was a brief silence, but Mowlam's instincts told her this was the right thing to do. The UDA wings at the Maze held some of the most notorious killers to emerge from the Troubles. She would take some flak for it, but if going into the prison meant the difference between keeping the process alive and its collapse, then she was prepared to do it.

The Secretary of State asked the UDP delegation to wait in the boardroom of her offices while she discussed the idea with her staff. As the Ulstermen waited, they were quietly confident they had convinced Mowlam that a potentially dire situation could be averted if she was prepared to take this momentous step. Several minutes later Mowlam returned to the boardroom to tell McMichael and his colleagues that she would go. There was a look of relief on McMichael's face as he and the others rose to shake hands and say their goodbyes. At least for the time being, the show was still on the road.

Later the same day, McMichael explained to reporters that his party had convinced the Secretary of State of the need to speak to the UDA prisoners directly. The press went into a frenzy at the prospect of a member of the Cabinet sitting down with terrorists who had been convicted of some of the most heinous crimes. The following day, Mowlam travelled to Downing Street to explain her decision to Prime Minister Tony Blair and Jack Straw, the Home Secretary. They were more understanding than she had anticipated: both accepted that, while the IRA had called a second ceasefire in July 1997 after the first was broken by a bomb at London's Canary Wharf 17 months earlier, it was the loyalists who now needed the Government's attention. Although she faced enormous criticism from the right-wing press, Mowlam's decision was made easier by the fact that David Trimble, the Ulster Unionist leader, had himself gone into the Maze to talk to loyalist prisoners earlier that week. At a time of extraordinary change in Northern Ireland, the idea was not totally incredible.

On Friday, 9 January 1998, Mowlam woke early in the London home she shared with her husband Jon Norton and his children by a previous marriage. She had slept well and as she dressed she knew that she was starting one of the most important days of her life. This was the day she was going to do her damnedest to kick-start the faltering Northern Ireland peace process. She would need all her powers of persuasion and her ability to listen if she was to convince the hard men of the UDA that they had made a mistake. Rightly or wrongly, they considered themselves soldiers and were not easily impressed by the rhetoric of politicians, especially British ones. She dressed in a neutral-coloured trouser suit, thereby avoiding any accusations of bias in the enclosed and ultra-sensitive world of an Ulster prison. She kissed Jon goodbye and, accompanied by her police bodyguards, left their house in the smart borough of Islington to catch the plane to Belfast.

An hour later the aircraft touched down at an airstrip behind Shorts factory in Belfast harbour, where Mowlam was met by her private secretary, Ken Lindsay. After the usual exchange of pleasantries, it was back on the road, this time the M1 motorway to the Maze. Mowlam had visited the prison in October 1996 but only as Labour's Northern Ireland spokeswoman in opposition, an event that barely made the news. On that occasion she had held exploratory talks with loyalist inmates, including Adair and Michael Stone. Some had been taken aback by her directness when she kicked her shoes off, put her feet on the table and asked one of them for a drag from his hand-rolled cigarette. This time, however, it was different. She knew that the mission was probably the biggest gamble of her political career, although she did not fully appreciate its significance until she saw the massive media scrum waiting outside the gates.

Once inside, Mowlam was met by Martin Mogg, the prison governor, who explained who she was going to see and ran over the procedures involved when meeting high-security prisoners. Mogg was clearly under immense pressure in the wake of Billy Wright's murder and was anxious to ensure that everything went as smoothly as possible. With the world's press parked outside his door, the last thing he needed was another fiasco. In the interest of balance, Mowlam decided she would meet prisoners from all the terrorist groups whose political representatives were part of the peace process. This meant not only the UDA, but also the UVF and the IRA. The LVF and the INLA, both of which were opposed to the peace talks, were outside the loop.

There was an air of expectation in H7 as Mowlam arrived at the prison. Sam 'Skelly' McCrory, Adair's oldest friend and the UDA's officer commanding inside the jail, had suggested a special dress code for the morning. Lycra shorts and tops – the normal garb for loyalist prisoners – were banned. Instead the five prisoners who would be meeting the Northern Ireland Secretary were told to wear shirts and slacks, presenting an image of respectability.

Determined not to give her critics an opportunity to accuse her of negotiating with terrorists, Mowlam had prepared a 14-point blueprint that set out the parameters of any political settlement and a reconciliation between Northern Ireland's two traditions. Most of the document was vapid and uncontroversial, with the exception of point 13. It declared, 'We are prepared to work on an account of what would happen in respect of prisoner releases in the context of a peaceful and lasting settlement being agreed.' It was a gigantic carrot for the prisoners, and the clearest indication to date that this would be inextricably linked to any peace deal. The document added, 'There would be no significant changes to release arrangements in any other context or for prisoners associated with a paramilitary organisation actively engaged in terrorist activity.'

In typical New Labour fashion, the language was measured and could be interpreted in several different ways, but there was no mistaking that a deal for prisoners could be on the table. The prisoners knew their political representatives had discussed the issue with London and Dublin, but now they were about to hear it from the horse's mouth.

Above the entrance to H7 Mowlam was greeted by the uncompromising message, 'Better to die on your feet than live on your knees in an Irish republic'. Waiting to meet her in the governor's office in the block were the authors of this slogan: Skelly, Johnny Adair, Michael Stone and two others – Bobby Philpott, who was serving a 15-year jail term for trying to murder two Catholics, and Glenn 'Titch' Cunningham, jailed for 25 years, also for attempted murder. Also attending the meeting was the UDP's John White, who had grown up in the same street as Adair and had come to know him again in his capacity as the party's prisons spokesman.

As Mowlam walked into the room, everyone introduced themselves and she shook their hands. Skelly, who in title at least was the most senior UDA man in the delegation, outlined the group's concerns. He said that the peace process appeared to be slanted to a Sinn Fein/IRA agenda and that working-class loyalists were worried the Government was slowly pulling out of the Union. As Mowlam recalled in her autobiography, *Momentum*, 'I did my best to convince them that that was not the case and that . . . everyone was going to have to swallow hard and make some tough decisions, including very much Sinn Fein and the IRA.' The loyalists sat in a circle round Mowlam, who stressed that there was no chance of meeting any of their demands unless their political representatives stayed at the negotiating table.

As the conversation broadened, everyone chipped in except Adair. As usual in formal discussions, he found it hard to concentrate and did not want to expose his lack of political analysis by speaking up. For years he had had to put up with his colleagues in the UDA waffling on about politics and exchanging intellectual positions about the future of Northern Ireland, but he had always been happy to ignore their discussions and reflect on the fact that he was a military man, not a thinker. As Mowlam spoke of difficult decisions for republicans, her hardline audience started to soften. Adair heard the words, and saw that his colleagues welcomed them, but they meant nothing to him. He sat looking at his hands and fiddling with a gold ring he wore with the initials 'UFF' engraved on it. Only he had nothing to say about loyalism, the Union or the future of the peace process. Not once did he address the Secretary of State. According to Michael Stone, the only interaction between the two came when, without warning, Mowlam rose from her seat, walked across the room, slapped him on the wrist and told him to stop biting his nails. His face turned bright red as his comrades burst out laughing.

If there was a single moment that pointed to Adair's subsequent fate, this meeting was it. As Northern Ireland moved tentatively towards peace, there were many articulate terrorists who used the same passion that had motivated them to commit acts of violence to become credible politicians. Johnny Adair was not one of them. As the peace lasted, Adair still wanted to be the centre of attention and continued to hanker after his spot in the limelight. But without being able to talk politics, there was no way for him to achieve this legitimately. As one senior loyalist observed, 'Johnny was afraid of being caught out in any intellectual interaction. He would have been embarrassed if he had been asked to explain his position or beliefs and his way of dealing with it was to say nothing. But he still wanted to be on loyalist delegations that were meeting important people. He loved being in the big picture, but he couldn't hack being asked questions and he was incapable of articulating a loyalist position in any meaningful way.' Adair had never felt anything but loathing for politicians, but he was smart enough to realise that the days of the early 1990s were gone forever and that he would have to reinvent himself. As time went on, it became increasingly clear that his plan revolved around gangsterism and money.

For now, however, the signs of Adair's subsequent degeneration were only just starting to become visible. Mo Mowlam gave him the benefit of the doubt, treating him, like his loyalist colleagues, as a man with sincere political beliefs. She spent a total of 50 minutes with the UDA delegation before shaking their hands again and thanking them for their honesty. She then spent 15 minutes with prisoners from the UVF and the IRA, though in reality this was mere window dressing. Later that day her decision to enter the Maze was vindicated. At 4 p.m., barely 90 minutes after she had left the prison, a clearly relieved Gary McMichael confirmed to the press that the UDA prisoners, impressed by the seriousness with which the Northern Ireland Secretary had listened to their concerns, were prepared to give the talks one more chance.

Despite his reticence at the meeting, Adair was delighted to be back in the newspapers. He was clearly excited when he phoned Jackie 'Legs' Robinson that evening: 'He said she [Mowlam] was a really nice woman, he really, really liked her because he phoned me when they'd had the meeting and he said, "Do you know what? I have to give her respect – she came in here and she met us. She's one hell of a nice woman." And he was genuine. Maybe to somebody else he's going, "She's a bastard," but to me he was genuine when he was saying she's a really, really nice woman. He couldn't get over the fact that she took the time to come in there and talk to them. He just told me that he thought she was brilliant and the meeting went really well. He didn't discuss what she said, he just said she was one hell of a nice woman and he really did have a lot of respect for her.'

But while Adair and his UFF colleagues were busy talking peace with Mowlam, the police were uncovering some disturbing evidence about the shooting of Eddie Treanor ten days earlier. Although claimed by the LVF, the murder had in fact been carried out by C Coy or, to be more precise, Stevie McKeag, its military commander. The attack had been ordered by Adair from inside the jail. Although he had always been deeply envious of Billy Wright, in the eyes of many loyalists the LVF leader was a cult figure and his murder had to be avenged. Sensing that Wright's death would leave a gaping vacuum at the top of loyalism, Adair moved quickly to prove his worth. His action did not, however, go unnoticed by his colleagues at the top of the UDA, who were alarmed by evidence of his growing links with the renegade terrorist group. Under pressure from his fellow brigadiers to explain the reasons for C Coy's breach of the ceasefire and its relationship with the LVF, Winkie Dodds pulled in McKeag and demanded answers. Unflappable as ever, 'Top Gun' had little to say to his boss. He quoted from a section of the loyalist ceasefire announcement, in which a permanent end to military activity was described as 'completely dependent upon the continued cessation of all nationalist/republican violence'. In true McKeag style, he then folded his arms and did not utter another word.

Two days after Mowlam's historic visit to the Maze, Terry Enright, a 28-year-old father of two and a popular community worker, was shot dead as he stood outside the Belfast nightclub where he worked as a bouncer. It had just turned midnight when Enright, whose wife's uncle was Gerry Adams, was hit four times by a masked gunman who stepped out of a red Ford Sierra car and fired over the top of it. The nightclub, which played rave music and had only just opened its doors, was owned by the sister-in-law of PUP leader David Ervine and was a popular venue with young people from both sides of the community. Enright was one of six doormen – including Ervine's brother-in-law – who were standing outside. In a call to a Belfast newsroom using a recognised codeword, a man claiming to represent the LVF said the murder was in retaliation for the killing of Billy Wright. The hijacked car was later found burnt out in a loyalist area of east Belfast. The UVF believes to this day that the gunman was Stephen Warnock, a drug dealer and a former UVF hitman who had defected to the LVF. But again there was assistance from other loyalists, this time a leading UDA figure in east Belfast who sold the murder weapon to Warnock for £150.

BACK TO THE BRINK

A week later, five days after the resumption of all-party talks at Stormont, Fergal McCusker, a 28-year-old Catholic civilian, was abducted and shot dead by the LVF in Maghera, Co. Derry. This time the murder was the sole work of the LVF. Ten hours later the cycle of death continued as two INLA gunmen, one wearing a wig, walked into a carpet shop owned by Jim Guiney, a 38-year-old UDA man, in Dunmurry on the outskirts of south Belfast. They shot him from point-blank range before escaping across a railway line at the back of the shop. Although Guiney had been a senior UDA figure for years, the father of four was said to have been fully supportive of the peace process and the UDA/UFF ceasefire. Within hours, the UFF retaliated. Larry Brennan, a 52-year-old Catholic who was engaged to marry a Protestant, was the seventh person to die in three weeks of tit-for-tat killings. He was shot four times in the chest as he sat in his red Toyota Carina outside the taxi firm where he worked on Belfast's Ormeau Road. Two days later the UFF struck again, shooting dead Benedict Hughes, a 55-year-old Catholic with three children, in the motor components store where he worked off the loyalist Donegall Road.

The following day, on 22 January, Ronnie Flanagan, Northern Ireland's Chief Constable, accused the UFF of breaching its ceasefire by killing Eddie Treanor, Larry Brennan and Benedict Hughes, and appealed for an end to the violence. His words fell on deaf ears. Within 24 hours C Coy was back in action, shooting dead Liam Conway, a 39-year-old Catholic, as he drove a mechanical digger in north Belfast. The killing came hours after the UDA/UFF claimed it had restored its ceasefire following 'a measured military response'. The next day the UFF murdered again, shooting dead John McColgan, a 33-year-old taxi driver from nationalist west Belfast. The father of three was shot five times in the back of the head and dumped at the side of a road on the outskirts of Belfast. Although the murders of Conway and McColgan were not claimed by the UFF, there was little doubt they were responsible. Even for the British and Irish governments, who had made an art form of turning a blind eye to ongoing acts of terrorism in their efforts to keep the peace process afloat, the fiction that the UDA remained on ceasefire could no longer be maintained. Three days later, as speculation mounted that the UDA's political representatives were about to be excluded from the negotiations, Gary McMichael led the Ulster Democratic Party out of the talks.

With Northern Ireland heading back to the brink, it wasn't long before the IRA joined in the act. On 9 February, it killed Catholic drugs baron Brendan 'Bap' Campbell and the following day it shot dead UDA member

Robert Dougan as he sat in his car at Dunmurry. Flanagan told Mowlam he believed the IRA had been involved in both murders and on 16 February Sinn Fein was formally expelled from the talks.

The security forces were also becoming anxious that dissident republicans were trying to exploit the tensions in the peace process. On 3 March, Irish police in Co. Louth discovered a 600 lb car bomb, prepared by the Continuity IRA, hidden on a farm under bales of hay and ready for an attack in the town of Armagh. That evening two LVF gunmen walked into a bar in Poyntzpass, Co. Armagh and opened fire. Two lifelong friends, Philip Allen, a 34-year-old Protestant, and Damien Trainor, a 25-year-old Catholic, were killed in the attack. Twelve days later, 23-year-old David Keys, one of four men charged with the killings, was found murdered on the LVF wing in the Maze. His attackers had beaten him and slit his wrists before stringing him up by a sheet from the window frame of his cell. The LVF, which accused Keys of giving information to the RUC following his arrest, ordered up to 20 inmates to be smeared with the dead man's blood to make it impossible for police to identify the killers. The grisly cycle of violence sparked by Billy Wright's murder showed no signs of abating.

Although Adair was pleased that his beloved C Coy had been at the forefront of the mayhem, he was still far from happy inside the Maze. After Wright's murder, the prison authorities became increasingly anxious that Adair could become the next republican assassination target. In June, RUC officers visited him inside the jail and warned him of a serious threat to his life from the INLA. One senior prison official explained, 'For a while after the murder of Billy Wright there was definitely a concern, a real concern, that Adair's life was in genuine danger and that he could be killed inside the prison.' According to INLA sources, the terrorist group even smuggled a quantity of the deadly poison strychnine into the Maze and was plotting to lace a body-building drink with the stuff in the hope that Adair would drink it. The plan was eventually abandoned because the INLA could not find a way to pull it off.

Although Adair likes to boast that he was close to Billy Wright, nothing could be further from the truth. Even in the early 1990s, when they shared a common goal of terrorising the wider Catholic community, they barely knew each other. A lean man with piercing blue eyes, Wright was a more complex figure than Adair. On the one hand he saw himself as a dedicated soldier who delighted in sowing fear and had the words 'King Rat' tattooed down his right arm. On the other he possessed a strong evangelical streak and habitually quoted from the Bible. Having grown up in the republican heartland of south Armagh, Wright also had an understanding of nationalism and a sophisticated political analysis that Adair lacked. Although he initially supported the loyalist ceasefire, within six months he became convinced that Britain was about to betray Northern Ireland's one million Protestants. Unlike Adair, Wright led an abstemious lifestyle. Just three years older than the Shankill UFF man, he never drank or smoked and did not allow his men to take drugs around him (though in later years he was happy to benefit from the LVF's drugs empire). Although the pair met several times in the early 1990s, they were instinctively distrustful of each other. Wright, who believed the UDA was run by unprincipled thugs, saw Adair as a dangerous maniac with no idea of the bigger picture; Adair, for his part, hated the UVF man because he was so articulate and commanded the type of cult following he had always longed for.

By the time Wright was jailed for eight years in March 1997 for threatening to kill a woman in his home town of Portadown, his newly formed Loyalist Volunteer Force had become the single biggest threat to the peace process. He had been forced to set up his own renegade terror group after UVF leaders ordered his mid-Ulster unit to stand down following the murder of Michael McGoldrick, a 31-year-old Catholic taxi driver, at the height of the Drumcree stand-off in July 1996. By the time he arrived at the Maze, Wright was under threat from both the UVF and republicans. Adair asked to see him but he refused. According to one close friend: 'Billy went into jail and Johnny sent word across to try and get Billy over to talk to him. Now Billy didn't swear or anything like that, but he told Johnny to do one – politely, in his way. Johnny got very agitated over that and it caused a row between him and another prisoner who would have gone back and forth to see him. Billy didn't like the fact that Johnny was a Judas – that's the way he said it. Johnny was just selling the country down the river and he had no time for him at all for that. The peace process was the thing that really did it between them. At first Johnny was dead against the peace process. He would say, "Fucking peace talks." And Billy Wright said that the only reason he went with the peace process was to get out of jail and that is one of the main reasons why Billy Wright hated him.'

But while Wright refused to have anything to do with Adair, several of his LVF colleagues drank and took drugs with members of C Coy. Even before he went to jail, Adair was friendly with Mark 'Swinger' Fulton, a heavily tattooed man who always wore a waistcoat, and his cousin Gary.

When Wright died, both Adair and Fulton realised they could help each other. According to the friend: 'Billy died and Johnny seen this gap and thought, "I'm in here." Swinger knew Billy didn't like Johnny and so he couldn't be too friendly with him [while Wright was alive] or it wouldn't have gone down well. Swinger and Johnny had been friendly from the early '90s and would have socialised a lot. And so when Billy died, Johnny got in touch with him and that's how things started from their angle. Swinger started to visit Johnny and that was the build-up of the drugs. With Billy gone, Swinger had a free hand, 'cause before Billy would have come down on him like a tonne of bricks.'

The first signs of an alliance between the LVF and C Coy were spotted not by police but by prison officers at the Maze. During a visit one day Mark and Gary Fulton, who were booked in to see a friend, switched tables to sit with Adair. It was the beginning of an arrangement that would give Adair money, kudos and another team of killers to call upon. As well as the Fultons, he also struck up a close relationship with several other leading LVF figures, including a 25-year-old assassin from Antrim whose influence extended into north Belfast. According to police intelligence, the man was part of an LVF team that abducted and murdered Sean Brown, a 61-year-old Catholic, at Bellaghy in Co. Derry on 12 May 1997. He was also suspected of the sectarian murders of Fergal McCusker in January 1998 and Ciaran Heffron, a 22-year-old Catholic, three months later.

But the main motivation behind Adair's friendship with the LVF was drugs. In the words of a senior Drugs Squad officer, 'By the time Adair went to jail, many senior figures in the UVF/LVF in north and east Belfast and in mid-Ulster were already well established and very successful dealers and importers. Although he was banged up in jail, Adair still held sway over C Coy territory and he was in a position to distribute huge amounts of drugs from his prison cell. Adair did not have the international contacts to import his own drugs and so he needed the LVF – and later a number of Catholic dealers – to bring the stuff in. We believe he bought into the LVF dealing as a wholesale buyer. This inevitably brought him close to that organisation and it also made him a lot more money.'

By the mid-1990s, the Shankill Road was right at the centre of Northern Ireland's illegal drugs trade. Although he tried to avoid getting his hands dirty, one of the biggest dealers was John White. Like Adair, who regularly took Es inside the Maze, White used drugs as a recreational pastime.

Adair inside H7, the C Coy block inside the Maze Prison, in January 1998. (Courtesy of PA Photos)

'Fat Jackie' Thompson poses with a fake AK-47 rifle and a large vodka and coke during a party inside the Maze. Thompson, who had a full head of hair in the early 1990s, went bald due to the stress of prison life.

The last photograph of Billy 'King Rat' Wright, leader of the renegade Loyalist Volunteer Force, before his murder inside the Maze in December 1997.

Adair emerges from jail in September 1999 showing off his new physique. He spent 20 minutes in the prison gym pumping iron to ensure his muscles looked their best for the media.

Adair in the Diamond Jubilee Bar with close friends William 'Winkie' Dodds (left) and 'Big Donald' Hodgen (right) shortly after his release.

Adair and Gary 'Smickers' Smith lead C Coy's march in support of Orangemen at Drumcree in July 2000.

Adair (far left) is one of seven masked terrorists who fire several bursts of gunfire during his 'day of culture' on the Shankill in August 2000. The firing party includes a mini-skirted Gina Adair (right).

Adair, dressed immaculately in brand new military fatigues, addresses the crowd during a short awards presentation. Jackie McDonald, the UDA's 'brigadier' for south Belfast, stands behind.

Stevie 'Top Gun' McKeag, Adair's most prolific killer.

McKeag is comforted by Adair not long after a serious motorbike accident in 1999. He never fully recovered and became increasingly dependent on cocaine.

Billy 'the Mexican' McFarland, the UDA's 'brigadier' for Co. Derry and north Antrim.

Jimbo 'the Bacardi Brigadier' Simpson.

Adair's fellow 'brigadiers' are among those who greet him on his release from Maghaberry Prison in May 2002. Around the cameras for the fake show of unity are (left to right) Jimbo 'Bacardi Brigadier' Simpson (partially seen), Adair's spokesman John White, Jim 'Doris Day' Gray, John 'Grug' Gregg and Adair. Two of the brigadiers, Jackie McDonald and Billy McFarland, are obscured by their colleagues.

The hero's homecoming, May 2002. John White welcomes his colleague and friend back to the Shankill at a street party outside Adair's house in Boundary Way.

INSET: An exclusive vintage, but one you can't buy in the shops. Dozens of bottles of C Coy champagne were opened as the godfather was welcomed back to his turf.

Adair takes his toddler son Jay, dubbed 'Mad Pup' by his father, for a spin on an expensive new toy.

From left to right: Adair, John White and Andre Shoukri arrive at a meeting with John Reid, the Northern Ireland Secretary, in July 2002.

Adair and some of his oldest friends enjoy a drinking session just months before the split which turned many of them against each other. From left to right: William 'Moe' Courtney, John 'Coco' White, John 'Paddy' Patterson, William 'Winkie' Dodds, Donald Hodgen and Johnny Adair.

The Shankill today: an eight-year-old and a seven-year-old pose during a game of 'punishment beatings'.

John 'Grug' Gregg lies slumped in a taxi minutes after his murder by C Coy gunmen in February 2003. His killing sealed the fate of Adair and his colleagues, who were chased out of Belfast days later.

A once-proud mural of Adair is defaced by mocking graffiti.

Alan McCullough, Adair's protégé and young military commander, who was murdered in May 2003 after returning to Belfast from C Coy's bolthole in England. Here he is pictured, just months before his death, in front of a mural to his father, who was killed by the INLA in 1981.

BACK TO THE BRINK

According to Jackie Robinson, 'When Johnny was inside he told John White to take me out for a good time. John White took me to Kelly's [nightclub] in Portrush one night. We stopped at a garage on the way up. He went in and bought some chewing gum. He handed me two Es and said, "There you are, if you need any more let me know." He had a great big bag of them.'

In the early 1990s, White's office on the Shankill was the dropping-off point for vast quantities of E-tabs imported to Belfast from England by boat every week. The drugs were packed under the hubcaps of a red Mercedes 230E and delivered to White every Friday by a dealer from Manchester posing as a respectable businessman. Concealing them behind the hubcaps meant that if police discovered the drugs, the driver could deny all knowledge and claim they had been put there by somebody else. Within minutes of arriving on the Shankill, the tablets were distributed to an army of small-time dealers whose job it was to sell the merchandise in pubs and clubs over the weekend.

According to RUC intelligence files, by 1995 there were no fewer than 26 main drug dealers in the area. In February of that year, the UVF's William 'Wuzzy' Paul, who was later shot dead by the loyalist gunman Frankie Curry, received a delivery of 30,000 E-tabs from Holland with a street value of more than £300,000. A police intelligence report, dated 16 February 1995, detailed the sordid web of relationships in the loyalist drugs world. It showed how protective both the UDA and UVF were of their criminal empires:

> Wuzzy Paul, although a member of the UVF, deals in drugs for his own benefit. Because of this, shortly before December 1994 he was fined by the UVF £40,000 which, if he failed to pay, would result in his execution. To date he has paid the UVF £20,000 and has been ordered to pay a further £20,000 by March 1995. Although he has been ordered not to deal in drugs by the UVF, he intends to continue supplying drugs to the UDA/UFF and trusted dealers. He does not get his supply of drugs (E Tablets) from the same supplier as the UVF – however, he does get them from England. As well as using his own dealers he uses Circle Taxis to deliver his drugs. This firm is owned by the UDA/UFF.

According to the document, Paul was making a personal profit of at least £5,000 a week from consignments posted to a safe house in the Shankill and stuffed in a cylindrical baby wipes container packed with coffee beans. The report named several of Adair's closest colleagues as drug pushers, including Stephen 'Dick' Dempsey, James 'Sham' Millar, Paddy Patterson and Winkie Dodds. Dempsey and Patterson sold at weekend discos at the Glenavna House Hotel on the outskirts of Belfast and the Kilwaughter House Hotel outside Larne. According to the RUC:

> On Saturday and Sunday nights, after the Glenavna disco is over, it has become common practice for the UDA and UVF pushers and dealers to return to a shebeen in 18 Midland Close, Belfast, and party all night taking drugs. This shebeen is run by the UDA, mainly Winky Dodds, Sham Millar and Dick Dempsey. Source believes that Winky Dodds supplies E-Tabs to [a hall on the Crumlin Road – authors' amendment to text] and also to the Diamond Jubilee Bar. This was done by John Adair prior to his arrest and remand in custody.

By the time Mo Mowlam visited the Maze, Adair's criminal empire had grown substantially and he was starting to make serious cash as a result of his blossoming relationship with the LVF. He even boasted to Jackie Robinson that he had stashed large amounts of money in four bank accounts in the Irish Republic and had invested heavily in legitimate businesses and property on both sides of the border. Despite extensive probing, the authors have been unable to uncover evidence to substantiate this and for now it must remain speculation.

What is certain, however, is that Adair had far more money than any other prisoner at the Maze. An examination of his 'tuck shop' account at the jail revealed that he was always in credit to the tune of several hundred pounds, while most other prisoners had little or no money in their accounts. Said one prison official, 'He always had plenty of ready cash – hundreds of pounds at a time lodged into his prisoner's personal cash account. People used to come in regularly to the jail to pay in money, and on several occasions a taxi driver came up from the Shankill with a list of accounts to put money into and a load of cash. His [Adair's] name was always first on the list.'

Another large, though one-off, source of income was a 36-year-old former soldier by the name of Keith Kenneth Winward. In April 1996, Winward was driving an armoured delivery van for Securicor when it was held up and robbed on the outskirts of Belfast. He was on a delivery run known as 'Route 15 – the Bookies Run', which involved taking a mountain of cash to the Post Office HQ in the city. Without telling his colleague why he was taking an unusual route, Winward drove to a derelict building on the outskirts of Belfast. As they pulled up, three masked gunmen jumped out and ordered them to hand over their cargo before handcuffing them to a window frame. They seized nearly £1.1 million.

Winward told police that he had been ordered to drive to the address after several armed men burst into his home and took his family hostage, claiming they were from the Provisional IRA. He was about to be released from Lisburn Road RUC station when Detective Sergeant Johnston Brown arrived. As soon as he started questioning Winward, the detective, who had been appointed to the robbery squad since helping to ensnare Adair, suspected he wasn't telling the truth. There were too many discrepancies and inconsistencies for his story to make sense. As Brown told him that he would be required for further questioning, the ex-squaddie flew into a rage and demanded of the police officer, 'Who are you?' Staring straight into Winward's eyes, Brown replied, 'Who am I? I'll tell you who I am. I'm your worst nightmare, that's who I am.'

Instead of being released, Winward was banged up in Castlereagh holding centre for a week, where he was quizzed in detail. As he made him repeat his story over and over again, Brown became convinced that he had been in on the act from the beginning, putting his wife and family through a terrifying ordeal. The Middlesbrough-born former soldier was convinced that he was smarter than Brown and arrogantly referred to the detective as 'Irish PC Plod'. He prided himself on being an expert in anti-interrogation techniques, the legacy of his days as an infantryman with the Green Howards. He also falsely claimed to have been captured and interrogated by the Iraqis during the Gulf War and to have fought in the Falklands conflict. As detectives appealed to his sense of decency in order to help recover the money before the UFF could use it to buy weapons, Winward made an increasingly bizarre series of utterances. According to police notes of his interviews in Castlereagh, he pretended to speak German, at one point emitting a phrase that was noted down as 'Nein grassen hi mein ficus'. He went on, 'Coconuts, Zanussi, you fat fucker,' before adding to Jonty Brown (who vaguely resembles the eccentric Uncle Fester from *The Addams Family*), 'Suck my dick Fester, ****** [Winward's friend] says you're a closet homosexual.' Told to settle down, Winward said his friend had told him that 'if I stick my dick in the fire it will hurt and that's the same thing as admitting anything to you boys. Would you eat yellow snow, Jonty?'

Winward was obsessed with the fact that Brown had helped to jail Johnny Adair. 'My [friend] knows you, he knows you put away Johnny O'Dair [sic],' he said. 'He has warned me that you are sleeked [sic] and if I trust you I will go to jail.' As the detective picked holes in his evidence, Winward dismissed his claims as 'fantasy, *Jackanory*'. At the end of his seven days' detention, however, he was charged with involvement in the robbery. Staring at him with his intense brown eyes, Brown told him, 'I have a promise to make to you. When you go down for 15 years, I want you to look to your left. You'll see a fat man waving you goodbye. That man will be me.'

Brown suspected that the robbery had been carried out by the UDA, not the IRA, and that Winward had helped to set up the ambush for a share of the money. His suspicions were confirmed when Maurice Gamble, a UDA man from Ballysillan in north Belfast, walked into Tennent Street RUC station several weeks after the robbery and asked for Jonty Brown by name. When the officer arrived in the reception area, Gamble said, 'Johnny told me to tell you, "Thanks a million."' It was Adair's two-fingered gesture to the man who had helped send him to prison.

On 27 October 1997, Winward was jailed for 15 years after a jury-free Diplock court found him guilty of aiding and abetting the UDA gang responsible for Northern Ireland's largest ever cash heist. As the sentence was being passed, he shouted, 'An innocent man is going to jail.' He then glanced furtively to his left. Standing there waving him goodbye was Detective Sergeant Jonty Brown. Police believe the cash from the Securicor heist was divided up among the UDA's leadership, including Adair. However, Winward's £78,000 cut ended up in the hands of C Coy. After he was admitted to the UDA block at the Maze, Adair befriended Winward with the sole intention of finding out where he had stashed his share of the robbery. Once Adair obtained this information from Winward he instructed his men on the outside to seize the money. He then arranged to have Winward beaten up and thrown off the wing.

According to one UDA brigadier: 'An arrangement had been made for Winward to receive his "commission" by instalments, but Johnny convinced Winward he was in a position to get the cash shipped back to England for him. Winward became so friendly with Adair that he even joined the C Coy wing in the Maze. But the minute the cash was handed over Adair dumped him. He ordered one of his close friends to beat him up with a pool cue and then he had him thrown off the wing.'

As Winward became increasingly desperate to retrieve his money, he telephoned William 'Winkie' Dodds, who had succeeded Adair as brigadier in west Belfast. Referring to his cut of the robbery, the Securicor driver said, 'My wife needs her cabbage.' Dodds replied tartly, 'I'm not sure if we can get her cabbage, but we'll send round a few carrots and turnips.'

After his painful encounter with C Coy, a devastated Keith Winward wrote to Mo Mowlam in her capacity as MP for his home area in the north-east of England. He requested a transfer to an English prison. His request was granted, but when it emerged that paramilitary prisoners in Northern Ireland were being released on licence following the signing of the Belfast Agreement on Good Friday 1998, Winward again wrote demanding he be included in the deal. Mowlam told Winward that in order to qualify, he would have to serve his sentence in a prison in Northern Ireland. Winward reluctantly agreed. After spending a short time behind bars at Maghaberry Prison in Co. Antrim, he was eventually released under licence. A broken man as a result of his encounter with Adair, he now lives quietly in the north of England.

13. The Boss

'Johnny started giving Billy McFarland abuse. He said he wasn't threatening him, but said he should get himself sorted out with the UVF. I told Johnny not to talk to Billy like that. He turned to me and said, "You think we're all equal here but we're not."' – *Jackie McDonald, UDA 'brigadier' for south Belfast*

WHEN JOHNNY ADAIR PUSHED HIS WAY THROUGH THE RICKETY TURNSTILE AT the Maze Prison on Tuesday, 14 September 1999, he became the 293rd terrorist prisoner to be released early as part of the Good Friday peace accord. He had served just four years of a sixteen-year sentence for directing terrorism, hardly much punishment for what he had done but part of the unpalatable price of peace in Northern Ireland. A small army of minders surrounded him as he emerged into the midday sun, while John White told the press that his colleague would be dedicating himself to cross-community work. He thanked 'Mr Adair' for his contribution to peace, knowing it was the first of many speeches he would make as he sought to reinvent the loyalist as a committed statesman. It was the start of a long and ridiculous charade. 'Mr Adair has given his unwavering support to the peace process, even through the various crises,' he declared. 'I know he will continue to support dialogue to resolve our difficulties.' Although it had been a long time since most of them had seen him, reporters couldn't help but notice that the C Coy boss had bulked out during his time behind bars. His diet of steroids and protein, mixed with hours of weight training, had paid off. Adair, who had also shaved his head, now looked the hard man he had always dreamt of becoming.

Wearing a Dolce & Gabbana T-shirt, a gypsy hoop in each ear and a back-to-front baseball cap, Adair gave a clenched-fist salute and grinned broadly. He did not utter a word as minders clutching walkie-talkies to their ears guided him through the crowd to a waiting Volkswagen Passat. Inside the car, he hurriedly slipped a bulletproof vest over his head.

As the UFF convoy headed from the Maze to the Shankill, Northern Ireland braced itself for the return of one of its most feared sons. Not everybody was celebrating. The RUC, aware that Adair had continued to direct terrorism from behind bars, had taken the unprecedented step of objecting to his release. Police suspected that C Coy was involved in the murder of Brian Service, a 35-year-old Catholic gunned down in north Belfast in October 1998 and claimed by an outfit calling itself 'the Red Hand Defenders'. Over the coming months the RUC would discover that the name was a flag of convenience for murders ordered by Adair, Gary 'Smickers' Smith, his military commander, and the LVF. Ronnie Flanagan, the Chief Constable, had warned Mo Mowlam that Adair would almost certainly seek to resume his terrorist career. Mowlam heeded the advice and objected to Adair's inclusion in the early release scheme. Of all the prisoners released up to this point he was the only one to have faced such a challenge. But she changed her mind after a UDP delegation led by John White told her the UFF ceasefire could be in jeopardy if Adair was not included. It was the supreme irony that the man flagged up by White as helping to secure the peace process was released because he had threatened to bring it down.

Flanagan was right. Even the day before his release Adair had been taped phoning a bank in west Belfast to make an appointment to go over C Coy's finances. His ego was simply too big to let him live a life of quiet obscurity. Back on the Shankill, he received a hero's welcome. As the cavalcade drove in, well-wishers waved and the drivers of passing cars tooted horns in his honour. Balloons and flags adorned Gina's house in Manor Court in the Oldpark, the first home the Adairs would share as a married couple.

After a reunion with his wife and children, Adair and his friends headed to the UDA's club in Heather Street for a 'men only' drinks party. That night he was guest of honour at another party, this time in the Diamond Jubilee Bar. The pub was packed. 'They came from all over the place, from Portadown and everywhere,' said one of those present. 'The place was bunged to the doors. I think the party lasted two or three days.' As he sat upstairs surrounded by old comrades, Adair, Winkie Dodds and Donald Hodgen were called onto the stage to receive a special silver plaque. Adair's read, 'In recognition of J. Adair, for showing leadership in our darkest days and showing us the way forward. UFF 2nd Battalion.'

Like a triumphant warrior returning home, the next day Adair toured the Shankill calling in to see old friends. By now he had fans way beyond his native west Belfast. A few days later Johnny and Gina were out shopping on the outskirts of Belfast when an incident occurred that confirmed his notoriety. 'Him and her had gone over to the Abbey Centre in Newtownabbey to buy clothes,' said Jackie Robinson. 'Johnny went into a shop to buy a pair of Levis, but he was a bit unnerved because the young man serving him kept staring at him. Eventually the shop assistant said, "You're Johnny Adair, aren't you?" Johnny was embarrassed. He just said, "Well, yeah." The young fella said, "I'll knock a tenner off for you." Johnny thought that was brilliant.'

In the run-up to his release, Adair had been paroled on several occasions. In May 1999, Winkie, Johnny and Stevie McKeag spent the weekend in Glasgow where they attended a dinner organised by loyalist friends of Skelly, who planned to move to Scotland when he was released from jail. Once again Adair was presented with a plaque, this one bearing the message, '28 May 1999, From All Your Friends in Scotland, Hands Across the Sea'. A month earlier Adair came within an inch of losing his life when, again out on parole, he and Gina went to a UB40 concert in Belfast's Botanic Gardens. Adair had booked the tickets as a treat for Gina's birthday, but as he entered the park he was spotted by a republican from the Markets district of the city. As Adair and his wife stood swaying with their arms round each other, a lone gunman walked up behind him, pointed a gun at his head and pulled the trigger. There was a loud crack and Adair slumped to the ground in agony. As a crowd of men started kicking him on the ground, it looked as though the loyalist folk hero was about to die an ignominious death to the strains of 'Red, Red Wine', one of his favourite songs. But suddenly he got up and started to run for his life, hotly pursued by Gina. With blood streaming from a large head wound, Adair summoned every ounce of strength and dashed for the exit. He was saved because the bullet, a .38 round, failed to penetrate his skull. It had flattened as it hit the skin, either because it was damp or because the weapon had been tampered with by the security forces.

The next day, after signing himself out of the Ulster Hospital on the outskirts of Belfast, Adair called in at Donegall Pass RUC station to make a statement about the attack, the seventh attempt on his life by republicans. John Kelso, a detective inspector who was on duty at the time, remembered: 'Word spread round the station that Johnny Adair had arrived. I wasn't dealing with him, but to tell you the truth I was very nosy to find out what happened. I walked into the office where Johnny and Gina were sitting. Johnny had a large bandage and a dressing on his shaved head. I said to him, "It's hard to kill a bad thing." He just looked up and laughed.'

In November 1999, Adair referred to the attack during an interview he gave to Kate Kray, former wife of the notorious London gangster, Reggie. She wanted to include a chapter on Adair in a book she was writing called *Hard Bastards*. He told her, 'When I came out of prison, I thought I was safe to go to a UB40 concert with my wife – I was wrong.' He added, 'I have no fear of the IRA or anyone else. If I did I would be living in England, but I'm not.' No terrorist group ever claimed responsibility for the murder bid, leading to speculation that it had been carried out by a member of the IRA but without formal authorisation.

The early release of paramilitary prisoners was a hard pill for relatives of victims to swallow, but it was an inextricable part of the 1998 Good Friday Agreement along with a commitment to decommission terrorist weapons. The newly created independent body on decommissioning, headed by Canadian General John de Chastelain, invited all paramilitary groups to appoint an 'interlocutor' to coordinate progress. The UDA was split down the middle on the issue and for months agonised over whether to comply. The biggest advocate for decommissioning was John White. Since his release from jail in 1992, he had been steadily building his profile as the respectable face of the UDA and a leading member of its political wing, the Ulster Democratic Party. White hoped to emulate Billy Hutchinson, a double murderer he had been friendly with inside the Maze who went on to become an articulate politician for the UVF's political wing. White himself was no angel. A bald man with small piggy eyes and a chilling stare, he had belonged to a Shankill UDA team known as 'the Dirty Dozen' in the early 1970s, whose members were linked to countless acts of petty crime, theft and even rape. In 1978, he was jailed for one of the most savage double murders of the Troubles, the 1973 killing of Paddy Wilson, a 40-year-old nationalist politician, and Irene Andrews, his 25-year-old companion. He stabbed Wilson 32 times and slit his throat from ear to ear. Andrews was stabbed 19 times and had her breasts cut off. White, who received a life sentence after admitting the murders, studied economics in jail and was determined to put his education to use – both to make money and to help his community.

By the time of Adair's release, White realised that decommissioning was an issue that could transform his political career. Having spent years befriending Adair, he knew it could also be used to win the Shankill man credibility as he attempted to build a new life outside prison. White wanted the UDA to carry out a major act of decommissioning. With the IRA defiantly insisting it would never surrender a single bullet, he believed such a gesture would win the UDA enormous goodwill and wrongfoot its critics and enemies. His problem was convincing the UDA's six brigadiers that he was right. Adair's support would be a giant step in that direction. When White explained the idea to him, he was instantly taken. According to a senior prison official, Adair discussed the plan on at least three separate occasions during monitored telephone calls from the Maze. It had Johnny Adair written all over it. He would go down in history as the man who persuaded the loyalists to lay down their arms. He also knew that handing over a big batch of weapons did not stop him from shopping for brand-new guns the very next day.

Adair and White were part of a five-strong UDA delegation that met General de Chastelain on 10 December 1999. The others were Winkie Dodds; John 'Grug' Gregg of south-east Antrim, whose claim to fame was shooting and wounding Gerry Adams in 1984; and Jackie McDonald of south Belfast. Afterwards, White told reporters that 'no loyalist guns will be handed over until the IRA makes the first move'. It was the usual tough talk, but in reality he and Adair were planning something more radical. At White's behest, Adair called a meeting of the UDA's ruling 'inner council' at which decommissioning topped the agenda. By now Adair was convinced that this was the issue that would propel him to greatness. Incredibly, he said he thought the time had come for the UDA to decommission not just a few of its guns, but its entire arsenal of illegal weapons. One of those attending the meeting was the veteran 'brigadier' for north Antrim and Derry, Billy 'the Mexican' McFarland. He could hardly believe his ears: 'Adair came back and called a meeting of the brigadiers where he said he thought decommissioning all our weapons was a great idea. His proposal was turned down point blank. But he pushed away and we agreed to return the following day to discuss it further. At the next meeting, it was obvious

Adair had managed to nobble a couple of people overnight. Jimbo Simpson, the "Bacardi brigadier", was one of them. It went to a vote and the result was three for decommissioning and three against. Adair said John White should be allowed to have a casting vote, but he was told to get lost.'

Later that day, after all the brigadiers had returned to their respective areas, they were again contacted and told to return to Belfast the following day because Adair had called an emergency meeting. During an extensive interview with one of the authors, 'the Mexican', who travelled nearly 100 miles to attend the meeting, said that, despite his insistence that everybody attend, Adair himself failed to turn up. The brigadiers sat in stony silence while White read out a statement on his colleague's behalf. It was highly critical of two brigadiers in particular. According to McFarland: 'I remember he said of me, "the Derry brigadier is a dinosaur with no forward thinking and he has nothing to offer this organisation". White went on to say Johnny had called a press conference in west Belfast where he planned to announce decommissioning on his own. Then White took a series of calls from Johnny, who was wanting to know if the other brigadiers were going over to the west to support him. All the brigadiers refused. White asked us all individually if we would go to support Johnny. When it came to me, I said, "No, I'm going back to Jurassic Park." I then looked White straight in the eye and asked, "Who's pulling your strings?" He didn't reply.'

Jackie McDonald, the UDA's brigadier for south Belfast, believes Adair was determined to go down in history as the visionary leader who saved the peace process: 'Johnny and I were the first ones appointed as interlocutors to the decommissioning body, but I said I wanted time to speak to the men. I didn't want people to think we were riding out with a white flag and surrendering. As far as I was concerned, if we were going to talk to de Chastelain it was going to be as much about not decommissioning as it was going to be about decommissioning. I mean, the fact that we were talking to him at all showed we were willing to progress the situation. We had a couple of meetings to discuss the matter, but Adair just wanted to go ahead with decommissioning and he and White attacked the other brigadiers for not showing leadership. He said that Billy McFarland was paranoid about the UVF and that John Gregg had never done anything in his life, apart from shooting Gerry Adams. We talked the thing through and it was put to a vote without resolution. The next thing was, Johnny called an emergency meeting, but he never turned up. He sent John White with a piece of paper.

THE BOSS

I told White to tell him to get down to the meeting and not to be sending bits of paper instead. It was all put on hold until he came down the next day. Johnny walked in and said he thought we should just forget about it. I said, "We'll forget about fuck all. What do you mean sending bits of paper down here accusing people of things?"'

According to McDonald, the meeting became increasingly heated as Adair once again attacked his fellow commanders. His version of events offers a remarkable insight into Adair's ego, which by late 1999 was ballooning out of control. As the mafia bosses all sat round the table, the west Belfast brigadier could no longer bite his tongue. It appalled him that these men – none of whom had fought the 'war' against the IRA as he had – were refusing to give him the respect he deserved. McDonald remembered: 'Johnny started giving Billy McFarland abuse. He said he wasn't threatening him, but said he should get himself sorted out with the UVF. I told Johnny not to talk to Billy like that. He turned to me and said, "You think we're all equal here but we're not." Things settled down and he asked us what we were doing. I said again that we would talk to the men. But I've no doubt that if we hadn't stood up to him, he would have steam-rollered us into decommissioning. John White kept saying that if we decommissioned it would put the Provies behind the eight ball. I said if we started doing it for the wrong reasons, then we would lose control and lose men to the loyalist dissidents. When I met de Chastelain, I explained all of that to him and he understood. I think he was just glad we were there. But the whole thing came about because John White was pushing Johnny to make them famous, like "we're the good guys here".'

Although Adair wanted to make an historic gesture on arms, he almost certainly had no intention of including C Coy in his plan. McDonald believes Adair was never serious about disarming, but simply saw it as an excuse to throw out a few old guns. The ploy was a sham. 'Johnny thought de Chastelain would give him a piece of paper which would allow him to travel around Northern Ireland in a lorry collecting UFF weapons,' he said. 'I've no doubt Johnny would have sifted through them, picking out the good stuff for himself before handing over the rest. In fact it would have meant he was better armed than ever before. It was all part of his plan to take complete control.'

McDonald was absolutely right. Over the course of several months in 1999 and 2000, Adair was seeking to rearm C Coy through a new supply route. He sent one of White's political colleagues in the UDP on a series of trips to Amsterdam to buy weapons. Adair paid for the north Belfast man to stay in a posh hotel and gave him several hundred pounds in cash. On one trip he even paid for the man's wife to accompany him for the weekend. The contact in Amsterdam was a former Official IRA man. He was living in the Dutch capital where he was posing as a respectable businessman buying and selling boats, though in reality this was purely a front. The contact held several meetings with Adair's representative and took him to a warehouse where he showed him a vast arsenal of weapons, including several types of handgun, assault rifles, pistols, rocket launchers and grenades. He also made it clear that he could ship large quantities of E-tabs back to Britain for Adair, though he could not deliver them all the way to Northern Ireland. Over the next few months the contacts continued and detailed price lists for guns and E-tabs, disguised in documents as various types of boat components, were faxed from Amsterdam to the UDA's offices in north Belfast.

It is not clear whether the Amsterdam link ever came to fruition and the north Belfast man, fearing an MI6 sting, refused to have anything to do with the handing over of money. By the start of 2000, however, one thing was beyond doubt: if there was a way to do it, Adair certainly had enough cash to finance a major arms delivery. One example of his money-making schemes reveals the full scope of his ambition at this time. Shortly after his release he decided to bank-roll a drugs importation scam in the very heart of the Shankill. Using Gary Marno, a convicted UDA extortionist who had set up in Spain as an international drug dealer, he arranged for cheap cannabis and E-tabs to be sent in bulk to Belfast. On Adair's orders, Stephen Harbinson, a convicted UFF murderer, opened a shop on the lower Shankill dealing in second-hand white goods. Harbinson started receiving fridges and microwaves by courier from Spain, but these were not ordinary household items: they were packed to the brim with cannabis and E-tabs. Although police found nothing during a raid on the shop, in a simultaneous swoop on Harbinson's home at Newtownabbey they recovered 20 kilos of cannabis, worth £200,000, in a car parked in the drive. Harbinson was arrested and charged with possession of drugs with intent to supply. However, after being released on bail he fled to Spain where he hooked up with Marno in the resort of Fuengirola on the Costa del Sol and set up a new drug-smuggling operation. They posted cannabis and Ecstasy to a garage in east Belfast where Harbinson's son, also Stephen, worked. Harbinson Jnr was caught with £250,000 of cannabis when police raided the garage. In January 2003, he was jailed for 21 months by a judge who described him as 'a patsy in an operation organised from Spain'.

By the time Adair was freed from jail, the cash was flooding into C Coy. Although estimates vary, James 'Sham' Millar, his most senior drug dealer, was said at this time to be earning up to £10,000 per week. It is not clear how much Adair was making, but he had enough to support an extremely comfortable lifestyle. He spent several thousand pounds renovating a new house he moved into in November 1999 after his colleagues persuaded him that Gina's place in Manor Court was too close to the peaceline. Just days after Remembrance Sunday, Adair and his wife moved into Boundary Way in the lower Shankill estate, known locally as 'Beirut'. His new next-door neighbours were Winkie and Maureen Dodds, while in the adjoining streets were Sham Millar, Donald Hodgen and 'Fat Jackie' Thompson. Although only a modest three-bedroom council house when it was provided to him by the Housing Executive, Adair paid for oil-fired central heating to be installed, an internal wall to be knocked down, black floor tiles to be fitted downstairs and a fancy fireplace put in. Within months he had transformed it into a luxury residence worthy of the Shankill's favourite godfather, with cream leather sofas and a matching television and hi-fi system.

But although he enjoyed his new house, he still felt unsettled. He badly wanted to be with Jackie Robinson, who he was again seeing intermittently. There were days when he wished he had never married Gina. After hearing story after story about his wife's extra-marital liaisons, he had even forced her to take an HIV test following his release from jail. On Christmas Eve 1999, Adair's first Christmas back on the outside, the couple had a major row after one of Gina's old boyfriends, who lived in Mount Vernon in north Belfast, was dragged out of the shebeen where they were all drinking and badly beaten by her husband's friends. When they returned home, both the worse for wear with drink, Gina challenged Adair about Jackie Robinson. He burst into tears as she held a kitchen knife to his throat and threatened to cut off his penis. On Christmas morning, when Adair was sober, he had his revenge by beating her. He then left the house with his nine-month-old son, Jay (whom Adair had nicknamed 'Mad Pup'), and spent most of the day with Jackie, who had moved to Florence Walk around the corner.

By the start of 2000, Adair also had other problems to contend with. On 10 January 2000, Richard Jameson, the 46-year-old leader of the UVF in mid-Ulster, was shot dead by an LVF gunman outside his home. The killing, two weeks after Jameson was involved in a fight with LVF members in a club in Portadown, signalled the start of a violent feud. Ill feeling between the two groups had been simmering since Billy Wright had broken away four years earlier to form the LVF. The next month the feud claimed two more victims. The bodies of Andrew Robb, a 19-year-old with a nine-month-old daughter, and his friend, 18-year-old David McIlwaine, were found with their throats slit on an isolated road near Tandragee, Co. Armagh. The murders were widely seen as retaliation for Jameson. Despite denials by the LVF that the dead teenagers had any links to the organisation, they were reported to have been minor drug pushers on the fringes of the group. Adair's appearance at Andrew Robb's funeral was further evidence of the close bond developing between C Coy and the LVF. On 26 May, the turf war claimed another victim. Martin Taylor, a 26-year-old UVF volunteer with two children, was shot dead by two LVF gunmen as he helped a friend build a wall outside a house in north Belfast.

On 3 July, Adair again showed his support for his friends in Portadown when he turned up with 70 members of C Coy to support Orangemen who had been prevented from marching along the Catholic Garvaghy Road. He led his men, sporting white T-shirts with the slogan, 'Simply The Best: Their Only Crime – Loyalty', down the hill at Drumcree to the British Army fortification designed to block the marchers' route. Later that night Adair, Smickers and several other colleagues attended an LVF bonfire celebration in the staunchly loyalist Corcrain estate. As Adair stood stroking his pet Alsatian, Rebel – also wearing a UFF T-shirt – two masked LVF gunmen stepped out of the darkness and fired shots into the air. Adair's presence at Drumcree worried the police. RUC Special Branch reports suggested he was considering murdering a Catholic a day until the Orangemen were allowed down the Garvaghy Road. When challenged about this by one of the authors at the time, Adair barked, 'Well, time will tell, won't it? I'm sitting here and I'm telling you I'm for peace.' In another interview he was dismissive about his presence at the LVF show of strength. 'It just so happened I was at a bonfire,' he said. 'You will find that in this country on bonfire nights most of the time, people do come out and fire shots into the air.' He insisted he was pushing for peace, declaring, 'I have been working tirelessly 24 hours a day, seven days a week, for peace in Northern Ireland.'

Adair's repeated visits to Portadown made several of his fellow brigadiers uneasy. For several months he and his closest colleagues, including Winkie Dodds, Stevie McKeag and Gary 'Smickers' Smith, had been travelling to mid-Ulster to attend LVF dinners and parties. Rumours started to circulate that Adair intended to create a 'super loyalist' organisation by bringing the UFF – or at least C Coy – and the LVF together under the same umbrella. For now they were just rumours, but before long his critics would have the proof they needed.

In August, Adair embarked upon a plan that was designed to do two things: to cement his friendship with the LVF and confirm his authority over the UVF in west Belfast. Ever since the early 1990s, when C Coy had challenged the UVF's financial supremacy on the Shankill, he had wanted to teach it a lesson. By summer 2000, the UVF suspected C Coy of carrying out attacks for the LVF in Belfast and the atmosphere between the two groups in west Belfast was poisonous. With the chance at last to rub the UVF's nose in the dirt, Adair came up with the idea of a day-long festival, to be grandly titled a 'celebration of Protestant culture'. Ostensibly it was to mark the completion of 19 new loyalist murals on the lower Shankill, including one to the late Princess Diana and another to the LVF's Billy Wright (whom Adair had hated when he was alive). But in reality the plan was little more than an excuse for a UFF show of strength that would show in graphic terms who was boss on the Shankill.

Ever since Adair walked out of the Maze he had been searching for a cause that would help to portray him as the defender of his community. He believed he had been his people's hero in the early 1990s and, although he knew that times had moved on, thirsted for the same approbation again. Throughout the summer he had been stoking sectarian tensions in north Belfast and had even ordered his men to attack Protestant homes to make it look like they had been targeted by Catholics. As a result of the UDA's devolved power structure, he was able to operate without having to account for his actions. With nobody to stand up to him, he seemed to be losing all sense of perspective. He seized upon the LVF–UVF feud as a chance to grab the initiative. Although he had been warned by his fellow brigadiers that there were to be no LVF banners or flags at the event, Adair was determined to antagonise the UVF by producing at least one LVF flag. The UVF was so worried that it had even sought and received assurances from the UDA that no LVF colours would be on display. Adair was one of those who personally gave that commitment. Despite this, on 18 August, the day before the celebration was due to take place, he had an LVF flag delivered to the Diamond Jubilee Bar.

By lunchtime on Saturday, 19 August, thousands of UDA members and supporters from across Northern Ireland and Scotland had descended on the lower Shankill. Most were gathered in front of the platform of a lorry, bedecked with Ulster flags and UFF regalia, that had been parked on waste ground at the bottom of the road. At around 2 p.m. they were addressed by John White and the Deputy Lord Mayor of Belfast, Frank McCoubrey, a leading member of the UDA-linked Ulster Democratic Party. To huge applause, White then introduced two men he described as 'loyalist folk heroes'. Johnny Adair was joined by Michael Stone, who had reluctantly agreed to appear on the platform alongside his fellow ex-prisoner. Before Stone could object, Adair grabbed his hand and lifted it triumphantly above his head. Minutes later, up to 4,000 men, most wearing black UDA ties and assembled by brigade area, set out on a march to the accompaniment of loyalist bands. They were led by around 80 masked volunteers in berets and full paramilitary uniform. Billy 'the Mexican' McFarland, brigadier for north Antrim and Derry, says he became aware that something was wrong even before his men left the starting point. 'The north Antrim section was the last to leave and a Belfast band tried to march with our people, but I told them to move up nearer the front. We marched off, but then another band suddenly tagged on at the end. We didn't know at the time but they had an LVF flag in with the UFF flags. Johnny had set up the whole thing.'

Shortly after 3 p.m., as the band was passing the Rex Bar, a known UVF haunt, a standard-bearer unfurled the LVF flag. The band was immediately attacked by UVF supporters who had been drinking outside the bar and saw the flag as a two-fingered salute to them. Within seconds the UVF men were embroiled in a fist fight with LVF supporters from Portadown, who had been invited to the rally by Adair. As word of the attack came back to the lower Shankill, Gary 'Smickers' Smith and Sam 'Skelly' McCrory led a mob of around 200 C Coy members up the hill. 'C Coy, fall in,' yelled Smickers, the unit's military commander. 'Up that road – now!' By the time they reached the Rex the door was firmly shut and crowds of UVF members had barricaded themselves inside. Footage from an Army helicopter captured the bloody scenes that followed. Sham Millar was filmed hitting a man four times over the head with what looked like an iron bar. Tommy Potts and a 14-year-old Shankill boy, David Coleman, were among a group seen kicking a man in the head and battering him with sticks and a drink crate. As Skelly tried to wrench off the security grills from the windows, up to three gunmen fired into the pub, wounding two men and a woman. The gunmen included Moe Courtney and Mark Whiteside, a 25-year-old from the mid-Shankill who later admitted firing 15 shots with a pistol and was jailed for four years for his part in the attack.

THE BOSS

Undeterred by the violence at the Rex, Adair was determined to press ahead with his day of 'culture'. After a short awards ceremony, he disappeared from view behind the platform. When he reappeared, his face was covered by a balaclava and he was wearing a khaki-coloured ribbed army jumper, cargo pants and a shoulder holster. In his gloved hand he held a new Austrian-made Glock 19 pistol. Adair was joined on stage by five masked men, three with sub-machine guns and two with AK-47 rifles. The final figure on the platform was a slim, mini-skirted female, also brandishing an AK-47. As British Army surveillance experts watched from nearby Divis Tower, it did not take them long to work out that the woman was in fact Gina Adair. To rapturous applause, the firing party knocked off the safety catches on their weapons and unleashed a long volley of shots into the air. The noise was so deafening that Adair's fellow brigadiers, seated at the back of the platform, were forced to cover their ears. But before Adair himself was able to fire a single shot, his gun jammed. As the smell of gunfire filled the air, he dropped to his knees and tried desperately to clear his weapon. While the remainder of the group acknowledged their adoring supporters, Adair, who was fitting a new ammunition clip to his pistol, gestured at them to wait. 'I've got her cleared,' he yelled as he scrambled to his feet, lifted his gun above his head and fired all nineteen 9mm bullets.

With the celebrations out of the way, Adair turned his thoughts to teaching the UVF a lesson. Just before 7 p.m., as the crowds were still leaving, C Coy attacked the homes of more than a dozen UVF members in the lower Shankill. Petrol bombs were thrown and windows smashed. Among those targeted was the home of Gusty Spence, founder of the modern-day UVF, whose family had lived in the area for generations. Shortly before 10 p.m., Adair was observed on the waste ground in a huddle with C Coy volunteers. He was clearly animated as he spoke to each member of the group, like a football coach motivating his team before a big match. Minutes later the young men raced off in different directions. A car screeched up, two masked men threw themselves into the back seat and several weapons, including an automatic rifle, were passed in. Adair looked pensive as they drove away. Two minutes later, the rattle of automatic gunfire again filled the air. Delighted UDA supporters, who had lingered after most of the crowds had gone, broke into raucous applause, whooping and cheering. Adair, who was ecstatic, ran among them like a hyperactive child and jumped up and down impersonating an ape. The reason for his joy

227

was that C Coy had just attacked the Rex Bar for the second time that day, raking it with gunfire in a drive-by shooting. Three men were injured as they left the bar.

Adair was jubilant. In a gesture designed to let his enemies know he was enjoying himself, he immediately gave the order for a fireworks display to begin, signalling the start of an open-air rave-style disco. Later that night he climbed on to the stage again and promised that the lower Shankill would be a 'UFF state by Christmas'. In addition to Gusty Spence, some thirty families were forced to leave the area over the next two days. Thanks to Adair's uncontrollable lust for power, he had sparked a mass exodus that would see up to 200 families leave the Shankill over the coming weeks and lead to a permanent change in the area's social fabric.

Two days later, on Monday, 21 August, the UVF hit back. Jackie Coulter, a 46-year-old father of four and commander of the UDA's illustriously titled 'C3A Commandos', died in a hail of gunfire as he sat in a Range Rover driven by his friend, Bobby Mahood. Shortly after 12.30 p.m. a lone gunman walked out of an alley and fired through the window of the car as it was pulled up outside a betting shop on the Crumlin Road. Coulter died instantly, while 48-year-old Mahood, a local publican, was critically wounded after being hit in the stomach. He died later in hospital. Coulter was one of Adair's drivers, while Mahood, a former UVF man, was known to be opposed to that group's support for the peace process. His brother Jackie had resigned from the Progressive Unionist Party, the UVF's political wing, because of its support for the Belfast Agreement and had survived several UVF murder attempts. Following the double murder, British troops were ordered back onto the streets of Belfast for the first time in two years. On the Shankill the tension was palpable. Within the space of 48 hours there were around a dozen shootings, including one on the offices of the UDA-linked UDP. Almost immediately, the UDA retaliated by setting fire to the PUP's offices. All bus services were suspended on the Shankill as the road, which had refused to be bowed even at the height of the IRA's campaign, was reduced to a ghost town.

Adair demanded immediate revenge. The man he wanted dead was Billy Hutchinson, a former UVF prisoner and now a member of Northern Ireland's power-sharing assembly. Adair hated him because he was clever and articulate. As Hutchinson discussed the feud on television, Adair picked up the phone and rang B Coy's Jim Spence. Unbeknownst to Adair, Spence's telephone was tapped and Special Branch heard every word.

THE BOSS

According to a senior Special Branch officer, 'Hutchinson was on TV and Adair got on the phone to Spence and said, "Shoot the fucker, go and shoot him. See where he is? Go out and shoot him right now." And Spence would say, "Aye, so I will." He was playing along with Johnny and saying he would do things, though really he wanted nothing to do with it.' To police there was little doubt that the main driving force behind the outbreak of violence was Adair. As they worried about what he would do next, Special Branch even considered planting listening devices on the waste ground in the lower Shankill, where Adair was regularly observed plotting with his men.

Adair was convinced that he could destroy the UVF on the Shankill, where he would use his power to achieve his dream of becoming Northern Ireland's supreme loyalist figurehead. According to the Special Branch officer, who monitored him for several years, 'He thought the lower Shankill was the centre of the universe, that the sun and everything else, the wee satellites, all went around it.' But his lust for power came at a price, as he soon discovered. The fight with the UVF split Adair's wider family, particularly on his mother's side. It also increased the chances of Adair being assassinated and put a limit on the places he could safely go. In one example of this, he was forced to abandon his plan to attend a skinheads' reunion party in a bar known as a popular UVF haunt. Luckily for Adair, as the threat on his life increased, the security forces stepped in.

Peter Mandelson, who had taken over from Mo Mowlam as Northern Ireland Secretary in October 1999, was in his London office being briefed on the weekend's events when news of the murder of Mahood and Coulter came through. For now the shooting war appeared to be isolated to west Belfast, with Adair's fellow brigadiers showing no interest in becoming involved. But it was only a matter of time before the dispute started to spread. As police officers assembled a dossier on Adair's activities at the RUC's headquarters in east Belfast, Sir Ronnie Flanagan, the RUC Chief Constable, cut short a holiday in South Africa to return to Belfast. Early on Tuesday morning, Colin Cramphorn, the Deputy Chief Constable, and Freddie Hall, the head of Special Branch, delivered the file to the Secretary of State at Hillsborough Castle. As well as chronicling his role in the weekend's mayhem, it presented other evidence of Adair's continued involvement in terrorism. It accused him of orchestrating attacks across the peaceline and stated that on one occasion in August he and a C Coy colleague had been messing around with a pipe bomb when it exploded. (Adair claimed the IRA had thrown the device at him, declaring, 'They

229

came from behind like cowards, as they always do.') It noted his growing closeness to the LVF and said he had been seeking to acquire weapons, controlled a lucrative drugs empire and had personally taken part in terrorist 'shows of strength' on the Shankill. As far as Mandelson was concerned, the dossier more than justified a decision to revoke Adair's early release licence and send him back to jail.

At 8 p.m. on Tuesday night, 22 August 2000, the arrest plan was put into operation. Adair was seized at a police checkpoint on the Shankill Road, some 300 yards from his house. He was in his Vauxhall Cavalier with Winkie Dodds when four armoured personnel carriers boxed him in and police in riot gear pulled him from the car. 'I think you've saved my life,' he said to the police officers, before telling Winkie to 'tell the lads I'll see them soon'. Fifteen minutes later, after being bundled into an armoured Land-Rover and whisked to a waiting helicopter, he was behind bars in Maghaberry Prison, 15 miles south of Belfast. Just 11 months after his triumphant release from the Maze, his quest to become loyalism's commander-in-chief lay in tatters.

With or without Adair, his C Coy colleagues were intent on revenge. The following day, as Adair was still going through the admittance procedures at Maghaberry, C Coy shot dead 22-year-old Samuel Rocket at his girlfriend's home in the Oldpark. From a well-known UVF family, he had just made a cup of tea and was sitting down to watch television when two masked gunmen burst in and gunned him down. It was the last fatality of the summer, and with Adair in jail there were rising hopes that the feud could be resolved. Then, on 28 October, it suddenly spread to north Belfast. David Greer, a 21-year-old UDA member, was murdered after a confrontation with UVF members in Tigers Bay. Three days later, on 31 October, Bertie Rice, a 63-year-old who had once been a senior UVF figure but was now a voluntary worker in Billy Hutchinson's office, was shot dead in reprisal. At 6.30 p.m. the same day, four UVF gunmen smashed their way into the Newtownabbey home of Tommy English, a 39-year-old former UDP member, and killed him as his children enjoyed a Halloween party. The next day, Mark Quail, a 26-year-old UVF man and father of two, was shot dead by the UDA in his flat on the Rathcoole estate. The murder brought to seven the number of victims since the feud erupted in August.

One death that was not linked to the feud, though at first it appeared to be, was that of Stevie 'Top Gun' McKeag, Adair's most prolific assassin. He was found dead at his home in Florence Court in the lower Shankill on

THE BOSS

Sunday, 24 September. Wearing nothing but his boxer shorts, and with the bath still running, the 30-year-old was found face down on the floor of an upstairs bedroom. His face and body were badly bruised and the house appeared to have been ransacked. A crossbow bolt, fired from inside the house, was sticking half-way out of a window. For more than a year, McKeag, the father of four children, had been on medication following a serious motorbike accident that left him in intensive care for several days. According to 'Pete', one of his closest friends, the first thing he did on regaining consciousness was signal to a nurse that he wanted a piece of paper. 'Stevie had been lying in hospital for days after the accident. He couldn't talk so the nurse gave him a pen and paper and the first thing he wrote was "Up the UDA".'

When he finally checked out of hospital, McKeag was a pale shadow of his former self. His injuries, which included a collapsed lung and damage to his stomach, were so severe that his girlfriend, Tracey Coulter, had to nurse him around the clock. He was forced to endure the indignity of urinating into a plastic catheter bag, which Coulter regularly changed for him. As he slowly recovered, McKeag continued to suffer excruciating pain and he started to abandon his medicine and turn to cocaine. As a C Coy drug dealer he had made so much money that he did not know what to spend it on, buying a caravan, a jet ski and even installing state-of-the art music mixing decks in his bedroom. But he had always been careful not to get hooked on hard drugs. Now, with his injuries causing him constant torment, he threw caution to the wind.

But even though his friends admit that his coke habit was becoming dangerous, the circumstances surrounding his death were so bizarre that many are convinced foul play was involved. The story of the final few months of his life is a sordid combination of sex and jealousy. Ever since he had known Adair, McKeag had worshipped him. Although his commander took pleasure in McKeag's friendship, deep down he envied his success as a gunman. According to Winkie Dodds, the three of them were at an LVF dinner in Lurgan shortly after Adair's release from jail when his feelings bubbled to the surface. 'They called Johnny up on to the stage and he got a plaque and there was lots of cheering,' said Winkie. 'Then the roof nearly came off when Stevie got called up – there was this look on Johnny's face, well, his face just dropped, you could see how he felt.'

Several C Coy veterans, Dodds among them, believe that Adair made his reputation on the strength of McKeag's killing achievements in the early

1990s, and that he was painfully aware of this. 'He made all the wee lads believe he was this hero that he wasn't,' said Winkie. 'Stevie McKeag gave Johnny Adair his name – he was the one who did it all.' When Adair came out of jail, the last thing he wanted was a reminder that he was not the legend he believed he was, and so long as McKeag was around this was always going to be the case. In the last few months of his life the pair fell out badly. Adair arranged for McKeag to be beaten after Jackie Coulter, Tracey's father, complained to him that Stevie had been hitting his daughter. According to one friend: 'Stevie was given a big beating. They took him out onto the green at the back of Florence Court and they beat him and told him he was out [of C Coy]. He spent a lot of time after that down at his caravan in Millisle. He came looking for me three weeks before he died. He was crying – he thought the world of Johnny. He was in tears. I says to him, "Go and speak to the Wee Man face to face, try and sort it out between you."'

The situation became further complicated when Adair started sleeping with Tracey Coulter. Adair and McKeag had a heated confrontation and both threatened to kill each other. 'Stevie threatened to put one in Johnny's nut when Winkie, Donald and a few others were there,' the friend recalled. 'Johnny said, "I'm putting one in your head," and Stevie said, "You'd better make it good 'cause I'm going to get you first."'

By the time of McKeag's death, the old friendship they had enjoyed in the early 1990s had vanished completely. His death remains shrouded in mystery, but some of his closest friends believe that Adair ordered it. They believe McKeag fired a cross-bow at his attackers after they entered his house and that the bruises to his face and body were sustained as they rammed cocaine down his throat. Others dismiss this as far-fetched and say that Stevie received the bruises from a beating earlier that week. They say he was probably just high, and maybe hallucinating, when he fired his cross-bow. Only his attackers and Johnny Adair know the truth.

14. Boss of Bosses

'He said he had 70 men up there [in mid-Ulster]. We said, "You can't have," and he said, "No disrespect to you, Jackie, but they want me as their brigadier."' – *Jackie McDonald, UDA 'brigadier' for south Belfast*

IT WAS STILL DARK AS BILLY STOBIE WALKED ALONG THE FROST-COVERED PATH to his car. As he pulled up his jacket to keep out the freezing cold, he thought about all the things he was going to do now the trauma of the last two and a half years was over. A fortnight earlier he had walked free from court when the case against him, accusing him of aiding and abetting the 1989 killing of Pat Finucane, collapsed. Despite the controversy it had caused, he had discussed the situation with his girlfriend Lorraine and they had decided to stay put in west Belfast. He had even been assured by his former comrades there was no threat against him and he was safe to keep living in the Glencairn estate at the top of the Shankill. As he reached into his pocket for the car keys, he gave a small sigh of relief. It had been a hard slog, but everything had worked out OK.

It was not until it was too late that Stobie saw the hooded figure striding towards him. At 6.15 a.m. on Wednesday, 12 December 2001, Lorraine Graham was getting ready for him to drive her to work when she heard three shots ring out. She knew instantly it was her Billy. As she rushed outside she saw him on the ground, a dark pool of blood under his bald head. Later that day the Red Hand Defenders said that it had killed Stobie because he had committed 'crimes against the loyalist community'. It was not a reference to his self-confessed role as a Special Branch agent (this was excusable), but rather his support for a public inquiry into the Finucane murder. Calling for an investigation into the activities of his former comrades was a step too far. Standing on the steps of Belfast Crown Court on his 51st birthday, Stobie had spoken of his joy at being free but also his belief that he was a pawn in a bigger conspiracy. Stating that the Finucane family 'deserves a proper inquiry', he added, 'I back that call for an inquiry. With this case at an end I can see no reason why that cannot happen immediately.'

Johnny Adair had personally given his blessing to Stobie's murder. Ever since his bungled attempt to kill him nine years earlier Adair had been patiently waiting for an excuse to have him shot dead. So long as Stobie was alive he was an unwelcome reminder of his failure to perform the simplest of executions. But Adair had also been the one who lied to Stobie by sending word from prison that he was still safe on the Shankill. 'What he [Stobie] was told was that so long as he didn't involve other UDA members, he would be safe,' said a senior Special Branch source. 'He was asked on the steps of the court if he thought there should be a public inquiry and he said yes. As soon as he did that all bets were off. That night the UDA decided to kill him. We went out the night we got the intelligence and warned him. He again contacted Adair and was given assurances by Adair and White that he'd be okay and he was killed two days later.'

Adair was delighted by the murder, though it was by no means the only occasion on which he continued to direct terrorism from inside Maghaberry Prison. On 4 October 2000, Johnston Brown and his wife Rebecca were scouring the Internet at home when they heard a noise at their front door. Assuming it was his father-in-law returning to collect something, Jonty went to reset the house's security system but was stopped in his tracks when the building shook with the force of an enormous explosion. A firebomb, consisting of explosives and petrol mixed with sugar, had gone off in the porch. 'Our lives were saved because the bomber was unable to get the device through the letter box, which had been sealed during a security review of the house. Otherwise we would have been incinerated,' he recalled. 'A fireball would have raced through the house and the sugar would have made sure the petrol found a surface to stick to. In the end the heat of the firebomb was so intense that it melted the front door frame and even the tarmac on the driveway.'

The murder attempt had been ordered by Adair, who had never forgiven the detective for his part in sending him to jail in 1995. He also believed, wrongly as it turned out, that Jonty had had a hand in his re-arrest. 'In August 2000, I had been sent to Tennent Street police station in the Shankill to assist with some inquiries,' said Jonty. 'This had nothing to do with Adair. But we later learned that I had been spotted going in and out of the station by the man in charge of the UDA's B Coy. He informed Adair, who took the view that I was part and parcel of his re-arrest. I had nothing to do with it, but he still ordered the attack on my home and my family.'

Despite these distractions, Adair's second big stint in prison was no easier than his first. The fact that Maghaberry was integrated – meaning loyalists and republicans had to share facilities with each other as well as with 'ordinary decent criminals' (ODCs) – deprived him of the authority he had enjoyed in the Maze. He felt insulted that a man of his stature had to share his space with rapists, thieves and conmen. His encounter with one particular ODC, Stephen McEntee, was particularly galling. In April 2001, McEntee, a 22-year-old fraudster who hailed from the Catholic Short Strand in east Belfast, was allocated the cell opposite Adair. He remembers clearly the day he moved in: 'I'll never forget it until the day I die. There standing straight in front of me was Johnny "Mad Dog" Adair, and what was he doing? He was mopping the floor. He was wearing a tight T-shirt to show off his muscles and a pair of tight lycra shorts. I nearly fell about laughing. I thought to myself, "Is this really Johnny Adair, the big-time UFF boss, or is it some wee boy who looks like him?"'

Adair was the most senior grade of prisoner, earning £15 a week on Maghaberry's 'enhanced' regime. As the wing orderly, his tasks included brushing and mopping floors and cleaning the kitchen and showers. A week after his arrival, McEntee was still adjusting to life behind bars when he went to the kitchen to make himself a snack. He was eating a slice of toast when Adair appeared at the door: 'He [Adair] looked at the toaster and the crumbs on the work top and said to me, "Wipe that!" It was the first time he had spoken to me. I told him to fuck off. I said that cleaning the kitchen was the orderly's job and Adair said he was the orderly and he was telling me to clean the mess up. Once again I told him to fuck off. Adair then asked me if I was a taig. I replied that I was a Catholic and that I was proud of my religion. I kept him in a fixed stare and then he said, "I'm Johnny Adair. I'll close that door and kick you up and down this kitchen." "Go ahead, Johnny," I said. Nothing happened and he walked out of the kitchen.'

McEntee's relations with Adair went from bad to worse when, a few days later, he turned down the loyalist's offer of money to help him murder Sinn Fein's Gerry Kelly. McEntee also made it clear that he was aware of the drug-dealing network Adair was running inside the jail. According to one friend familiar with the situation, 'All the prisoners went to church on a Sunday and that's when the drugs and money were passed over. All the transactions were done in church. Gina always visited Johnny on a Sunday and she would take the baby with her. She would put the money down the child's nappy and take it out. I thought it was a total disgrace. But she was also taking the drugs into the jail the same way, down Jay's nappy.'

Adair was so astounded that a small-time crook like McEntee had dared to stand up to him that he decided to make an example of him. One day, using his forefinger and thumb to make the shape of a gun, he pointed to his temple and shouted to the fraudster, 'You'll get that!' On 3 January 2002, McEntee was listening to the late-night news on the radio when a pipe bomb attack was reported on a house in Manor Street in north Belfast. His stomach turned. 'When the word came back that the attack had been at my house, I felt sick in the pit of my stomach,' he said. 'But I also knew that Johnny Adair had ordered his men to do it.' The attack, just the other side of the Oldpark peaceline, came disturbingly close to killing McEntee's baby son, Sean. As the bomb was hurled through the window he was struck above the eye by a piece of shrapnel. Doctors said it was a miracle that he had survived the blast at all.

On 15 May 2002, after 21 months in Maghaberry, Adair was released for a second time. As he jumped out of a white prison van, he punched the air in celebration and shouted the only Latin words he had ever known, '*Quis Separabit*'. Over the next eight months the UDA's slogan, meaning 'Who Will Come Between Us?', would become a bad joke. But for now there was unrestrained jubilation as up to 300 supporters cheered and let off fireworks. Before returning to a triumphant reception outside his home in Boundary Way, where the bottles of champagne were decorated with his picture, he was welcomed by his fellow brigadiers. The media captured the show of unity as Jackie McDonald and his colleagues gathered round him to shake his hand. What reporters did not know, however, was that most had been reluctant to go. Looking back, Billy 'the Mexican' McFarland of north Antrim and Derry explained: 'I regret going to meet him. John White begged all the brigadiers to come to the jail to meet him coming out. I said I didn't want to go, but then I said that if all the other brigadiers were going then I would go as well. In the end the five brigadiers went and out of those five, no one wanted to shake hands with him. White played the line that it would be a show of unity. There had been stories in the papers about splits in the UDA and White argued that this would show unity.'

Even though McDonald had reservations about Adair, he believed he deserved the opportunity of a fresh start. He said: 'We were trying to let everyone see the wee man was welcomed back into the organisation. People look at it now and reflect and say I was the first over to shake hands with him and then look at the way things ended up. But we gave him a chance to get back in and just be part of the thing. We kept saying to him, "Don't try to be it, just be part of it." But before too long he was back to his old ways. It was the Johnny Adair show.'

Within weeks, Adair and White were again contriving to persuade the world that the Shankill loyalist was a changed man. He took up a £16,500 post as a prisoners' welfare coordinator, a position funded by the British taxpayer. When news of his job emerged, the Northern Ireland Office faced a storm of protest and insisted Adair had only been employed for five weeks. Adair was defiant. 'For years people were complaining, asking what I did to earn money and now they can see that I'm legitimately employed and pay taxes just like everyone else,' he said. 'People complain no matter what I do.'

Throughout the summer he continued to pretend that his interests now lay in community work and politics. Although the majority of the political initiatives came from White, Adair willingly went along with them. Although some observers have suggested he may have been manipulated by White, all the evidence suggests that he knew exactly what he was getting into. 'It was a relationship where they both realised they needed each other,' said one senior police officer. 'Adair needed White to give him some semblance of credibility, precisely because White was the softer face of loyalist terrorism. White needed Adair because he was Johnny Adair. He had power.'

On 2 July, a snappily dressed Adair was part of a loyalist delegation that met John Reid, Tony Blair's third appointment as Northern Ireland Secretary. 'Has the man from the UDA become the Man at C&A?' asked a Sunday newspaper as it pored over his costume. In fact Adair was considerably more up-market. As he stepped into the East Belfast Mission Hall for the meeting he was wearing a pinstriped Hugo Boss suit, a yellow tie with a fashionably large knot, and a baby-blue shirt. He looked every inch the stylish mafia boss. Only Jim Gray, the UDA's brigadier in east

Belfast, and Andre Shoukri, its new leader in the north of the city, came close to him in the dress stakes. As one of those present recalled, 'Jim Gray was wearing some bright Caribbean shirt and Shoukri and Adair were in city suits, but the rest were in drinking-club garb.' The meeting, which took place under the mantle of the newly formed Loyalist Commission, lasted two and a half hours as Dr Reid urged the loyalists to abandon violence for good. He took off his jacket and sat on a table in front of around 60 members of the Commission – Protestant churchmen, community workers and paramilitaries – who sat before him in the shape of a fan. Amid a backdrop of rising sectarian violence in east Belfast, he said that all sides – republicans and loyalists – had to work to stop the clashes. 'He played the crowd without being patronising. I talked to people and they thought it went well,' said one official. 'The questions were very sensible and John Reid gave them very frank answers. They were telling him what their position was and seeking assurances.'

It was the second time Adair had met a serving Secretary of State. But just like the previous occasion, when he had met Mo Mowlam inside the Maze, he never opened his mouth. Jackie McDonald, who was among those at the meeting, recalled, 'Johnny didn't say anything, not one word. After it was all over John Reid pointed outside and said, "I'll go out and talk to the reporters now – there's about 40 cameramen out there, but if you want to go for a cup of tea, go in that way. The cameras are that way." So myself and others headed for the tea, but of course Johnny headed for the cameras.' Reid was well aware of the media interest in Adair but refused to comment on his contribution to the talks. The Glaswegian left a lasting impression on many of those who met him, including McDonald. The south Belfast brigadier said he enjoyed chatting to the Secretary of State over a cup of coffee. 'He was a very plausible wee man. He says, "I'm just a wee taig from Glasgow," and I said to him, "Aye, you are like fuck!"'

But probably the most memorable image of the afternoon came as Rev. Mervyn Gibson, the Commission's chairman, closed the meeting with a prayer. 'Every head was bowed, they were all locked in prayer,' said one participant. 'It was like Sunday School. I looked up and saw the top of Johnny Adair's bald head shining back at me. It was one of life's experiences.'

Sectarian tensions had been high since June 2001, when Protestant residents in north Belfast began a 12-week picket of Catholic schoolgirls and their parents as they walked up the Ardoyne Road to the Holy Cross

Primary School. Although both his brother, Archie, and his friend, Gary 'Smickers' Smith, were sent to jail over the trouble at Holy Cross, Adair did not support the protest and saw it as a public relations disaster for loyalism. On his release from jail he used his influence to make sure it did not blow up again. On the surface, he was trying to present himself as a mature peacemaker trying to build bridges to his old enemies. With Adair's blessing, John White and two fellow loyalist politicians took part in a meeting designed to portray the Shankill UDA as progressive and non-sectarian. In June, Sinn Fein's Alex Maskey, who Adair had repeatedly tried to kill in the early 1990s, made history by becoming the first republican to be elected Lord Mayor of Belfast. After several gestures reaching out to Unionists, he made another on 12 August when he met White and two political colleagues, Davy Mahood and Frank McCoubrey, in his private parlour at Belfast City Hall. During more than two hours of talks the men discussed the need to tackle sectarianism and interface violence. Describing the talks as 'frank' but 'positive', White said afterwards, 'We are prepared to play our part in any initiative aimed at defeating sectarianism. We are eight years into a peace process and sectarianism is as bad as ever.'

The meeting was a turning point for the UDA's public image, but it caused enormous strife inside the organisation. The UDA leadership told White and Adair before the meeting that it was unacceptable. According to Jackie McDonald, many rank-and-file UDA members saw it as a step too far. 'The meeting with Maskey was specifically against the wishes of the inner council,' he said. 'Johnny and John White were told in no uncertain terms that it wasn't to happen. But they just went ahead and did it and I said to them, "I know what's coming next here." I said, "You'll be standing in north Belfast getting your photo taken with Gerry Kelly." It never got to that stage, but that's where they were heading.' At the next meeting of the inner council White and Adair were taken to task by their fellow brigadiers, but White claimed he had met Maskey in a personal capacity and not as a UDA man. 'John White said he went just as John White the person,' said McDonald. 'I said, "You can't be John White the person. You can't say I'm not a UDA man today." He was told straight, he shouldn't have fucking done it. He said we weren't showing leadership, but he should have been sacked on the spot.'

By now Adair was so obsessed by the media that he was starting to irritate even his closest friends. There was nothing he loved more than being on television. Maureen Dodds, Winkie's wife, recalls, 'Any time he was on TV no one was allowed to speak. He used to record all his TV appearances and just sit on the edge of the table playing the video over and over again.' Even before Adair's release from jail, White was briefing reporters that his colleague was considering standing in elections for the Stormont assembly. Like most of their ideas, it was little more than a publicity stunt designed to boost Adair's profile and flatter his ego.

Although the seeds of Adair's downfall were already visible by the time he went to jail in August 2000, the real turning point came on 10 June 2002. Adair, who had just returned from a beach holiday in Benidorm, was sitting in his living room with the LVF's Jackie Mahood when he heard about the death in jail of Mark 'Swinger' Fulton. His friend and fellow drug dealer, who was on remand in Maghaberry, had been discovered in his cell with a leather belt around his neck. The fact that he was lying on his bed when he died led to lurid speculation that he had been engaged in an act of auto-erotic asphyxiation, starving the oxygen supply to the brain to enhance and prolong orgasm. Whatever the cause of death, Fulton was genuinely suicidal. He had never fully recovered since the murder in 1997 of Billy Wright, his LVF commander and close friend, while he was also convinced that he was dying of stomach cancer. Although he had taken over as leader of the renegade terrorist group, in the weeks before his death his colleagues had become increasingly concerned about his mental stability and it was even reported that he had been stood down.

While Adair was upset at his friend's death, he also saw it as an opportunity. According to one close associate, 'I was talking to Swinger four months before he died and that was the first time I realised what Johnny was up to with the LVF. Johnny was running up and down to Portadown and he would have gone to all these different dos. So my reckoning was that he was definitely working deals with them on the drugs. And I think what happened was that when Swinger died, Johnny saw that as his move to take over the whole patch and that's exactly what he was doing.'

The strength of Adair's relationship with the LVF was confirmed on Sunday, 21 July 2002, when Gerard Lawlor, a 19-year-old Catholic, was shot dead. The murder followed the shooting of Mark 'Mousey' Blaney, a 19-year-old Protestant, earlier that evening. Although Blaney was not killed, the fact that he was shot in broad daylight across the Ardoyne peaceline was seen as a deliberate republican provocation. Within two hours, teams from C Coy and the UDA in north Belfast were dispatched to kill a random Catholic, shooting and injuring a man in the Oldpark and opening fire without success on the Ligoniel Road. Shortly after midnight, Gerard Lawlor was walking home from a pub on the Antrim Road when a motorbike pulled alongside him and a gunman shot him twice in the back with a .38 revolver. Summoning its favourite choice of words, the UFF said the killing was a 'measured military response' and warned of 'further military action'. The credit for the operation went to north Belfast, though in reality the murder was a 'help-me-out' carried out by Adair's friends in the LVF.

Adair had called in a favour from the LVF because he wanted to impress Andre Khaled Shoukri, who in June had replaced Jimbo 'Bacardi Brigadier' Simpson as the UDA's leader in north Belfast. One of three brothers with an Egyptian father and a Northern Irish mother, Shoukri was an unusual candidate for a hardline Protestant terrorist. He and his brothers were brought up in the Coptic Christian faith of their father and attended Lagan College in east Belfast, an integrated school dedicated to improving understanding between Catholics and Protestants. Six feet tall and with natural good looks, Shoukri had the build of a professional football player and briefly tried his hand as a male model at the aptly named Pharaohs International Modelling Agency in Templepatrick, Co. Antrim. However, going straight was never going to sustain the sort of lifestyle he had envisaged for himself. While still in their teens, Andre and his elder brother Ihab joined the UDA's K Coy in their home territory of the Westland estate in north Belfast. At first glance it seemed a strange decision for the simple reason that the UDA is not known for its racial tolerance; indeed, before long their colleagues had dubbed them 'the Pakis'. However, the pair's motivation was money. At the age of just 20, Andre Shoukri was jailed for eight months for malicious wounding after knocking to the ground the Dublin tennis ace Gareth Parker. The 23-year-old was run over and killed seconds later by a passing car. While on bail Shoukri was caught attempting to smuggle cigarettes into Northern Ireland and was jailed for three months. Two years later he was again back behind bars, this time with his brother Ihab, after demanding protection money from a café owner.

While in jail, the Shoukris became friendly with Adair, helping to extend his influence in prison and dealing drugs on his behalf. After their release, they formed an informal business alliance with Moe Courtney, Gary 'Smickers' Smith, William 'Muggsy' Mullan and Alan McClean, commander of C9 and Adair's welfare officer. They traded drugs and took over the running of a brothel on the outskirts of north Belfast, which earned them each in excess of £500 per week. When Adair was released from prison he immediately set about installing Andre Shoukri as brigadier in north Belfast, where Jimbo Simpson was becoming increasingly difficult to deal with on account of his four-day drinking binges. After testing the opinion of UDA commanders across north Belfast, Shoukri decided that the time was right to move and borrowed several guns from Adair to make his point. The takeover was surprisingly easy: two major drug dealers were stripped of their merchandise and beaten, while Simpson, who in reality was relieved to be going, stood down without a shot being fired. At 25, Shoukri became the UDA's youngest ever brigadier and a welcome new ally for Adair on the inner council.

On the lower Shankill locals began to notice a change in Adair during the summer of 2002. Although he had always been an obsessive cleaner, he became increasingly fanatical about making sure the area was tidy in case television crews came up to film. According to Maureen Dodds: 'He had Belfast City Council tortured about it, always on the phone demanding that the wee cleaning cart with the brushes was sent up to sweep the place. When the cart arrived, Johnny was out on the street ordering everyone to move their cars to let the man drive it into every corner. I'm surprised nobody ever touched for him [tried to assassinate him] on a Sunday night. Every Sunday night without fail he would have taken everybody's bins out in Boundary Way, took them up the front, brushed up, hosed down and brought the bins back down the next morning. He used to fine you £1 in Boundary Way if you didn't keep your front clean.'

Adair was so obsessed with cleanliness that he refused to shower at home because he didn't want to mess up the bathroom. Instead he would wash in the local community centre, nicknamed the 'Big Brother House'. 'You'd see him crossing the square with his toilet bag and towel,' said Maureen. 'He'd always shower in the community house and him and Gina used to keep the kids' toys there so their own house wasn't untidy. He bought a sunbed but he didn't keep it in their house – that went in the Big Brother House as well along with his weights.'

By the summer it wasn't just the behaviour of Adair Snr that was attracting attention, but also Adair Jnr. To his father's growing anger, Jonathan Adair was rapidly gaining a reputation as a thug and a troublemaker. In June, his father's men beat him with baseball bats and iron bars after he broke into the home of an 84-year-old pensioner and stole her purse. In another incident, Adair himself gave his son a beating after he took his car without asking. In August, Adair had little choice but to consent to a more severe punishment after Jonathan hit a female shop assistant in a filling station on the Crumlin Road. Shortly before midnight on 7 August, 'Fat Jackie' Thompson, who as C Coy's 'Provost Marshal' was in charge of knee-cappings, dragged the 17-year-old into the middle of Florence Square in the lower Shankill and shot him twice in the legs with a 9mm pistol. As punishment-shooting victims go, Adair Jnr was lucky. By shooting the teenager through the calves, Thompson ensured that there would be no permanent damage to his legs. For anybody else the attack would almost certainly have been more severe.

'Johnny had no choice other than to give his blessing,' said one of Adair's friends. 'There was a whole catalogue of things. Johnny beat the fuck out of him a couple of times. When he got beaten with iron bars, he had to get a skin graft. He [Adair Snr] knew it was only a matter of time before he was going to get shot.' Although the shooting surprised few on the Shankill, to the outside world it was a harrowing insight into the brutality that ruled in Adair's mafia fiefdom. Even by the harsh standards of Belfast's battle-hardened ghettos, the idea of a father authorising a gun attack on his own son was savage. As Jonathan recovered the following day, Adair was indignant at suggestions that he had sanctioned the shooting or even pulled the trigger himself. 'What man in his own mind would do a thing like that to his own son?' he told one of the authors. 'Had I known prior to this, I would have had my son on a ferry away from here as fast as possible. I haven't got to the bottom of it and why this happened. I've tried to speak to my son but he's traumatised and drugged up with morphine.' Maintaining that he had 'no idea' why the shooting took place, he added, 'He's a quiet boy. He never smoked, never drank, he loved his wee pushbike. Every day he was down the job centre looking for work, he was always doing the old age pensioners' gardens for nothing.' In an extraordinary claim, he even said that his son was planning to join the Police Service of Northern Ireland.

Adair was fast becoming a caricature of the terrorist godfather, a cult figure whose face was rarely out of the newspapers. It was only a matter of time, it seemed, before his thirst for power and celebrity drove him into open confrontation with his fellow loyalists. In September it became clear that he was trying to promote a far closer alliance between C Coy and the LVF than the rest of the UDA had realised. On his release from jail the LVF had presented him with a commemorative mirror bearing the message,

'UFF–LVF Brothers In Arms', but it was now obvious that the links went far beyond personal friendship. To its astonishment, the UDA leadership learned that Adair viewed the mid-Ulster LVF as an extension of his paramilitary empire and claimed to have up to 70 men under his control there.

Jackie McDonald could hardly believe his ears when one of his commanders told him that the LVF in Lurgan, Co. Armagh, had asked to borrow some camouflage equipment on the basis that they were 'all part of the same organisation now'. McDonald, whose south Belfast brigade stretches into mid-Ulster, was determined to confront Adair. He drew up a list of LVF figures in mid-Ulster and went straight to the Shankill to ask Adair about their relationship with C Coy. 'I got half a dozen names and went to see him up the Shankill, myself and another fella,' he recalled. 'We challenged him about these people who now said they were part of the west Belfast UDA, although they were in the south Belfast area. We said this can't be and he said he had 70 men up there. We said, "You can't have," and he said, "No disrespect to you, Jackie, but they want me as their brigadier." I said, "If they want you as their brigadier they should go and live on the Shankill Road, 'cause you're not living in south Belfast."'

The row with McDonald marked the beginning of a sharp deterioration in Adair's relations with his fellow brigadiers. McDonald, a convicted extortionist, was an old-style UDA boss in his early 50s whose views about running the organisation were dramatically different from Adair's. While Adair believed it needed a single charismatic leader (and that he was the man for the job), McDonald was convinced that the UDA's strength came from the fact that each brigade area was autonomous. Adair despised McDonald because he had been in prison during the early 1990s and had never taken part in the 'war'. In a rant from his prison cell, he described McDonald as a 'nothing and a nobody' who had 'never once been on the battlefield'. He told the authors, 'Use your contacts in the Branch – they're no idiots – to find out what Jackie McDonald and those others were doing back then and who were the true loyalists. Ask them what kind of a man this is. He's into fake clothes and fake perfumes and contraband cigarettes. That's what he's involved in.'

But it wasn't just McDonald whom Adair secretly loathed; it was all his fellow brigadiers with the exception of Shoukri. He saw Billy McFarland, of north Antrim and Derry, as a hillbilly, and John 'Grug' Gregg, of south-east Antrim, as a waster who had contributed nothing since shooting and failing to kill Gerry Adams 18 years earlier. Last but not least was Jim Gray of east Belfast, for whom Adair reserved special contempt. Gray played off a golf handicap of three and was a part-owner of the Avenue One Bar on the staunchly loyalist Newtownards Road. A flash dresser, he enjoyed the high life, eating and drinking in the best restaurants and bars and rubbing shoulders with Glasgow Rangers footballers during regular trips to Ibrox Park. His detractors dubbed Gray and his cohorts 'the Spice Boys', while at every opportunity Adair referred to him mockingly as 'Doris Day' because of his bleach-blond hair. He was also jealous of Gray's money: he and McDonald were believed by police to be the two wealthiest racketeers in Belfast.

The spark that set in motion Adair's showdown with his fellow commanders came on Friday, 13 September, when Stephen Warnock, a senior LVF drug dealer, was shot dead. He was killed as he sat in his BMW in Newtownards, Co. Down, with his three-year-old daughter. According to police sources, he was murdered because he had borrowed £10,000 from a local drug-dealing cartel and had refused to pay it back. A friend of Adair's from jail, the two had become increasingly close following the death of Mark 'Swinger' Fulton, triggering speculation that the Shankill godfather intended to install him as his leader in east Belfast in a new loyalist terror group. The LVF was stunned by Warnock's murder, and Adair was immediately convinced it had been carried out by the UDA on the orders of Jim Gray. Although press reports suggested the killing was the work of the UVF-linked Red Hand Commando, Adair's suspicions appeared to be confirmed when a man was abducted and questioned by the LVF in a shop in east Belfast. He told his interrogators that Gray was directly responsible for Warnock's murder. As far as Adair was concerned, it was all he needed to hear.

Three days after the shooting, Gray called at the home of one of Warnock's brothers in east Belfast to pay his respects to the murdered 35-year-old. He was leaving and about to get into his BMW when he heard a voice say, 'This is for Stephen.' As he turned to see who was speaking, a bullet pierced his cheek, shattering his jawbone and teeth before exiting the other side. Gray recoiled in agony, but he instantly knew that had he not turned his head he would have been dead. The assassin then turned his gun on Gray's UDA colleague who was about to get into the passenger seat. He lent across the car roof and pulled the trigger, but the gun jammed and Gray's friend took to his heels. Despite his injuries, Gray also had the presence of mind to run. After finally clearing his weapon, the gunman fired several more shots at the fleeing UDA men before disappearing into the night. With blood streaming from his face, Gray staggered to the nearby police training depot at Garnerville, where he received first aid from officers before being whisked away to the Ulster Hospital at Dundonald. He was lucky to survive the assassination bid, although he now faces an £11,000 dental bill to have his mouth rebuilt.

Gray's fellow UDA brigadiers were livid at the attempt on his life. But it was nothing compared to the anger they felt when they discovered that Adair, John White and Andre Shoukri planned to attend Warnock's funeral. McDonald thought it was a sick joke: 'I heard from a mate that Jim Gray was shot. I heard he was dead and then he wasn't and I didn't know what was happening. So I phoned John White and said, "What's happening?" He didn't sound at all surprised and he says, "We have a funeral to go to tomorrow," and I said, "How the fuck can you? Whoever shot Jim Gray will be at that funeral." This was on the phone about midnight that night, the night Jim was shot. I came over to east Belfast the next morning and they were on the phone to John White saying, "You can't go to the funeral." White was told Jim Gray specifically asked from his hospital bed that they didn't go. He said, "Well, we're going, do you want to have a meeting afterwards?" I said, "If you go to the funeral, there will be no meeting at all."'

Gray's colleagues were sure he had not been involved in Warnock's death. As they pieced together the events leading up to his attempted murder, they uncovered a disturbing piece of information. They learnt that Adair had been attending the wake shortly before Gray's arrival and had been moved to a neighbouring house where he was able to watch the shooting from a window. They believed Adair had deliberately encouraged the attack and had even told the LVF he would be able to sort out any trouble with the UDA following Gray's murder.

To the consternation of McDonald and the other brigadiers, Adair, White and Shoukri went ahead with their plan to attend Warnock's funeral. On Friday, 20 September, Adair was summoned to explain himself at an emergency meeting of the UDA's inner council in a community centre in south Belfast. The day of reckoning had at last arrived. In a gesture of defiance, Adair gave the go-ahead that morning for a joint UFF/LVF mural bearing the message, 'Brothers In Arms'. As he paced up and down the front room of his offices in Boundary Way, he was determined not to back down. He was furious that a group of middle-aged men who had done next to nothing during the early 1990s was about to sit in judgement over him. He could barely believe it had come to this: Johnny Adair, the loyalist hero who had brought the war to the IRA's front door, who had survived countless assassination attempts and a long stint in jail, was being ordered to explain his actions to the leadership of the Ulster Defence Association. As he became increasingly agitated, his mind churned through a range of possible scenarios but began to settle on one in particular. There was only one course of action, it seemed, that could salvage his authority and teach McDonald and his cronies a lesson.

As he prepared to travel across Belfast to the meeting in Sandy Row, a police listening device picked up the basic outline of Adair's plan. 'Adair had this idea to walk in and shoot them all,' said one Special Branch officer. 'Special Branch heard him discussing it. He was saying, "I'll just walk in there and shoot all those fuckers. I'll pull a gun on them and shoot them all."' This version of events is confirmed by one of Adair's closest advisers, who was in the office that morning: 'Everything blew up that day. I was in the house when he went ballistic. He was so berserk he punched a hole in the door downstairs. John White was trying to calm him down. He was saying, "It's all right, Johnny, calm down, calm down." But Johnny was saying, "I'm going to stiff every one, I'm going to stiff that big girl McDonald. I'm going to kill them before they kill me." John tried to calm him before the meeting but he couldn't get him calmed down.'

Realising what he had to do, Adair sent one of two young brothers to fetch him a pair of black leather gloves. 'I was there when he sent one of the wee lads out to get a pair of gloves, but they were too big so he sent him away to get another set. He wanted them nice and tight,' said the source. 'Then they went down to Sandy Row, carloads of them. Fat Jackie and Big Donald – the usual crew – were in charge of the men. They took a load of weapons down and had the men detailed to take over certain streets.'

As Adair arrived in a jeep with blacked-out windows, several dozen men from the UDA's other brigade areas were already waiting on nearby street corners. The police were also there in numbers, though they deliberately kept their distance. As Adair walked into the building he was accompanied by 'Fat Jackie' Thompson and James 'Sham' Millar, both of whom were armed. In the gents' toilet, Thompson pulled a 9mm chrome Ruger from under his jacket and handed it to Adair, who tucked it under his waistband and covered it with his fleece. He then walked into the meeting, making it painfully obvious that he had a gun. Seeing this, McDonald deliberately sat next to Adair, believing he could overpower him if he produced his weapon. McDonald was later told by another UDA man attending the meeting that Adair had warned him what to do if shooting started. 'If I pull this out, hit the deck,' Adair had said. As the meeting wore on, however, he realised that there were other guns in the room and that it would be madness to chance his arm. This was not the time or the place, and he knew there would soon be other opportunities to kill his old comrades. But the meeting, which lasted two hours, became increasingly heated as Adair continued to justify his allegations against Gray. According to McDonald: 'Johnny had this thing about east Belfast. The east Belfast thing had been ongoing for a long time. Even when Johnny was inside there was a problem and he kept talking about this criminal element. So right away when Stephen Warnock got shot, Johnny assumed they had something to do with it. It suited him to believe that and then he saw that as an opportunity. But the evidence produced against the east Belfast UDA was totally ridiculous. I said to him, "Would you like to get shot on that evidence?"' The meeting broke up abruptly after Adair received a call on his mobile phone. The mainstream UDA later discovered that the caller was a member of the LVF. Recalled McDonald: 'Johnny's mobile phone went. He was speaking to an LVF man and then he said, "I'll have to go." He and John White left and everyone else left at the same time.' All the brigadiers headed off, fearing that they could be ambushed by Adair and his men if they hung around.

As Adair and his C Coy minders drove away from Sandy Row it was clear that it was only a matter of time before the tensions inside the UDA erupted into a vicious shooting war. He had cooled down enough to stop him from pulling a gun, but he intended to make his old colleagues pay for challenging him. Within minutes of leaving the meeting he was kicking up a second storm. He went straight to Ballysillan in north Belfast where he told senior members of the LVF what had just happened. Unbeknownst to him, however, he was being monitored by a team from the mainstream UDA. They were one step ahead of him. 'We knew everything that happened,' said Billy 'the Mexican' McFarland, who believed that Adair's terrorist career was now finished. 'He walked straight into the LVF meeting and told them, "I've just met the puppets."'

15. Who Will Come Between Us?

'We were talking about going to Newcastle. Truesdale says, "Aye, Newcastle." Truesdale was leading the attack, but he didn't know a fuck where he was going. Nobody had a clue where to go or what to do.' – *James 'Sham' Millar*

JOHNNY ADAIR DIDN'T KNOW IT AT THE TIME, BUT WEDNESDAY, 25 SEPTEMBER 2002 was to be his last day as a member of the UDA. Another emergency brigadiers' meeting was called, but this time Adair and White were not invited. Although still badly wounded, Jim Gray signed himself out of hospital to attend the meeting, at a bar in east Belfast. Jackie McDonald says it was probably the most important, though shortest, inner council meeting in the organisation's history. There was only one item on the agenda: the dismissal of Johnny Adair as brigadier in west Belfast. In two minutes flat he was found guilty of treason. McDonald recalled, 'There was no other option for us but to dismiss him. He was involved in the attempted murder of two members. The reality is, Johnny Adair dismissed himself from the UDA.' A short time later the UDA issued a statement to the press. 'As a result of ongoing investigations, the present brigadier in west Belfast is no longer acceptable in our organisation,' it declared.

Ripping up the dismissal notice in front of television cameras, Adair told reporters, 'It's not worth the paper it's written on but you'd better ask the UDA what it's all about.' Two days later the UDA ejected White as well, saying it had no choice but to 'expel the former commander's close ally and media spokesperson'. Twelve years after seizing control of C Coy in a bloodless coup, everybody but Adair could see that the game was up. 'It didn't seem to sink in,' said Sham Millar. 'Johnny didn't seem to know the importance of what was happening. He was out, but he didn't accept it. He just sort of went, "Fuck them 'uns."' Even his young protégé, Andre Shoukri, had seen sense and decided to side with the mainstream brigadiers. Adair's only hope was that A and B companies would stick with him and that the UDA in west Belfast would remain defiant to the last.

Shortly before midnight on 4 October, Geoffrey 'the Greyhound' Gray, a 41-year-old LVF member, was blasted to death with a shotgun as he made his way home from a local pub. The killing, on Ravenhill Avenue in east Belfast, was the UFF's retaliation for the shooting of Jim Gray. Three days later, the LVF shot 22-year-old Alex McKinley, a Protestant with links to the UDA in east Belfast. He died of his wounds on 13 October. The following day the LVF held out the white flag, saying that it wanted to 'mediate a settlement' and 'get the UDA leadership to the table to talk'. Following intervention by Protestant clergymen, senior members of the LVF and UDA met on 18 October in a bid to reconcile their differences. After a flurry of meetings in early November, both sides agreed a truce. In a thinly veiled swipe at Adair, the LVF issued a statement admitting it had been wrong to blame Jim Gray for the murder of Stephen Warnock. 'It has now become obvious that erroneous/false information was furnished to both organisations, which resulted in this unfortunate conflict,' it said. It had cost three murders and seven attempted murders, but the feud with the LVF was over.

The stage was now set for the final confrontation, an all-out war between Adair and his old colleagues. On 1 November, in the first sign of the coming storm, Davy Mahood, one of Adair's political advisers who had tried to keep himself right with both camps, was shot in the legs behind a community centre in Ballysillan. In a statement read by Sammy Duddy, who had replaced Mahood as the group's spokesman in north Belfast, the UDA said the attack followed a four-month investigation into Mahood's activities. It blamed him for staging an attempt on his own life, which Mahood had claimed was carried out by republicans. Duddy, a former drag queen once known as 'Samantha', said that 'Mahood's life was spared, largely because of the intervention of the new regime'.

On 8 November, the UDA said that eight families had been attacked over the past two weeks and blamed Adair for the incidents. Calling on rank-

and-file members in west Belfast to walk away from their leader, it said, 'The loyalist people of west Belfast do not want this. The west Belfast UDA must take action to distance themselves from these individuals. They have caused enough suffering.' Not to be cowed into submission, Adair and White insisted that their support was as strong as ever and claimed that 2,000 west Belfast UDA men had turned out for the 2nd Battalion's Remembrance Sunday parade. They even claimed that they had formed three new units – one in north Co. Down, one in mid-Ulster and another in Scotland.

The build-up to a new feud began steadily over the next few weeks with a series of threats and attacks, including the shooting of Sammy Duddy's pet Chihuahua, Bambi. On the lower Shankill, Adair started to scent treachery everywhere. He turned on some of his oldest friends, including Alan McClean, his welfare officer and head of C9, who was driven off the Shankill. McClean was blamed for stealing C Coy money, though in reality Adair believed he was conspiring with the Shoukri brothers in north Belfast. But the clearest sign that Adair was losing the plot came when he fell out with his old friend and ally, Winkie Dodds. After learning that Winkie's brother-in-law, William 'Muggsy' Mullan, was still dealing drugs with the Shoukris, Adair went mad and ordered him to pay a fine of £10,000 or leave Northern Ireland. Mullan's family scraped together £7,000 and Winkie offered the payment to Adair, but he refused to accept and Mullan fled to England. After the parade on Remembrance Sunday, Winkie's brother Milton 'Doddsy' Dodds was standing next to some of Adair's colleagues at the bar when he asked them why they were giving his brother such a hard time. Donald Hodgen responded by hitting him, while later that night 'Fat Jackie' Thompson led a C Coy punishment squad to Milton's house where they broke down the front door and beat him with baseball bats. For Winkie and his wife it was the final straw. On 21 November, after living on the Shankill all their lives, they moved to the loyalist White City estate on the outskirts of north Belfast where they were given protection by the UDA's south-east Antrim brigade.

The defection of Winkie Dodds – a living legend in the eyes of many loyalists – should have been a wake-up call for Adair. But to his twisted mind it only hardened his belief that he was doing the right thing.

On 6 December, an incendiary device was found outside John White's luxury £300,000 home at Carrickfergus on the outskirts of Belfast. Two days later a sophisticated booby-trap bomb was discovered under the car of

John 'Grug' Gregg, the UDA's south-east Antrim brigadier. It was a revenge attack by C Coy, but with an extra twist: the device was said to have been made by the same LVF bomb maker responsible for the booby-trap that killed Catholic solicitor Rosemary Nelson in 1999. As far as the UDA was concerned, it was a declaration of war. Five nights later, 17 shots were fired at the Ballysillan home of C9's Ian Truesdale and his wife's barber shop on the Crumlin Road was destroyed by arsonists. Truesdale, whose wife had refused to pay £25 per week in protection money to the north Belfast UDA, immediately moved to the lower Shankill where Adair gave him £4,500 to help decorate his new home. Just a week before Christmas the stakes rose again. Adair himself was the intended target of two gunmen, who had planned to kill him as he dropped his 11-year-old daughter at school. Henry Smith, from the UDA in Rathcoole, and Daryl Coulter, from north Belfast, were arrested with an automatic pistol as they made their way across north Belfast on a motorbike.

By the middle of December, the UDA had launched a concerted propaganda campaign against Adair. It seized on the fact that he had briefly abandoned his beloved C Coy to spend a weekend with Gina in Lapland, a trip that did not go down well with ordinary volunteers in west Belfast. It also encouraged speculation that there was a £10,000 bounty on his head, to be doubled if he was killed by Christmas. Adair remained defiant. Wearing a black Diesel sweatshirt and surrounded by cheering young men in designer tracksuits, he told *The Observer*, 'The Adair family will have a normal family Christmas. I'm not going anywhere.' Exaggerating as always about the number of murder attempts he had survived, he went on, 'The IRA and INLA tried to kill me. I survived 15 murder bids and I have bullet fragments in my head and side, so I'm hardly worried about a couple of bully boys who sat on their hands and did nothing when loyalists from the west Belfast brigade were taking the war to the IRA.' In a direct reference to Gregg, he added caustically, 'If I was to wait for these people to do anything, I would die of old age.' It was the clearest indication to date that Adair saw the feud as a personal battle between himself and the 45-year-old south-east Antrim brigadier, who had consistently blocked his initiatives at inner council meetings and had been one of his harshest critics.

Despite two pipe bomb attacks on Gregg's house and a gun attack on the home of his friend, the loyalist councillor Tommy Kirkham, Christmas came and went without serious violence. All that changed at 7.30 a.m. on 27 December. Jonathan Stewart was standing chatting to a friend at a house party in Manor Street when a hooded gunman strode into the kitchen and shot him several times in the head and body. The 22-year-old was killed for the simple reason that he was a nephew of Alan McClean, who had sided with the mainstream UDA since being thrown off the Shankill. But in a cruel example of how paramilitary feuds could divide families, he was also the boyfriend of Ian Truesdale's 19-year-old daughter, Natalie. Her father almost certainly knew his killers.

It was not long before the UDA retaliated. Three days after Christmas, a decision was taken to execute Roy Green, a convicted drug dealer and the UDA's former military commander in the Donegall Road area of south Belfast. A close friend of Adair, Green believed he was playing a clever game, pretending to set him up while in reality keeping him briefed about the UDA's plans to kill him. He even agreed to lure Adair to the Village district of south Belfast and to murder him personally. He was lying through his teeth. As the UDA watched his movements, it became apparent that he was phoning Adair several times a day and sending him text messages saying where Jackie McDonald would be. He was also suspected of helping to set up Jonathan Stewart. Shortly before 7 p.m. on 2 January 2003, the 32-year-old was shot dead as he left the Kimberley Bar off the Ormeau Road. In a statement, the UDA apologised to the Green family for the execution, but said that he had been a 'double agent'. Among his 'acts of betrayal', it said that he had tipped off Adair about an intended attempt on his life. 'Green may as well have pulled the trigger himself,' it concluded.

On the morning of 8 January, a blast bomb exploded in the back yard of Adair's home, though it was not even loud enough to wake him. Branding his former cohorts 'criminals', Adair said, 'If they have something against me, bring it to me. I'll face them as individuals one on one, these five brigadiers at a place of their choice. What they are doing is cowardice.' Two days later Paul Murphy, the new Northern Ireland Secretary, decided that enough was enough. In a dossier broadly identical to the one presented to Peter Mandelson two and a half years earlier, he was shown police intelligence accusing Adair of continuing to direct acts of terrorism, involvement in drugs and extortion, membership of a banned organisation, and acquiring and distributing weapons. This time it had taken Adair a mere eight months to land himself back behind bars. Shortly after 5 p.m. on Friday, 10 January, he was arrested on Murphy's instructions at his home in Boundary Way. As he arrived at Maghaberry Prison, White protested that his friend was a 'peacemaker' who had done nothing to justify his re-arrest. 'Here we have a man who did not want to see any violence and who did not want to see anyone losing their lives,' he said. 'Yet we have these UDA brigadiers ordering the death of Johnny and myself and they are running around free. I think many loyalists will be very angry.'

With Adair back in jail, the security forces hoped that the worst of the feud was over. They were badly mistaken. At 10.10 p.m. on Saturday, 1 February 2003, John 'Grug' Gregg was sitting in a red Toyota taxi at traffic lights near Belfast docks after returning from a Rangers match in Glasgow. He was talking to his 18-year-old son, Stuart, who was also in the car, when it was suddenly rammed by another vehicle. The sound of crashing metal and automatic gunfire filled the night air as two gunmen concentrated a stream of bullets on the cab. Gregg died instantly when a bullet entered his brain, his bald head slumping to one side and his face covered in blood. Killed alongside him was Robert 'Rab' Carson, a 33-year-old UDA colleague. The taxi driver, who was also hit, was seriously injured. Gregg's son was unhurt.

By any standards it was a spectacular gangland 'hit', and Adair was delighted. Although the gunmen were two young volunteers in their early 20s, the planning had been done by the old Dream Team of the early 1990s. It was the work of 'Fat Jackie' Thompson, who had taken over as brigadier, and Sam 'Skelly' McCrory, who had returned from Scotland to visit Adair in jail the previous day. The plan had been meticulously prepared. C Coy had intended to kill Gregg as he returned from a Rangers–Celtic match a few weeks earlier, but on that occasion he had felt too unsafe to go. This time, however, he had been confident about his safety. On the same day that Skelly was visiting Adair inside Maghaberry Prison, Gregg discussed a non-aggression pact with Mervyn Gibson, the Presbyterian minister who chaired the Loyalist Commission. The clergyman was hopeful that both sides were moving towards a truce. It was only when Gregg was already in Scotland that C Coy withdrew its support for a deal.

While Adair was celebrating in his prison cell, John White, who had personally blamed Gregg for the bomb attack on his house, pretended to be surprised. 'I felt shocked as I held the phone,' he said. 'Then I thought – well, he was planning my death, so the shock went. It was like a film – a gangster movie. What struck me was the recklessness of it: the hit. It was like they didn't care about getting caught. The main target was to get to Gregg and take him out, and getting away was secondary. It was a risky hit. Wide open. That's what happens when you're dealing with a team that has been involved in a war situation for years. The professionalism takes your breath away. Pure 100 per cent professional.'

While the UDA warned that the feud was about to go 'nuclear', it also started to receive signals that several leading UDA figures in west Belfast were unhappy. Although they had been reluctant to put their heads above the parapet, the murder of a brigadier put this in an entirely different perspective. Gregg was the most senior UDA figure to be murdered since John McMichael in 1987, but this time the killers were not republicans but loyalists from his own organisation. The cracks were slowly starting to appear. Adair had arrogantly believed his power base to be indestructible, but this time he had gone too far. By Tuesday, A and B companies, who had never supported him in the feud with the UVF, had defected. The UDA warned C Coy members that they had just 48 hours to follow suit. Setting a time limit of midnight on the day of Gregg's funeral, it warned, 'After this deadline, if they have not decided to move to A or B company, they will be identified as Red Hand Defenders and treated the same as the enemies of Ulster.' The same day the UDA stepped up the pressure by briefing reporters that it planned to mobilise up to 15,000 men for a march on the Shankill at the weekend.

First to jump ship was Moe Courtney. By the time Gregg was dead he had already defected, claiming in an interview that Adair was a 'treacherous bastard' who had tried to have him murdered. Courtney had been C Coy's military commander at the time of Jonathan Stewart's murder, though early in the new year he was stood down and replaced by Alan McCullough, a 21-year-old who until then had led Adair's youth wing, the Ulster Young Militants. Although Courtney claimed to have fallen out with his old friend over two weapons exchanges with the Continuity IRA, in fact their relations had been strained ever since a BBC *Panorama* programme in June 2002. The documentary, which produced new evidence about collusion in the murder of Pat Finucane, rekindled old speculation that B Coy's Jim Spence was a high-ranking police informer. For Courtney, who had long suspected Spence was a tout, it was enough to justify his murder. He wanted him killed but was overruled by Adair, who refused to believe that his old brigadier had spent all these years betraying him. But the real turning point in Moe's disintegrating friendship with Adair came when Winkie Dodds was driven off the Shankill. Courtney started to believe that his boss had become mentally unhinged. As Adair's paranoia intensified, he became convinced that Moe was plotting with the Shoukris and was trying to kill him. In January 2003, Adair sent a hit team to his house to murder him. He would almost certainly have been dead had it not been for a tip-off from Donald Hodgen, who was appalled by what was going on but was too loyal to Adair to challenge him.

By the evening of Wednesday, 5 February, Adair's empire was starting to fall apart. An eerie atmosphere settled over the Shankill as commanders from A and B companies met at the UDA's club in Heather Street to consider their position. They were joined by members of D Coy, former Shankill men who had moved to north Down but remained in close contact with Adair. As they were debating what to do, a steady trickle of volunteers from C Coy arrived at the club to turn themselves over. As the evening progressed, the trickle turned into a deluge. UDA members who had never addressed a meeting suddenly found voices to express their anger. Although they had initially gathered to discuss whether people wanted to move from the Shankill, the atmosphere suddenly changed. A television appearance by John White, in which he said he was 'indifferent' to Gregg's murder, tipped them over the edge. 'The plan was originally for up to 1,000 men to come into Johnny's area after Gregg's funeral, but what with the adrenalin and the drama, the defectors took it into their own hands,' said one UDA veteran.

Sensing that something was afoot, 'Fat Jackie' Thompson and Sham Millar slipped out of the lower Shankill estate and called to see William 'Woodsie' Woods, a member of Adair's robbery team who lived in nearby Manor Street. His wife explained that he had already cut his losses and left. They then contacted Ian Truesdale and John White only to discover that they too had bolted. In an instant, Thompson and Millar realised it was time to run. They telephoned home to say they were going to Scotland. Thompson told his wife to book furniture removal vans for the following day and said he would meet her coming off the boat. In a series of mobile phone calls, they arranged to meet some of their colleagues on the road to Larne, where they would catch a ferry to the mainland.

In the end, Adair's fiefdom collapsed with barely a shot fired in defence. Shortly after midnight, more than 100 men piled out of the Heather Street bar and into their cars. They drove straight to Boundary Way, where they started smashing windows and kicking in doors. Although most of his friends had already fled, a young C Coy volunteer involved in Gregg's murder was seized and badly beaten. He was about to be shoved into the boot of a car when a phalanx of police and Army Land-Rovers arrived, almost certainly saving his life. Within minutes, a convoy of seven cars carrying around twenty people, including Gina Adair and her four children, left the Shankill for the last time. They fled so quickly that Adair's two Alsatians, Rebel and Shane, were abandoned in the street. Under police escort, they headed to the cross-channel ferry terminal at Larne where they met up with White, Fat Jackie and the others.

As around 7,000 UDA supporters descended on the Rathcoole estate for Gregg's funeral the next day, the exiles were adjusting to a harsh new life outside Belfast. After arriving in the port of Cairnryan, Fat Jackie and White were questioned by Special Branch officers from the Dumfries and Galloway Police. The police had found £69,000 in cash in one of the cars, but although it belonged to Gina Adair, White claimed it. The money, in separate white envelopes containing £1,000 each, had been stuffed into a shoebox. Police also discovered that Fat Jackie was carrying £7,000 in cash, the takings of a sandwich shop he and Sham Millar had just opened and a fruit machine they had looted in the 'Big Brother House'. While Thompson and White were quizzed, the others set off up the coast in the direction of Ayr. They arranged to tie up with Skelly, who had promised them free food and shelter from Scottish loyalists sympathetic to their plight. But even this did not go according to plan, as Millar told one of the authors: 'Skelly kept phoning me and saying, "How many is there? Right, we'll need so many houses." He was acting as though he had houses and all for us. But then he said, "Youse would be better going into a hotel." So we went to the hotel in Ayr and Skelly just went about his business. He said he'd call back to see us. And then the fucking next minute, fellas I knew from years ago who had moved over to Scotland were calling round. It was supposed to be secret, but Skelly must have been phoning everyone in fucking Scotland. He landed down that night, but I never went anywhere near him. He didn't really take much to do with us. He wasn't a great help and I said, "I'm not staying anywhere round here with him like that there."'

Following their release later that afternoon, White and Thompson rejoined their colleagues. After a night in Ayr, the group reviewed its position. But without maps and very little money, Scotland was a confusing and frustrating place. Said Millar: 'We were talking about going to Newcastle. Truesdale says, "Aye, Newcastle." Truesdale was leading the attack, but he didn't know a fuck where he was going. Nobody had a clue where to go or what to do. So he just says, "Why don't we try Newcastle?" So he was trying to get us to Newcastle and he got us fucking lost.

Everybody was just a bit pissed off, and we said, "Fuck it." So the nearest place to where we were was Carlisle, so we just went to Carlisle and booked in there for a couple of nights, because we actually had more families from Belfast wanting to come over and join us.'

While Adair contemplated the ruins of his empire from his cell, his old comrades faced the harsh new reality of life on the road. After spending a few days in Carlisle, a collective decision was taken to head further south, this time to the more densely populated town of Bolton. It was chosen at random as a place with few loyalist connections and where they hoped they could lie low for a while. The 120-mile journey straight down the M6 would take them a few hours at most. But as they neared their destination, the exiles again found themselves heading in the wrong direction. Tempers flared as bitter words of recrimination, in thick Belfast accents, raced from car to car by mobile phone. In a foreign country and with nobody to turn to, the remnants of Johnny Adair's elite C Coy were well and truly lost.

Epilogue – From 'Beirut' to Bolton: Where Are They Now?

'As Ulster's young men we looked up to Johnny. We idolised him.'
– *Wayne Dowie, a young C Coy volunteer*

FAT, BALDING AND MIDDLE-AGED, THE REMNANTS OF C COY WERE A SORRY sight as they walked into the foyer of the Travel Inn in Bolton. Jackie Thompson and Sham Millar sank into a couple of armchairs while Ian Truesdale loitered behind them. After fetching a seat from across the room, Herbie Millar pulled a crumpled sheet of paper from his pocket and started reading out loud. Looking round to make sure nobody else was listening, he began, 'In response to the statement issued yesterday by the Ulster Defence Association stating the reasons for abducting and brutally murdering Alan McCullough, the opportunity should be taken to set the record straight – not only to the UDA leadership but also the ordinary people of the Shankill and those further afield who want to know why Alan McCullough was murdered by those who guaranteed his safe return. Firstly, Alan McCullough played no part in the murder of Jonathan Stewart at a party in the Oldpark area at Christmas 2002. Moe Courtney, who has been questioned about Alan's death, was at that time military commander for C Coy and would have known about any attack carried out during this time. Secondly, Alan McCullough had no knowledge of nor played any part in the execution of loyalist John "Grug" Gregg. It is widely believed that Moe Courtney had a hand in Alan McCullough's murder. And why? To deflect from Courtney the fact that he knew about Jonathan Stewart's death and possibly John Gregg's as well.'

It was nearly 1 a.m. on 6 June 2003 when Herbie, without the mask he usually wore for these occasions, finished reading and looked up at the bleary-eyed journalist in front of him. 'Did you get all that?' he asked. The reporter nodded. Barely 24 hours had passed since the discovery of McCullough's body in a shallow grave on the outskirts of north Belfast and his old comrades wanted to have their say. The 21-year-old had been shot in the head and back, the latest casualty of Johnny Adair's war with his fellow UDA commanders. Three weeks after venturing back from Bolton, McCullough had been led away from his mother's house in Denmark Street in the lower Shankill by three senior loyalists. They included Moe Courtney, who assured his mother that her son would come to no harm. According to C Coy sources, they took him to a restaurant in Templepatrick, near Belfast International Airport, for a 'chat'. He was then taken to a field, where he believed he was going to be kneecapped but was shot dead. After he failed to return home, his mother telephoned a mobile number she had been given and spoke to one of his abductors, a former member of Adair's C9 team. When she asked where her son was, she was told bluntly, 'He's sleeping with the fishes.'

For nearly four months, McCullough had lived in Gina Adair's house in Bolton, sleeping on a camp bed in the same downstairs room as Jonathan Adair, C Coy's Wayne and Benjy Dowie, and two other brothers. But he had been so desperate to return home to his girlfriend and young daughter that he had even helped to organise a drive-by gun attack on Gina's house on 30 April, when up to 12 shots were fired at the house from a 9mm Browning. The tiny community of the lower Shankill was all he had ever known. At the age of 16 he had joined the Ulster Young Militants, Adair's youth wing, and rose to command it with one aim only: to murder the republicans who had killed his father nearly 20 years earlier. Billy 'Bucky' McCullough was shot dead by the INLA in October 1981 as he left his home in the lower Shankill. He was the UDA's brigadier in west Belfast and a hero to his fellow loyalists. Although his son had never known his father, he wore an etched image of his face on a thick gold chain that never left his neck. 'He always grew up thinking about what happened to his dad and he wanted revenge,' recalled one former colleague. McCullough was one of Adair's most fanatical supporters. 'He was 200 per cent behind Johnny. He looked up to him,' said the friend.

EPILOGUE

Even on the lower Shankill, where for 30 years life has been cheap and violence commonplace, Alan McCullough's death angered many residents. Moe Courtney, who had replaced 'Fat Jackie' Thompson as brigadier, was so afraid for his life that he went into hiding. 'Moe Courtney wasn't 100 per cent trusted by the inner council and he needed to win confidence and get in with south-east Antrim [John Gregg's brigade area],' said a former C Coy gunman. 'All Moe was ever interested in was money. That was the real reason he jumped ship from Johnny, because he knew there was more money on the other side.' Within days of the killing both Courtney and Ihab Shoukri of north Belfast were charged and remanded in custody.

McCullough's grisly murder was confirmation that the feud between Adair and his rivals was far from finished. In July, when Gina Adair returned briefly to visit her husband, a hoax device was left in a car outside her mother's house on the Shankill, where she was staying. It was left by two young volunteers, one from C13 and the other from C17. 'They were supposed to get a pipe and tape it to a five-gallon container of petrol,' said one C Coy veteran. 'They even wanted shots fired into the windie.' The following day the UDA warned that future visits by the exiles would not pass 'without incident' and that anybody associating with them would 'not be tolerated'.

After the security alert at his mother-in-law's house, Adair telephoned his old comrades in England and asked them to organise a retaliation. Aware that officials at the jail were monitoring the conversation, he said slyly, 'You wouldn't let that go, would you?' He was told by one old friend to 'Go and look in the mirror. You're finished.' At the time of writing, his most senior allies in Bolton say they have had enough of him. They believe that he has blamed them for the feud with the UDA in a cynical attempt to persuade his rivals to allow his family back to Belfast.

Adair's old cohorts in England – the 'Bolton Wanderers', as they have been dubbed – appear resigned to the fact that they are not coming home. For Gina in particular, who is used to living in style and making others pay, it has been a humiliating comedown. She has even had to go to court to beg, unsuccessfully, for a council house. Up to 50 former members of C Coy and their families are now living in the Bolton area, while several others are in Manchester. Like Gina, they are all pleading poverty, claiming to have sold their cars and pawned their jewellery in an attempt to survive. A handful of them are genuinely broke, but for Gina, 'Fat Jackie' Thompson and Sham Millar (who are brothers-in-law), the claim is a little far-fetched. They are probably not as wealthy as newspapers in Belfast have speculated, but the cash is almost certainly there, stashed away and waiting for them to lay their hands on it. The police, for one, are convinced that Adair still has money. The real reason Gina and her fellow exiles have yet to access it is because they know they are being monitored by a new government agency with the power to confiscate the illegal assets of Northern Ireland's paramilitaries. John White, who has severed his links with Adair and become a born-again Christian in the north of England, is also being watched.

If or when the exiles try to return to Belfast, there will be more blood spilt. The only small cause for hope is that none of Adair's old friends has the energy to carry out further acts of violence for a man who is already busy betraying them. Adair's most prolific hitman, Stevie 'Top Gun' McKeag, is in the grave. The rest are getting old. 'Fat Jackie' Thompson will be 40 in November, Sham Millar is 37 and his brother Herbie 38. Ian Truesdale is 42. Donald Hodgen, who turned 40 in May 2003, has had virtually no contact with Adair since his old friend was returned to prison. All he wants is to stay out of the way, and he is rumoured to be living with his partner, the sister of C Coy's Tommy Potts, in the fishing village of Portavogie on the Co. Down coast. Even Sam 'Skelly' McCrory, Adair's closest friend, appears to have gone to ground. Nobody knows where he is. Since the early 1990s he has been flitting between the west coast of Scotland and Northern Ireland, but he has not been sighted in Belfast since the day before John Gregg's murder. Scotland suits him better, and he feels more comfortable pursuing a gay lifestyle without the baggage of his past. He was 38 in March 2003.

Although many loyalists across Northern Ireland still quietly admire Adair, only two of his old friends are still prepared to show him unquestioning loyalty. They are Truesdale and Gary 'Smickers' Smith, who would literally throw himself in front of a bullet for his old commander. He is expected to join his old colleagues in Bolton this autumn following his release from prison.

As for Adair himself, he has experienced bouts of black depression since returning to jail. He turns 40 in October 2003. With middle age upon him he cannot comprehend how his reputation and empire have fallen apart. Even C Coy itself, for so long synonymous with Adair, has been disbanded as a UDA unit. 'See, republicans have their heroes and they stay heroes, but loyalists build you up and then they knock you down,' he said in one telephone conversation from jail.

EPILOGUE

As well as dealing with the collapse of his old power base, he will also have to come to terms with this book. His secret – that although he tried to be an 'operator' he was never successful as a gunman – is finally out there. The overwhelming evidence from his enemies and friends alike, and also from police officers who knew him best, is that he has killed just one person, 26-year-old Noel Cardwell, who he shot in the head in December 1993. He tried to kill many more but always failed. What set Adair apart was his energy for the job and his brilliance at planning operations, moving weapons and volunteers, and motivating his men. The full extent of his boasts to police, which enabled them to make him a casual (though unpaid) informer, is also now known. While his close friends are aware of his messy personal life, the squalid details will shock many outsiders. It will come as no surprise, though, to learn that Adair has at least one illegitimate child, a son who is now on the threshold of his teens but maintains absolutely no contact with his father.

In one telephone conversation from jail Adair suddenly became dejected when talking about his UDA rivals. Sounding like a child, he muttered quietly, 'They all hate me.' Although there are moments when he feels responsible for what has happened, most of the time he is defiant. 'I'll be honest with you,' he said, totally seriously, 'my only crime is loyalty, that's what it is.' While many of his old allies, including Jim Spence, have wondered what it was all for, Adair comforts himself with the thought of the man he was in the early 1990s. 'I had my hand on my heart,' he insisted to the authors. 'I was a dedicated loyalist who stood firm and fought for my people and my country. I tell you I've no regrets – our country was slowly and surely going down the tubes and it was only right that people like me stood up and did something to stop it.'

While nationalists continue to believe that Adair was a sectarian bigot unleashed with the formal collaboration of the security forces, there is no evidence to suggest that collusion with C Coy, though occurring at low level, was ever a thought-out British policy. Back on the Shankill, Adair will leave a mixed legacy. 'He took the war to the IRA but he also turned the Shankill against itself,' said one former friend. In the front room of Winkie and Maureen Dodds, who moved back to the lower Shankill after the C Coy exodus to the mainland, the devastation is evident. At 44, Dodds is like an old man. The veteran gunman walks with a stick and talks with difficulty, the result of a stroke and a brain haemorrhage in the aftermath of the feud with the UVF. When asked about his old comrade, he has just four words to say: 'He's a fucking wanker.' His wife is even harsher. She still has five bottles of C Coy champagne, all with Adair's face on the label, which she has kept from the day Johnny was released from jail in May 2002. 'We're saving them,' she says. 'We'll pop them when we hear he's dead.' Less than half a mile away in the Oldpark, there is an atmosphere of unspoken desperation in the small terraced house where Mabel Adair, Johnny's mother, lives with two of his sisters, Lizzie and Etta. Although Mrs Adair still worships her son, she, too, has suffered poor health and had a stroke shortly after he was sent back to prison in January 2003.

Of all the people to come into close contact with Adair, few have escaped unscathed. The press is right to portray him as a caricature – 'Mad Dog', 'Daft Dog' and 'Sad Dog' are a few of the headlines – but he is capable of extraordinary harm. After a nervous breakdown, Jackie 'Legs' Robinson, his long-term girlfriend, made a break with the past by telling her story to the *Daily Mirror* in October 2002. She has not spoken to Adair since May of that year and she feels stronger every day. The one individual who has emerged with enhanced credibility as a result of his contact with Adair is Detective Sergeant Johnston Brown. Jonty, who was arguably the finest Northern Irish detective of his generation, is the real hero of Adair's story and a credit to the Royal Ulster Constabulary. But even he still lives in dread that the former C Coy chief has enough remaining influence to order another attack on him. As a result he and his wife, Rebecca, have decided to move abroad.

Enough violence has already emanated from the small maze of streets at the bottom of the Shankill Road. As a director of terrorism, Johnny Adair controlled a dangerous clique and ordered around 40 murders by C Coy and the west Belfast UFF. He was the UFF's most influential figure throughout the early 1990s, when it claimed the lives of nearly 90 people in Northern Ireland. When he is finally released from jail, probably in January 2005, Adair will face a stark choice. Does he go back to the Shankill and try one last throw of the dice? Or does he settle quietly away from Belfast, hoping he can avoid assassination and live in peace with his family?

Although he appears to be written off, only the very foolish would take this for granted. His mother and sisters, who are well aware that he may be murdered, have already expressed anxiety about whether his rivals would allow his funeral to set off from his mother's house in the Oldpark. Few people would bet on him ever drawing his pension. In a small suburban house in Bolton, however, a new generation of militant young loyalists is

EPILOGUE

waiting for the day when they can return to Belfast. 'From when I've been growing up he's been the biggest loyalist in my eyes,' says 23-year-old Wayne Dowie. 'As Ulster's young men we looked up to Johnny. We idolised him.' So long as Adair believes he can still be a hero to young volunteers like Dowie and Alan McCullough, he will find it difficult to live a life of obscurity.

Glossary

A Company or A Coy: The upper Shankill 'company' of the west Belfast UDA.

Anglo-Irish Agreement: Signed in November 1985. Unionists believed it was selling them into a united Ireland because for the first time it gave the Irish Government a say in the affairs of Northern Ireland.

Apprentice Boys: Apprentice Boys of Derry. A Protestant male marching order which commemorates the siege of Derry in 1689.

An Phoblacht/Republican News: The Sinn Fein/IRA weekly newspaper.

ASU: Active Service Unit. A paramilitary cell, normally consisting of between four and six volunteers.

B Company or B Coy: The mid-Shankill 'company' of the west Belfast UDA.

'Brigadier': The title given to the head of each of the UDA's six 'brigade' areas.

Buff's: Short for Royal Antediluvian Order of Buffaloes. A charitable organisation mainly supported by the Protestant community in Northern Ireland. It runs a number of drinking clubs in loyalist areas of Belfast.

C Company or C Coy: One of three 'companies' in the west Belfast UDA. At the peak of its violent campaign under Johnny Adair, C Coy stretched from the bottom of the Shankill Road to Tennent Street half a mile up the road.

C8: Johnny Adair's old C Coy 'team'. One of around 18 teams of up to 60 men, which together made up C Coy.

CIRA: Continuity IRA. A dissident republican terrorist group opposed to the peace process. It is the military wing of Republican Sinn Fein, which split from Sinn Fein in 1986.

CLMC: Combined Loyalist Military Command, an umbrella group that spoke for the UDA, the UVF and RHC at the start of the peace process.

Dail: The parliament of the Irish Republic.

GLOSSARY

DUP: Democratic Unionist Party. Hardline Protestant political party founded and led by the Reverend Ian Paisley.

Fenian: A derogatory term for a Catholic.

Good Friday Agreement: Also known as the Belfast Agreement. Signed in April 1998 by the British and Irish governments and all the major political parties in Northern Ireland except the DUP.

Hallion: A peculiarly Ulster word meaning 'savage' or 'lowlife'.

Inner Council: The ruling body of the UDA/UFF. The council hears representations from the UDA's brigade areas across Northern Ireland. They are represented by 'brigadiers', who command the organisation in each area.

INLA: Irish National Liberation Army, a republican terrorist group.

IPLO: Irish People's Liberation Organisation. A maverick republican paramilitary group which broke away from the INLA. It was forced to disband by the IRA.

Loyalist Commission: An umbrella group comprising well-meaning clergymen, community workers, Unionist politicians and loyalist paramilitaries. It endeavours to exert a restraining influence on militant loyalism.

LPA: Loyalist Prisoners' Aid. Welfare group linked to the Ulster Defence Association.

LVF: Loyalist Volunteer Force. Volatile loyalist terrorist group founded by the loyalist icon Billy Wright in 1996 after he was forced out of the UVF.

Maze: Northern Ireland's largest prison for holding terrorists, which closed in 2000.

NF: National Front. The largest group of the British fascist and racist movement.

NIO: Northern Ireland Office.

Orange Order: The largest of the Protestant marching orders. It has close links to the Ulster Unionist Party and holds its meetings in Orange Halls.

Peeler: A policeman.

PIRA: The Provisional Irish Republican Army. The largest republican terrorist group, more commonly known as the IRA. It is the military wing of Sinn Fein.

Provos (or 'Provies'): A term for the Provisional movement. It describes both Sinn Fein and the IRA.

PUP: Progressive Unionist Party. Fringe loyalist political party linked to the UVF.

Quis Separabit: the UDA's Latin motto, meaning 'Who Will Come Between Us?'

RIRA: Real IRA. A small republican terror group which broke away from the IRA in 1997 because it disagreed with the IRA ceasefire.

MAD DOG

RHC: Red Hand Commando. A small loyalist terrorist group closely linked to the LVF.

RHD: Red Hand Defenders. A flag of convenience used by both the UDA and LVF.

RUC: Royal Ulster Constabulary. The police force of Northern Ireland until it was replaced by the Police Service of Northern Ireland in 2001.

SDLP: The moderate mainly Catholic/nationalist party formerly led by John Hume.

Second Battalion: The west Belfast UDA.

Shebeen: An illegal drinking den.

Sinn Fein: The political wing of the Provisional IRA.

Taig: A derogatory term for a Catholic.

Tout: A police informer.

UDA: Ulster Defence Association. The largest loyalist paramilitary group. Formed in 1971 as an umbrella group to replace vigilante organisations which sprang up in Protestant areas in reaction to IRA violence. At its peak it claimed to have a membership of over 40,000. Its small but ruthless military wing is known as 'The Ulster Freedom Fighters', and has been responsible for some of the most despicable murders of the Troubles. Only a small minority of UDA members are active in the UFF.

UDP: Ulster Democratic Party. The political wing of the UDA. Disbanded in 2001.

UDF: Ulster Defence Force. A corps of specially trained UDA volunteers intended to make the UDA more professional. Set up and disbanded in the 1980s.

UDR: Ulster Defence Regiment. A section of the British Army locally recruited in Northern Ireland and amalgamated into the Royal Irish Regiment in 1992.

UFF: Ulster Freedom Fighters. Nomme de guerre of UDA members involved in paramilitary attacks; first used in 1973.

UR: Ulster Resistance, a shadowy loyalist umbrella group established in 1986, following the Anglo-Irish Agreement.

UUP: Ulster Unionist Party, the largest Unionist party in Northern Ireland.

UVF: Ulster Volunteer Force. The oldest loyalist terrorist group. Took its name from the organisation which was set up to oppose home rule in 1912. It was reformed in 1966 under Augustus 'Gusty' Spence.

UYM: Ulster Young Militants. The UDA's youth wing.

WDA: Woodvale Defence Association, also known as B Company.

Index

INDEX

MAD DOG